PRAISE FOR M. L. BUCHMAN

The first...of (a) stellar, long-running romantic suspense series.

— Booklist, The 20 Best Romantic Suspense Novels: Modern Masterpieces. *The Night is Mine*

Top 10 Romance of 2012, 2015, and 2016.

— Booklist: *The Night Is Mine*, *Hot Point*, *Heart Strike*

One of our favorite authors.

— RT Book Reviews

Buchman has catapulted his way to the top tier of my favorite authors.

— Fresh Fiction

A favorite author of mine. I'll read anything that carries his name, no questions asked. Meet your new favorite author!

— The Sassy Bookster, *Flash of Fire*

M.L. Buchman is guaranteed to get me lost in a good story.

— The Reading Cafe, Way of the Warrior: NSDQ

I love Buchman's writing. His vivid descriptions bring everything to life in an unforgettable way.

— Pure Jonel, Hot Point

MID-LIFE CRISIS ON WHEELS

A BICYCLE JOURNEY AROUND THE WORLD

M. L. BUCHMAN

Buchman Bookworks

Copyright 2019 Matthew Lieber Buchman

Published by Buchman Bookworks, Inc.

All rights reserved.

This book, or parts thereof, may not be reproduced in any form without permission from the author.

Receive a free book and discover more by this author at: www.mlbuchman.com

All images by author except as noted.

Cover image:

Matt and Junior in Kupang © Ondine

As I rode the market in Kupang, Timor, Indonesia. Sticking up behind me is an Australian didgeridoo. I became, like on so many instruments before, barely acceptable at playing it. However, its low, buzzing honk was an amazing goodwill ambassador until I lost it in Surakarta, Indonesia.

Other works by M. L. Buchman:

Thrillers

Dead Chef
Swap Out!
One Chef!
Two Chef!

Miranda Chase NTSB
Drone
TBA

Romantic Suspense

Delta Force
Target Engaged
Heart Strike
Wild Justice
Midnight Trust

Firehawks
MAIN FLIGHT
Pure Heat
Full Blaze
Hot Point
Flash of Fire
Wild Fire
SMOKEJUMPERS
Wildfire at Dawn
Wildfire at Larch Creek
Wildfire on the Skagit

The Night Stalkers
MAIN FLIGHT
The Night Is Mine
I Own the Dawn
Wait Until Dark
Take Over at Midnight
Light Up the Night
Bring On the Dusk
By Break of Day
AND THE NAVY
Christmas at Steel Beach
Christmas at Peleliu Cove

WHITE HOUSE HOLIDAY
Daniel's Christmas
Frank's Independence Day
Peter's Christmas
Zachary's Christmas
Roy's Independence Day
Damien's Christmas
5E
Target of the Heart
Target Lock on Love
Target of Mine
Target of One's Own

Shadow Force: Psi
At the Slightest Sound
At the Softest Word

White House Protection Force
Off the Leash
On Your Mark
In the Weeds

Contemporary Romance

Eagle Cove
Return to Eagle Cove
Recipe for Eagle Cove
Longing for Eagle Cove
Keepsake for Eagle Cove

Henderson's Ranch
Nathan's Big Sky
Big Sky, Loyal Heart
Big Sky Dog Whisperer

Love Abroad
Heart of the Cotswolds: England
Path of Love: Cinque Terre, Italy

Other works by M. L. Buchman:

Contemporary Romance (cont)

Where Dreams
Where Dreams are Born
Where Dreams Reside
Where Dreams Are of Christmas
Where Dreams Unfold
Where Dreams Are Written

Science Fiction / Fantasy

Deities Anonymous
Cookbook from Hell: Reheated
Saviors 101

Single Titles
The Nara Reaction
Monk's Maze
the Me and Elsie Chronicles

Non-Fiction

Strategies for Success
Managing Your Inner Artist/Writer
Estate Planning for Authors
Character Voice

Short Story Series by M. L. Buchman:

Romantic Suspense

Delta Force
Delta Force

Firehawks
The Firehawks Lookouts
The Firehawks Hotshots
The Firebirds

The Night Stalkers
The Night Stalkers
The Night Stalkers 5E
The Night Stalkers CSAR
The Night Stalkers Wedding Stories

US Coast Guard
US Coast Guard

White House Protection Force
White House Protection Force

Contemporary Romance

Eagle Cove
Eagle Cove

Henderson's Ranch
Henderson's Ranch

Where Dreams
Where Dreams

Thrillers

Dead Chef
Dead Chef

Science Fiction / Fantasy

Deities Anonymous
Deities Anonymous

Other
The Future Night Stalkers
Single Titles

SIGN UP FOR M. L. BUCHMAN'S NEWSLETTER TODAY

and receive:
Release News
Free Short Stories
a Free book

Get your free book today. Do it now.
free-book.mlbuchman.com

CONTENTS

About This Book	xi
A Word on Measurements	xiii
Prologue	1
1. United States of America	7
2. Japan	49
3. South Korea, Singapore	95
4. Australia	107
5. Indonesia	161
6. Singapore	205
7. India	211
8. Israel	243
9. Greece	253
10. Macedonia, Bulgaria, Yugoslavia, Hungary	271
11. Austria, Czech Republic, Germany, Luxembourg	287
12. France	303
13. Getting Home	313
14. Afterthoughts (2000)	319
15. Afterthoughts (2019)	323
Appendix I	337
Appendix II	353
Appendix III	361
About the Author	365
Also by M. L. Buchman	367

To Mac and Ruth, the best friends anyone could ever ask for, my definition of home for so many years.

To my wife and stepdaughter for expanding that definition a thousand-fold.

ABOUT THIS BOOK

Cutting-edge computer systems designer. Crisis project manager. Consultant to the Fortune 100. Utter workaholic.

Before he became a writer, M.L. "Matt" Buchman had dreamed of traveling the world by sailboat or small plane. Not once did he think about doing it by bicycle — not until he lost everything: career, house he'd been remodeling for the family he never had time to find, sense of self, all of it.

Broke and burned out at thirty-five, he sold everything, climbed on his bicycle Junior, and together they headed out on a journey of unknown duration.

His one guide? Following the setting sun west.

11,000 miles through eighteen countries. A voyage of adventure, discovery, and rebuilding a life. But mostly? A journey of discovering hope and the unexpected possibilities of the future.

A WORD ON MEASUREMENTS

For reasons passing understanding, the US is the last country in the world to officially use English measurements (feet, yards, miles, pounds). The other two holdouts, Liberia and Myanmar, converted in the mid-2010s. Even the US military is using the far more sensible metric system. Most of this trip happened to me in metric, so I'll use the measurements of that time and place. For my non-traveling American readers: a meter is a fat yard and a kilometer is fat half-mile. A kilogram (kilo) is two pounds, a really heavy two pounds.

As I never got the hang of Centigrade temperatures (and in the early 1990s many places hadn't, even though they were metrified) I list both.

PROLOGUE
THE ON RAMP

When did my journey around the world begin?

Did it begin when I was twelve and filled the blank ceiling of my room with dream images of sailing single-handed around the world?

Or perhaps at the age of twenty-five when I stood, feet braced wide against the pitching of the *Lady Amalthea?* She was a lovely, though rather run-down, fifty-foot, wooden ketch I had just purchased and barely knew how to handle. The journey certainly didn't start when I sold her three years later, though perhaps it came a little closer. I'd finally learned that she'd never been designed for deep sea and perhaps I hadn't been either. (Though I still miss her every single time the wind ripples the water.)

The journey drifted a bit nearer when a new assistant at a law firm where I was a paralegal introduced himself with, "I'm Christopher. Sell it all and go now." My reply was some lucid comment on the order of, "Um, hi." I had no idea what he meant.

Now I do. I've received worse advice often, but only rarely have I received better.

The best advice I ever received was a few years *after* the journey chronicled here.

It came from *every single one* of my friends upon their first meeting with the girlfriend who would eventually agree to become my wife. Every single one of them, including my sister, delivered it in almost identical words: "If you fuck this up, we're going to kill you." My wife is awesome and engenders that kind of loyalty from people with an ease that still shocks this socially awkward boy despite twenty-plus years together.

The first turning point that I can truly identify after Christopher's introduction was five years later on August 23rd, 1992. (In a few moments you'll see how I can pinpoint that date.)

I'd just flown into Seattle for four days. It was the longest I'd been back at home in six months. I'd taken a half-partnership in a small, but very high-end, computer consulting firm. A dot-com before there were dot-coms or even a public Internet. I slept on planes. I ate in restaurants, sometimes in three different cities for three consecutive meals. At home was a computer network for 3:00 a.m. testing of software I'd be installing the next day in Calgary or Houston. The only ones using my bed were my cats and an ex-girlfriend and her fiancé who were my regular house sitters. Honestly, they lived there more than I did.

On that cool evening of August 23rd, a pounding on my front door dragged me from a hurried bowl of chili I was trying not to slop over my latest printout. Silhouetted against the late summer sun stood a specter that thankfully resolved itself into my friend George. I offered him a glass of wine; in return he assaulted me with a question.

"Why are you doing this to yourself?"

I was wholly unable to answer.

For the following four nights, rather than sleeping, rather than attending to the urgent programming I needed to do, I repeatedly flung myself upon the poniard of his question. I didn't even understand what he was asking, nor could I find an answer he'd accept no matter how I twisted and turned. Yet for some reason, each evening I agreed to meet—sometimes at my house, sometimes at his—like a Shakespearian tragic hero.

The fourth night, as I left his house, I looked aloft at the stars shining impossibly bright against the midnight sky. Understand that I love astronomy and the stars. I ran the college planetarium for four years and presented hundreds of shows there to thousands of students from schools all around the area. I often wonder why I didn't pursue that field of study.

As I breathed in, the heavy green of late summer filled my lungs. Summer was near gone. I'd missed an entire season (two of them actually as I'd missed spring as well). I was missing *my life*. I had become a workaholic, one of the ones whom I'd always considered "deluded." The ones I'd jeered at (quietly, I'm not a rude sort). Worse, I now saw that I'd been that way for at least a decade.

I was thirty-four, burned out, I'd thoroughly scared off the few girlfriends I'd found out of the women who didn't just avoid me to begin with. I worked hard on my career and I thought that working just as hard, with just as intense a focus on a relationship, should work just as well. Right? Of course right! ...or not.

I began to laugh.

It was like all the folly of all the choices I'd made since roughly, oh, the day I graduated from...uh, kindergarten (?) became clear in that single expanse of brilliantly starry sky.

And couldn't stop laughing.

I collapsed in hysterics on George's front lawn, soaked in a chill dew, filling the night with my howls. The laughter continued so long and hard his wife almost called 911 before I recovered.

I faxed in my resignation the next day.

I was now the proud owner of:

- a house that I'd spent every spare minute and dollar of seven years remodeling for a family I'd never had time to find
- just one very expensive consultant-type suit (the rest were shredded by my ex-business partner)
- a disconnected cell phone (to have one at all in 1992 was a great anomaly; to make it work, I had three accounts with three different companies in my three major cities and had to change my phone's settings from one number to the next every time I flew)
- about five months' worth of mortgage in my savings account. Due to a small legal loophole that my ex-business partner had slipped in, my departing share of my company was worth $3,000 rather than the mid-six figures I knew to be its value.

I spent the first three months' of my savings: watching TV, eating, and rereading old science fiction (one month each). I couldn't even face new books.

I certainly couldn't return to my career. Even if I could tolerate doing so, every connection I'd built over the prior decade got burned in the collapse of my personal dot-com disaster. Seattle, Calgary, Denver, Oklahoma City, Houston, anything to do with the corporate offices of Microsoft, Oracle, Compaq, the Association of Systems Managers... The list of broken connections goes on.

"You could sell your house. That would open up your options."

"I could *what?*"

I'd finally called Mac, my best friend, late one night just past Christmas in a fit of depression. I was so far down that I had started the conversation with, "Just so you know, I'm not considering suicide, but I don't have any brilliant ideas either."

Selling my precious house, and the dream of family I'd built into it, was not the sort of irrelevancy I wanted to hear.

"If I sold the house..." (insert loud scoff). "Not a chance!"

But if I did...

I could go back to school.

In what?

I could start a new career once freed of the overwhelming mortgage. But I couldn't imagine anything that would be different enough to be tolerable. I had always loved my work, now all it gave me was dry heaves when I thought about it too much.

For two weeks that broken sentence followed me about like a needle stuck on an old phonograph.

I could...tick!

I could...tick!

I could...with no one kind enough to lift the needle. Actually, my friends tried, but I couldn't find any verb-object combination that completed that phrase.

January 10th, 1993, I was walking in the chill sunlight along the pedestrian path around Seattle's Green Lake Park when a bicycle whizzing by me nearly clipped my elbow.

I spun around at the last second, probably all that saved me from being thrown to the ground on the otherwise empty walkway. Looking the other way on the path was like looking at a whole new landscape.

I could...bicycle around the world.

It was ludicrous.

It was insane!

...but what if it wasn't?

My last vacation had been three weeks cycling through New Zealand. The one before that was a five-day, three-hundred-mile charity ride across Washington State. Before that, a group ride with one of those companies that takes care of hotels, meals, and luggage for a week along the Oregon Coast.

My weekends, back when I'd still been able to occasionally etch one out of the hard corporate clay, had been things like riding a century (a cyclist's term for a hundred miles) around the steep canyons of the fourteen-thousand-foot dormant volcano Mount Rainier, including a ten-thousand-foot-high pass.

I *could* bicycle around the world.

Actually, it was the first thing that had made sense in ages.

My journey had begun.

Total Distance: 0 miles
Elevation Climbed: 0 feet

1

UNITED STATES OF AMERICA

27 MARCH 1993 – 20 MAY 1993

English: *I'm going around the world by bicycle.*
Translation: *I must be nuts.*

Kicking the Pedal High

March 27th, 1993, shortly after my thirty-fifth birthday, I kicked my right pedal high and tried not to look too closely at the small cluster of friends circled about me. Finally, I focused on their faces because I couldn't bear to look at the house behind me—now empty of every single thing.

No furniture, no spices in the gourmet kitchen that I'd designed and built and from which I'd thrown so many "come all ye chefs" dinner parties, no car in the garage. The new owners were an hour away, so now even my dreams would need a new residence. Inadvertently I'd eased up on the brakes and rolled backward down the hill just far enough that my foot had swung past high-center and dropped down.

Again, I kicked my right pedal high and clicked my bike shoe into the cleat with a sharp snap. Hugs would be completed after breakfast at a nearby restaurant, but first I had to start the journey.

Eleven weeks from concept to action.

After seven years of work, I'd finished the house—for someone else to inhabit. The electrical had passed inspection only three days earlier. The plumbing the day before that.

But now I was free.

Now was the time.

I lifted my weight, released the brakes on my heavily loaded touring bike. My friends' applause rattled around that chilly morning like so many lost robins hunting worms in the hard ground who had arrived too early for the spring and didn't know what else to do on that chilly March day. I had planned to start in the warmth of May, but the house had sold too quickly, the new owners wanted to move in too soon.

It was time to go.

I drove downward with all my weight.

The handlebars twisted left.

The front wheel twisted right...

| Kicking my pedal high.

As I lay upon my back in the middle of the street, I noted

that the sharp blue sky looked very unusual from this position. I'd never lain in the middle of the street to observe it before.

"Wow, Matt! That was amazing. Can you do it again?"

"Is it too late to buy back your house?"

"And you're going to ride around the world?"

They helped me swing the heavy bike upright. In the final weeks, I'd had no time to maintain my poor machine. Instead I'd dragged it to a bike shop for a tune-up and they'd missed tightening the handlebar bolt after they were done.

"I have the wrench here somewhere." I emptied the front-left pannier in the middle of the street. T-shirts, guidebooks, a bag of rice, and one sandal.

"I saw it just last night." I unearthed my right-front pannier and disgorged it onto the growing mound: spare tubes, a pair of pants, a set of nested cookpots with a tiny stove, and my rain gear.

There had been no time to pack for the trip while I was finishing the house and selling most of my worldly possessions. I'd simply thrown things I might need into one corner, from tents to toiletries, until I'd buried the actual bike.

The previous night these friends and more had come to drink champagne in the echoing cavern of a living room that was a single night from no longer being mine. I'd sorted through everything.

"Too many T-shirts in the pile. Anyone want one?" Nope. Garbage.

"Extra flashlight?" Paul allowed as he could fit a second one in his glove compartment.

"Room for one novel, who wants the other two?" A few friends departed at this point leaving tears on my shoulder. At least in the morning they'd still have each other. I fought my own tears back for their sake. I was the brave adventurer and if I let my fears show, I'd never be able to depart. (I was also half afraid that like the laughter of the prior August, if I started to cry in March, I might not stop until the August following.)

At the bottom of the right-rear bag I unearthed the hex-wrench beneath another layer of clothes, a spare fuel canister for my cookstove, a wide variety of other tools and parts, and the missing sandal. A quick twist, a hasty yet equally disorganized repack, and I was ready.

I kicked the pedal high once more and, amidst as much laughter as applause, I ground my way slowly *up* the steep hill in first gear while my friends walked easily alongside.

Ride Through It

I remember nothing of that breakfast except that we all sat very close, buffing our memories against each other to shine them up so they'd last. I had a tentative route in my head, which would take me through four years, five continents, forty countries, and at least thirty languages.

When next would we gather together over our shared joys and sorrows? When next would we make each other laugh? (Yes, I do actually wax that poetic in my head sometimes... often. And this was *before* I became a writer.)

As I rode away from that little restaurant, a roar of applause rose behind me, impossibly loud for the six friends come to see me off. It rose and soared like a wind against my back until it washed over me like a benediction that perhaps I wasn't insane after all.

I didn't look back.

I *couldn't* look back.

I turned my bike mirror so that all I could see was my knee going up and down as it moved me away from everything I knew. Upon my return a year-and-a-half later, my friends told me that the patrons waiting in line outside the crowded restaurant had burst into spontaneous cheering when told that it was the first day of my solo journey around the world.

It was a fair wind.

Out of sight, past the first rise, I stopped to clean my riding glasses. The long streaks of salt had made the road ahead blurred and splotchy. Cleaner glasses did little to aid the view.

As I cranked north out of Seattle along a busy suburban street mostly given over to stores and apartment buildings, I searched for something to be happy about.

Here I was setting off around the world while the lawyers continued to earn money on the dissolution of my business partnership (something that I would finally conclude nine months in the future with a Washington State judge by phone at 2:00 a.m. from a Singapore phone booth).

My friends were in their cars and headed on with their own lives. A rental truck filled with someone else's belongings was being emptied even now into a house that was no longer mine.

My father could no longer find me.

Ah! *That* was a good feeling—sad, but good.

Our relationship had never been better than when I was climbing my way up through the computer industry. His entire life had been dedicated to computers. He had worked with their design since the 1950s, when they were barely called that, right up to his retirement just a few years before my trip.

I'd implemented things he'd helped develop in the research labs of IBM.

We discussed at length the evolution of monitor technology from RGB to VGA. Of large-server implementation in the PC environment, including work I was doing on the very early practical applications of client-server architecture. The intense challenges he'd faced sending a 5 kHz signal down a piece of wire that was now 100 MHz. And I even had a 1 GHz fiber-optic backbone in my 1989 system design, another item he'd helped develop years before.

Then I quit.

It didn't take long to learn that we had *nothing* else to talk about. He assumed that I'd get over my funk and return to my career.

Instead I sold my house.

He suggested that I get an apartment and get back to work.

Instead I began planning a bicycle journey around the world.

He sent me the names of IBM-recommended psychiatrists in the Seattle area.

I stopped answering the phone and began to fear each knock on the door.

My father wielding commitment papers became the bogeyman of my waking hours. I was struggling, but I'd finally found a path toward a future. It was a narrow path, barely wide enough for one bicycle, but at least it seemed to be leading somewhere.

Suddenly the old family joke about the little men in white suits coming to take us away—far too often repeated (typically as a cruel tease my father had trained us kids to aim at our mother)—did not seem so humorous. How hard would it be for him to declare me incompetent because of a nervous breakdown? I guess it shows how close I was to such a state that I could imagine it so clearly.

Each stroke of the pedal, slow though it was due to lack of training time, took me farther from my LKP, Last Known Point. When I turned off that first stretch of road, that would make it even more difficult for some state patrol to find me if he set them to search for me. When I turned again for Whidbey Island, I began to breathe more easily despite the sweat now streaming down my face.

After I crossed the ferry, I had other concerns. I'd never ridden here before. It was my first new road and I might as well have been on another planet. The busy Seattle streets no longer hummed with the traffic I'd become used to over a dozen years of living there. The air now smelled of the sea and the trees, a deep rich scent that took me back to days hiking through the woods of Maine where I'd gone to college.

Mental checklists fell by the roadside as I climbed the first hill by the ferry. The few items that I hadn't wanted to sell were now in storage, paid a year in advance. My arms, sore from all of the vaccinations I'd needed to travel through long stretches of the tropics, were now to be spared for six months until my next booster was due.

No need to look for a job in the morning, my daily task was now to literally, and perhaps ironically, make my wheels spin.

No mortgage.

No car, so no car payments.

No phone (disconnected or not).

My sole monetary needs were medical insurance and the expenses of my trip.

The bike began to wobble. I checked the front tire, but it spun smoothly if slowly beneath me as I climbed. Sweat poured off me. I decided that it must have more to do with the hill than anything as prosaic as stark terror; at least that's how I would choose to think about it.

"Ride through it."

Little did I know how often I'd use that adage over the next eighteen months. "Just ride through it." That had propelled me over aching climbs before. It had sustained me when I chose to do the 200-mile Seattle-to-Portland group ride while suffering from the flu.

Now it was a mantra to sustain me the last miles to my first stop.

The Stars Will Be There

I hadn't seen this friend in three years, but then I hadn't seen much of anyone. The night before I'd called on a whim.

"Around the world? That is wild. Come on out. I'll drag you out to a friend's birthday party if you want."

I rolled into his back yard an hour before he returned from work. Work. Already a somewhat strange, even foreign concept. I parked my bike against his picnic table and emptied the panniers.

My belongings covered the picnic table, both benches, and the cheap lawn chair leaning precariously against the side of his house. Novels (I'd unearthed a second one that I hadn't given away) tumbled against guidebooks. I found the small monocular inside my underwear and my bag of extra nuts and bolts in the cookpot. Bike gloves, spare tubes, T-shirts, two bottles of fuel, spices, pots and pans, PowerBars, string, straps, tent, sleeping bag, knapsack for day hikes, camp shoes, rain slicks, sunscreen, a really scary medical kit including antibiotics, Band-Aids, and hypodermic needles just in case...

No wonder it had been so hard to climb the hills today. I broke it down into piles and ladled it back into the bags. All of the tools and parts were in one place. All the cookware in another. All the clothes in a third. I didn't want to lose something on the bike again. I mean, it wasn't that big a space after all. (There's a complete list in the appendices.)

Then I sat.

Too wound up and physically exhausted to read or nap, I watched the neighbor's newborn lambs frisking about in the field. In the last five days I'd had two electrical inspections, a plumbing inspection, meetings with banks, attorneys, people who wanted my furniture, my house, my car. I'd even spent an entire day at a hearing as my ex-business partner worked to shaft me out of a final six thousand dollars. (She didn't succeed, but the lawyers got half.)

From my point of view, she and I had very different definitions of integrity. In future years (thank you, Google, which was still a long way off as I departed), she would go on to destroy a major company, be named the worst IT manager of the year, and finally end up as a business motivational speaker. Her family cowered whenever she came home from a trip—though I can only see that in retrospect. Her daughter was a particularly gentle, lovely, and deeply skittish girl and to this day I hope that she eventually found a way out.

Even though we had different ethics, my business partner and I did share the same intense focus on work.

Thankfully, I didn't manage to push my friends away as I had been pretty manic in those last few years.

Quite how manic?

It was something I wouldn't understand until my friends would meet my future wife when we were first dating—and warn her at length about "Type A Matt." In fact, over twenty years on, they still check in with her from time to time to make sure that I haven't regressed.

What *was* I like back at the start of my trip? I don't even know. Lost? Going through adrenaline detox? I'd certainly been hooked on the growing cycle of tackling impossible projects, pulled off by Herculean efforts, making people tell me how amazing I was before I went off and repeated the cycle elsewhere.

But on that March day in 1993, I was just sitting and watching lambs play in the late afternoon sunshine. I had *nothing* more important to do.

Type A personalities like mine don't take easily to such changes. While the newborns gamboled about the field, discovering the wonder of being alive, I repacked my bike *again*, distributing the weight more evenly between the packs. (In bike touring, you want the heavy weight low, forward, and equal on either side.)

As the Olympic Mountains melted from snow-capped peaks into silhouettes against the reds and purples of a sunset sky, my friend arrived home. After a hot shower and an amazing meal of mahi-mahi and new asparagus that we cooked together, we wandered off into the dark in search of a birthday party. The party: a dozen people grouped around a campfire blazing in a small meadow surrounded by hundred-foot Douglas firs. I couldn't have found a greater change.

Exactly twenty-four hours before, I'd been pacing around a house swept clean of everything except echoes and unfulfilled dreams of family.

Now I was with a crowd of people I didn't know who welcomed me with open arms. They were all beating on drums, eating marshmallows and birthday cake, and circulating a pitcher of lemonade like a jug of moonshine.

"Matt, can you play?"

"Guitar a little bit, but not well."

"Can you sing?"

"Well, that's debatable. I sing flat." (I do, always, about a quartertone. I'm told that's very irritating. My inability to make music, despite years of lessons on a variety of instruments including voice, is one of the great regrets of my life.)

"C'mon. You're going around the world on a bicycle. You have to be able to sing something."

I tried to unravel this curious equivalency after an emotionally and physically exhausting day but was unable to find a flaw in the logic. I started softly on an old Cherokee Indian peyote chant that I'd learned a decade before from a Brewer & Shipley record.

> *What a spirit spring is bringing round my head,*
> *Makes me feel glad that I'm not dead.*

Witchi Tai Tai, kimarah...

A drum joined in soft and low. A second joined in on a counter-beat slowly swelling to fill the night. There might have been a flute eventually. I looked up from the firelight past the towering Douglas firs and focused upon the stars peeking between the topmost branches as I sang.

Whoa Ron-nee Ka...

They would be the same stars for all my journey. Old friends from when I was a child lying on a stack of the neighbor's freshly harvested hay bales. Companions of many late college nights as we members of the astronomy department aimed our telescopes heavenward.

Hey-ney, hey-ney, no-wah...

There would be other campfires and other journeys, but there would never be another first night for this trip. My hands, frenetic through the day, were finally at rest in my lap.

What a spirit spring is bringing round my head...

My eyes drifted closed as an alto raised a harmony to my rhythmic baritone.

Makes me feel glad that I'm not dead...

For the first time in what seemed forever, I *was* glad to be alive.

Type A All the Way

I rode north the next day. My plan called for riding from Seattle to Los Angeles as a warm-up ride in "friendly" territory—meaning somewhere they spoke English. For at least the first six weeks of my journey, I would know how to find food and a bike shop.

But first I wanted to visit my friend George and his wife at their new home on an island in northern Puget Sound (the same George who'd arrived at my door with wine and a question, and thankfully not called the ambulance the prior August). I'd bought undeveloped property next to them but only visited it a few times in the last year. He and his wife had finally pulled off their dream of moving there.

As I ground north up the length of Whidbey Island, a bald eagle came to circle overhead. I thought about stopping for my camera, but knew that though it seemed so close, it would be little more than a black speck against a gray sky. It continued to circle overhead as I rode. With great lazy loops it led me over hills I didn't notice and around quiet bends in the country road. For nearly an hour it led me onward.

When I finally stopped for lunch, a peanut butter-and-jelly sandwich with water, it perched and watched me from the highest branches of a maple just barely brushed green by the spring. I left the tail end of the sandwich as an offering and rode on. The bird took wing and, ignoring the small gift, led me for another mile before soaring away on an updraft.

I never thought of myself as a spiritual person, but if a bald eagle was going to guide the beginning of my journey, I wasn't going to be filing a complaint with the spirit-guide bureau. In fact, I'd keep an eye out for any future emissaries.

I dragged north. I didn't want to damage my undertrained knees, so I stayed in an easy gear and just kept the pedals spinning. Six, seven, maybe eight miles per hour. But I had a goal, so I kept riding.

I walked and cursed my bike up the final monstrous hill—our small, side-by-side properties had amazing views, so they were near the top of the highest paved road on the island. Three hundred feet may not sound like much (though it is the same elevation as the highest point in the entire state of Florida), but it was horrendous when I realized what I'd done.

Eleven hours and sixty-five miles on the second day of my trip had taken everything I had…and then I'd pushed a hundred-and-twenty-pound bike up a three-hundred-foot hill, one limping step at a time.

"Dumb," I thought. "Really dumb."

I crawled into George and Jodi's yard and collapsed in a way all too reminiscent of that dewy August night. I lay on the ground still wearing helmet and gloves, too weak to care that they were laughing at me. Every muscle cried and moaned except the ones that were throbbing too loudly to do even that.

"Still trying to move like that old corporate Type-A-Plus. One day that's really going to tear you up."

I was leaving behind everything and everyone I knew. If I could be any more torn up than I already was, I didn't want to know.

They shoved a beer and a plate of pasta into my hands and I lay back against the bike as I wolfed both down. Shortly afterward they must have coaxed me into my sleeping bag, as that's where I woke sixteen hours later.

The next night we sat around a small campfire.

"I think this is a great thing you're doing." Jodi, rarely effusive, leaned in and stared intently at me through the flames. "I mean, Christ, Matt, you were a mess. Anything that fixes that is alright in my book."

"I just can't believe that I'm out here. I want a family—yet I haven't had a girlfriend in two years. I want a home life—yet I've always lived alone. I want..."

"You're a nut," George entered the conversation with his normal subtlety. "You've never slowed down enough for your own sweat to catch up with you, never mind any of the women who were chasing you."

"Which women?"

George slapped his forehead and Jodi simply huffed in exasperation. As they named names, I felt dumber and dumber. I'd been so damn busy remodeling a house for a family and so damn busy building a career to support it that I'd missed any number of chances to actually have one.

"And building a house for a family *before* you have one struck us all as a bit odd."

"All who?"

They proceeded to name most of my friends, who were only too glad to confirm this later when I asked. As a matter of fact, even two and a half decades later it is something I still get teased about.

Perhaps the road ahead would be smoother.

Effing Cool

I turned south the next day. Finally headed in the right direction.

March 31st, a day early for an April Fool's joke, so I feared that the weather was actually real and not a dose of someone's twisted humor: 41°F (5°C) and a mizzling rain. As the Eskimos have a hundred words for the vast panoply of snow, Seattle residents have at least that number for rain. Summer "misting rains." Winter "torrentials." A mizzle is heavier than a mist and, you guessed it, not quite a drizzle. (Okay, maybe I made up mizzle myself, but it sounds right, doesn't it?)

I'd thought to sell my house in late May or early June and

hadn't intended to be mizzling my way south in March. It took three days to retrace the path of my heroic ride north before I reached a ferry across Puget Sound to the Olympic Peninsula and truly turned south. (Irony Vista Point Number One: the next day I rode within five miles of the home of my future wife, whom I wouldn't meet until several years after my return. Thankfully, the ironic nature of the moment escaped me at the time for obvious reasons.)

I hadn't ridden much since my daily high school commute (a couple miles each way)—my solution to escaping school bus teasing dynamics. I worked 363 ½ days in 1990 in Seattle, three years before my trip; I took off Thanksgiving and half of Christmas. (But, oh no, I *wasn't* one of those workaholics. No, ma'am.) I was rotting at my desk, no matter how fast the million-dollar computer system I'd designed was going in.

Unable to stand it anymore, I simply left work in the middle of a Friday afternoon and within three hours had purchased a top-quality mountain bike and all the rain gear a person could want.

I began riding six miles each way to work that December and never looked back. For half an hour twice a day, no one could find me. My pager was in my saddle bag. I turned it off just to ensure it wouldn't disturb my ride. It was just me and several tens of thousands of stressed-out commuters in vehicles weighing a hundred times more than mine. At other times I rode home at midnight in the rain and rode back at 5:00 a.m. in the sleet.

I didn't care.

This led me to the longer rides I mentioned in the prologue. It turned out I had been building up to this crazy adventure after all. Who knew?

For distance riding, especially with a load, you have to work up to it slowly. A blown knee would end all of my fantastic plans very abruptly. Other than that misguided second day, I rode a maximum thirty miles each day, which took me about four grinding hours. By lunch I would have my tent erected in some park. Crawling inside, I'd listen to the rain for the next twenty hours.

Mizzle had long since given over to varying levels of drencher.

On one particularly damp day, I slogged into a little general store that dark afternoon about a week from home. As I came out with an orange juice and a bag of Fritos, a couple of bikers rolled in on their Harleys.

I looked at their road machines that could cover my last week of splashing about in mere hours.

I looked at their helmets that actually kept the rain off their heads rather than funneling it through the air-cooling slots like mine.

I looked at their heavy foul weather gear that was fine for sitting but would never work on a bicycle—even if it did keep them warm and dry (cheaters).

As I struggled to swallow this sad state of affairs along with the water sliding off my mustache and into my Fritos, one of the bikers was inspecting me equally carefully. He looked at my heavily laden bike. My fingers had ached with the cold in my padded, fingerless riding gloves until I'd thought to buy some latex dishwashing gloves. My bright yellow fingertips poked out into the world. Stupid-looking but warmer. My mud-spattered riding slicks and little booties completed the drowned-rat look.

The biker pulled off his helmet and let his long hair, dry I noted, hang down his back.

"Where you headed, man?"

"Week two of four years around the world." This comment stopped most people. They had no point of reference to continue a conversation begun with such a foreign concept.

"Alone?"

As I nodded, a stream of water that had been collecting in

one of the airholes of my helmet shot forward, ran out of my hair, created a small torrent off my forehead, and diluted my open orange juice even more than the rain had already done.

"That is so cool!" The biker started to dance around me like a mad leprechaun. "Shit, man. I have to be back at the bank in two days. And you just said, 'screw all that corporate kiss-ass shit' and you're doin' it, man. You're doin' what people only dream about. That's just the sweetest thing I've ever heard, man. So effing cool, man!" (Having a hairy Harley biker, complete with beard down his chest say "effing" just added to the mad leprechaun image.)

Those were the most encouraging words I'd heard in a long time and I certainly needed them when a few miles later I passed the road sign: "Seattle ferry – 6 miles." A whole series of ferries cross Puget Sound. I'd taken the northernmost one onto the Olympic Peninsula and now I was passing the last sign for the southernmost.

After eight days in the rain, I was just six miles from friends who would let me use their dryer and be glad to put me up on the couch under a blanket that didn't smell of week-old bicycle rider. If it hadn't been for the war dance offered by that biker, I might have made that oh-so-easy turn and given up the journey.

Even with his help, that sign pulled at me for days.

Another day riding in the rain. Are those socks tied to the back getting drier or wetter? Either way, I'd be wearing them tomorrow no matter what condition they were in...and I look so happy about it.

On the Tracks

Bike tracks.

There were definitely bike tracks in the mud-spattered shoulder of the road from Shelton to the coast. At first I'd discounted them as local kids. But they continued for mile after mile, sometimes washed away, but always returning. These were cycle-tourists.

People!

For the first time, I began to push my pace.

Right before I'd become a partner in the IT firm that was to end my climb up the business ladder, I'd taken three weeks off in March and gone to New Zealand on my bike. For twenty-one glorious days, I rolled up and down the roads of that country, definitely one of the finest and friendliest places it has ever been my privilege to ride. And New Zealand in March is filled with cycle-tourists. I always had someone to ride with and the campsites often boasted dozens of us. Bicycling there was a very social event.

After two weeks on the road alone in forsaken drenchers (that's where downpour meets the suck), I was ready to ride with some people. I followed those bike tracks into a bakery parking lot even though I could see they departed as well.

"British couple. About half a day ahead of you. How'd you know?"

"Bike tracks." Okay, so maybe the baker thought I was insane or some sort of a demented gumshoe in rain slicks, but his Danish was good even if the hot cocoa was powdered.

Two days later, after thirsting along their tire tracks like a dying hound, I caught up with Jo and Henry. They were in month fourteen of their eighteen-month tour and had recently entered the US from Vancouver, Canada.

We rode together for five days and with each passing one I grew more excited about my trip.

"Four days on, one day off. That's the rule everyone follows. The fifth day on is always a horror." Henry was adamant.

I declined to mention that I had caught up with them after seven straight. By the way, he's absolutely right: four on, one off. Trust me.

"Your butt hurts? Ours don't. Well, not like that." Jo hopped on my bike and climbed right back off without pedaling a stroke. "What's wrong with your seat? It's awful."

Just before I'd left on the trip, I'd put on a new bike seat. My reasoning was that my hard-and-narrow commuting seat designed for fast riding would become painful doing long touring. What I hadn't realized is that I'd acquired a seat that was shaped nothing like a person's bottom.

The next day we passed a bike shop and I was able to find a much more comfortable ride. As a result, my attitude brightened immensely, and it added ten to twenty miles to my typical riding day.

"No alcohol or heavy beef if you're riding the next day. It slows you down too much."

I was eating vegetarian plus fish, so I wasn't very worried.

As they introduced me to the wonders of rational bike travel, I sought to introduce them to the joys of American living. If there is one thing we do to the level of mastery, it's junk food. Our supermarkets are the biggest in the world and are filled with numerous, uniquely American products. Above and beyond inundation with a dozen brands of twenty types of soup, far and away from the hundreds of pounds of meats in long refrigerators which fill the entire back wall of megamarkets, we Americans adore our junk food. We have numerous wonders unique to our country: Fig Newtons, Oreos, Cracker Jacks, and Jiffy Pop popcorn.

Henry was intrigued beyond reason with the silvery circular disk prefilled with popcorn and oil. I made them a batch on my camp stove and the rattle of popping kernels had his six-foot-plus frame nearly shaking with anticipation.

The next night, in the midst of another inundation from above that had sent me screaming for my tent, Henry squatted over his tiny white-gas camping stove. An enormous flash of light and a curse brought Jo and me running back out into the drist (drizzle and mist mixed together).

He'd forgotten to shake it and the hot flame had melted the bottom out of the pan, dumping all the superheated oil onto the stove, creating a fireball and removing bits of his eyebrows.

Jo preferred her from-scratch tapioca pudding, though she did allow the difficulty of determining what was a simmer and what was raindrops attempting to dilute her efforts. Jo's two luxuries were a small cutting board and a good chef's knife. I'm a pretty fair cook, but I could only watch in wonder at the meals she produced from a single burner. Clearly, however, I had unleashed a monster as Henry purchased another Jiffy Pop the next day to go with the Slim Jim beef jerky I'd had him buy.

I was finally getting into shape and easily kept up with their casual southward pace. They continued to offer their cycling wisdom.

"The great advantage to cycling is that if someone smiles at you, you can stop. Tour buses don't do that very well."

"For the best advice on what to see? Ask a local. They always know about the special places that we'd never have found or weren't even in the guidebooks."

"Remember to stop occasionally, or you might as well be riding at home."

I had to reach LA before my plane departed and they were on the see-America-as-you-go plan. So, the next morning I shifted into a higher gear, waved farewell, and pushed south.

Little did I know that a year would pass before I found another cycling companion along the road.

Circles of Cycles

While driving through Oregon a few years before my trip, I'd stopped atop Cape Foulweather, the highest point of the Oregon coast road perched upon the edge of a vertiginous cliff. I'd pulled over at the scenic lookout to watch the sun glitter off a shining sea far below. It's a popular spot and a number of drivers had pulled over to enjoy the fine weather.

As we did so, a lone cyclist pedaled her road bike up the hill. Laden with little more than a water bottle and a windbreaker, those of us standing atop the crag were terribly impressed. She earned a fair round of applause for her amazing achievement.

Now, I climbed Cape Foulweather alone in a driving rain (drrain) on a bicycle weighing over a hundred and twenty pounds. The wind slapped me about on the road as I struggled upward. At the top I stood alone, precisely where the woman had stopped. I stared down the cliff to the breakers so far below. I shot my arms upward in triumph. I had been so impressed by her achievement, and though alone, I had now surpassed it. Perhaps, just perhaps I could survive the rigors of the journey ahead.

Irony Vista Point Number Two happened nearby.

Just before Cape Foulweather, I spent two miserable, drenched nights alone in a campground in Lincoln City, Oregon. My bicycle was having severe mechanical problems, I didn't have the right tools to fix it, and the next bike shop was thirty miles south. Mixed together, the depression, fear, and chilling headwinds were wearing me down badly.

Almost exactly twenty years later, shortly after I became a successful full-time writer, my wife and I would move into a cozy apartment overlooking a lovely lake in this small coastal town. It would take me months to realize that our view, looking out across the narrow neck of the lake, was of that exact same campground.

In twenty years, I had shifted my position perhaps a thousand feet, yet what a difference it made.

First Moment of Fame

My short distances and easy pace were finally beginning to pay off. Seven miles per hour had risen to twelve, nearly twice the distance for the same amount of time. The main trick to long distance riding is not strength or endurance. It's patience. When a bike weighs thirty pounds, you can stomp down on the pedal and go. Do that with a bike weighing over a hundred and you'll blow out a knee, or, if lucky, merely fall over sideways.

The trick is spinning fast in easy gears. Cycle tourists, and racers for that matter, rarely spin their pedals below eighty rpm. Clap your hands a little faster than once per second and you'll have a feel for it, try for about seven times every five seconds—that's the healthiest way to ride.

Now do that for four hours with only a couple short breaks.

So for three weeks, except that insane day on Whidbey Island, I'd spun fast in an easy gear, taken frequent breaks, and sat for unending hours in a tent staked out in a swamp that would be filled with RVs as soon as the rains stopped and the soil drained.

One day I discovered that my target campground was closed for another month and was mostly underwater anyway. I should have stopped and camped in the woods but rather chose to power through twenty more miles to arrive at the next campground near sunset. A small problem, the only store in the area had closed; dinner consisted of my last half cup of rice with a bit of salt. I rode another ten miles in the morning before I found breakfast. Despite that, I had achieved my first athletic breakthrough.

After years of always being the last kid chosen for any team, my body had crossed some threshold. Though my journal entry that night was miserable, wet, and lonely, it also records 74.8 miles for the day rather than the more typical 35-45. It set a new standard that expanded my options. I didn't have to go farther, but now I could if I wanted to.

And my appetite was better. Frankly I could eat like a horse (i.e. constantly). On a typical day I'd eat four meals and at least as many snacks and still my weight was dropping. I later calculated that I needed six-to-ten thousand calories a day to keep my weight stable. (Office life was below twenty-five hundred.)

This meant a lot of shopping; at least once or twice a day I'd hit a grocery store. At a store in Raymond, Washington, a young reporter stood doing exit interviews of shoppers, trying to generate material for his weekly article.

"Where are you headed now that you've done your shopping?" He pinned me with his riveting key question.

"Over there," I pointed to a bench lit by a rare sun break, "To eat lunch."

"And after that?"

"I'm going to LA as the warm-up for a bicycle trip around the world."

His pencil hovered over his clipboard desperately seeking the proper little checkbox in which to plant its blunted nose.

We spent an hour together before he looked at his watch. He leapt to his feet, pumped my hand several times, and sprinted away mumbling about a deadline. Somewhere in the archives of the newspaper of Raymond, Washington, I'm sure that the beginning of my travel resides, and the shoppers had to wait another day for their moment of fame. A version of this would happen a few more times that I'm aware of, but I suspect there are other equally obscure snippets of me scattered around the world in one form or another.

A Day in the Life

As I rode south toward my goal, I fell into a pattern that was to define my life with little variation for the next eighteen months.

- 7:00 up and puttering about with the sunrise.
- 7:30 breakfast, usually yogurt and granola with honey and a mug of hot cocoa if I had the energy to fire up the stove.
- 8:00–9:00 pack up camp, minor bike work (air in tires and such), fill the water bottles.
- 9:00ish sprinkle talcum powder liberally into bike shorts to reduce chafing, then kick the pedal high.
- 11:00 eat first enormous lunch of the day. (Elevenses in Hobbit-speak.)
- 2:00ish buy groceries close to camp. Don't want to carry them outside my belly any farther than I had to. Large snack / second lunch. (I was definitely communing with the hobbits.)

- 3:00–5:00 get off the road (2 earliest, 7:30 latest). Eat another meal.
- 5:00–7:00 goof off, shower, read, walk the beach, see the sights, bigger bike stuff (tighten bolts, true wheels, lube, adjust), set up camp, write journal and letters.
- 7:00–8:00 dinner, such an important thing takes a lot of time.
- 8:30 finally do my yoga. I sought to be kind to my body, but generally did it after dark to diminish my embarrassment as I fumbled about.
- 9:00 go to bed.

Compared with my former lifestyle of sleep from 3:00–6:00 p.m. on the plane after working thirty-seven straight hours in Calgary so that I'd be "fresh" for the evening meeting and midnight installation crew in Houston, I was doing great.

Spa Day for Junior

Junior, my bike—to this day I don't know how he acquired the name—simply showed up in my journal one day as Junior, always written out, never Jr (which I always think should be pronounced *jerr*, not *junior*). And it's not like he was a younger version of anyone, it was just his name.

Anyway, Junior was not doing very well. He'd survived thousands of miles since I'd purchased him to start bicycle commuting three years before. The stresses and strains finally set in seriously at the Oregon-California border.

I ground my way into Brookings, Oregon (that's Or-e-*gun*, not Or-e-*gone* by the way), literally ground my way in.

My bottom bracket (where the pedals attach and which contains a set of bearings that allow your pedals to spin), was filled with road grit and sand. All the protective grease I'd been able to jam in was no longer enough.

I pulled into a sports shop, but it was the mechanic's day off. After a little bit of begging and pleading, the owners agreed to let me use his work area.

In moments I had Junior unloaded and up on the rack. A real bike shop instead of a muddy puddle—I almost chanted a Viking warrior battle with my joy (I might have if I knew any other than the Ho-yo-to-ho chorus of the Valkyries from the Wagner Ring Cycle of operas).

I opened the bottom bracket…and bits and pieces of its innards sprinkled across the concrete floor.

I prowled through the mechanic's parts shelf and stumbled upon something called a sealed bottom bracket. Checking out that the two store clerks were busy up front, I read the directions. This was a new development. It was truly sealed; no greasing, no adjustment, just put it in and away you go.

Almost.

Bottom brackets are more tightly sealed to the bike than anything—mostly because pedals falling off would really suck. I found the two-foot-long adjustable crescent wrench I knew all bike mechanics had for just this moment. But this is the one situation where two feet of leverage still isn't enough. I prowled around the shop once more. Sure enough, in-between the main bench and a rack of drawers rested a long pipe. I slid the four-foot pipe over the two-foot handle of the wrench just as one of the clerks, Julie, surfaced.

"Is your bike okay?"

"Almost," I replied as I swung my weight against the lever. With a distinct pop, the bottom bracket spun loose, the wrench slipped off, and with a loud clatter, everything fell to the floor.

"Great." I stowed the pipe and spun the bracket free.

Julie was white as a sheet. As she sought some way to revoke her invitation to use the shop despite the scattered state of my bike, someone came in with a flat. I grabbed a pair of tire wrenches from their cubby I'd spotted earlier and taught him how to fix it himself next time as I did his tire repair.

Julie staggered away to the front of the store to ring up tire wrenches and a patch kit for the man. She didn't come back into the workshop again until after I was gone.

I slid in the new bracket as sweet as could be and went over every system on the bike: truing wheels, cleaning cogsets, and other long-neglected projects. I actually may have started to sing, I don't recall, but I'm sure I was humming a merry tune (though probably not Wagnerian). I've always found fixing my bike a relaxing thing to do.

After two hours, I left a nice note for the mechanic, paid Julie for the parts, and wandered away. Two days later, fixing a snapped spoke in the near-freezing rain, I sent some thanks to that shop. If you're ever in a little sports store in Brookings, Oregon, go past the rows of wetsuits for surfing and the moisture-wicking jogging shorts, and thank the man at the well-equipped bicycle repair counter in the back for Junior and me.

Lost in the Woods

I roved south along the West Coast, feeling pretty pleased with my pace. The sun put in a brief appearance as I rolled into the California redwoods. It turned the wet roadway into rainbow swirls broken by shadows of the behemoths towering for seeming miles above me.

I lost awareness of the bike, my sore butt, my tired knees, and simply...rode.

The Avenue of the Giants slopes for mile upon mile ever so slightly downhill. A child wizard on his broomstick could have had no lighter feeling than I through that long gliding afternoon. I turned at long last into a hiker / biker site along with the fading sun.

Perhaps "hiker / biker site" requires a bit of explanation. Other than China, the US is probably the most stringent about prohibiting camping except in approved campsites. Stories of forest arrests or awaking at 3:00 a.m. to gun-wielding farmers who want you to move out of the far corner of their thousand-acre pasture, and so on, are rampant among cycle-tourists.

But campgrounds are expensive. A thirty-foot RV and a cyclist often pay the same camping fee. When the daily budget for food is $3–4, a $12 campsite is harsh. (Nowadays the tariff is more like $30!)

Hiker / biker sites are usually in some remote corner, where they couldn't fit an RV anyway, but then were only $2–4 per night. Some are tucked on small clearings in the center of a dense thicket of brush, others are on the back of sand dunes where it is impossible to use a tent stake, and every once in a while they're on some beautiful field right next to the beach or along a quiet meander in a river.

The hiker / biker site in the Avenue of the Giants is several miles from the main campground and its amenities. It has running cold water, a toilet, three old picnic tables, and trees towering two and three hundred feet above the forest floor until you are sure they can scrape the clouds from the sky.

In mid-April it was stone empty.

For three days I sat and relaxed.

For three nights I alternately listened to the rain and watched in wonder the crystalline stars winking between the swaying trees.

I had not seen such a sky in years as the one above the clearing just outside my tent. I was always in the city; even then I'd been too busy to look upward from the rut I was so busy digging. Here, I was miles from the nearest light source. I couldn't see my hand before my face except when I blocked out the stars.

One night I slid out of my little tent and went to relieve myself against a convenient tree. I stood in the cool spring night clad in nothing more than my camp sandals and watched the sky. Leo, the great lion, ruled the sky, shining like the giant question mark he really was. Cygnus, the swan, was poking his beak over the eastern horizon foretelling the arrival of spring to wash clean the blossoming earth. Soon, the transformed Orpheus would once again play the music of summer on his harp, Lyra.

How long I stood thus entranced, slowly turning beneath the heavens, I don't know. They've always affected me that way.

But when I looked back down to Earth, I had absolutely no idea where my tent was.

None.

My skin, heated from the sleeping bag and cooled by the spring night, was now cold. My flashlight was nestled carefully under the edge of the jacket I used as a pillow somewhere within twenty feet of me.

I began a stooping walk in slow circles, swinging my arm in front of me in hopes of finding the tent before a stake found my toes. Other than running into a tree square-on and tripping over innumerable roots, it was a tie. With images of curling up into a huddle and covering myself in a pile of wet pine needles for warmth, I jammed my toe into a stake at the same moment I touched the back of the rain fly.

Dumb, but I do muddle through.

In those few days, as I alternated between the damp picnic table and the pattering of rain upon my tent, I seemed intent upon solving a lifetime of issues with my father—as if in three days I could resolve the last thirty-five years.

One thing I knew for certain: I had never been good enough for him.

"You're smarter than that; you just aren't trying."
"No, that's not how you do it. Do it this way."
"That was a dumb thing to say."

When I was old enough, our time together consisted of doing things together...in silence. I am my father's son. I love to sail. I enjoy building and fixing things. I think that a hike in the woods is time well spent. We simply never found a common ground that included the use of vocal cords.

Then I started building computer networks. The higher I rose, the more we had to discuss.

"I helped design that from 1977. We had a team that spent ten years coming up with VGA." I'd never known that my father's team had overseen computer monitor technology at all. We talked every weekend, sometimes more often if I was on a particularly exciting project.

When I'd quit, I suddenly wasn't good enough again.

"You haven't earned the right to travel. You haven't put in your dues. Sometimes you dislike your job, sometimes I did, but you just have to get through that. I had a family to support."

"I don't."

"You are going to die alone in poverty, and it is going to hurt me terribly to watch you do it. You'll never again have a job better than bagging groceries."

I'd actually hung up the phone on that conversation. When I called my sister for some form of support, she told me she'd received precisely the same barrage from him a decade before —except that she'd only ever be good enough to pump gas. (This trip brought my sister and me quite close together despite continuing to live on opposite sides of the country. It was a real surprise to discover just how much we liked each other as adults.)

I lay there in my tent, staring up at the mighty trees, struggling to convince myself that I had not ruined my life by doing this "stupid, ill-advised trip." On the third day I wrote a long letter, working on it well into the night by the flickering light of my candle lantern.

"I'm seeking to learn who I am and why I'm alone before another 35 years pass me by. I am seeking 'self'."

I remember when I was just entering teenagerhood, my sister, four years older and whole worlds wiser, called a "family meeting" to talk about how we lived together. Dad shut down the conversation from the get-go with "I gave up introspection thirty years ago and never missed it." My sister walked away, and I went to the dictionary. Yup, introspection meant what I thought it did. Dad was just living his life; how could I explain that I was trying to *understand* it?

I left at sunrise the next day, apparently freed of the angst that had kept me motionless in the tall redwoods for three days. I rode like a demon until I reached the nearest mailbox. I wanted to mail it before I tore it up or it burned my fingers. For the first time I had told Dad how much I feared him and how much I respected him.

How many thousand miles would pass before I understood him? Would he ever understand me? For that matter, would I?

Let the Sun Shine In

Now one of my pet peeves is stereotypes. I don't know why, it just is. I've despised them as long as I can recall. My first corporate job after working for five years in theater, managing a fast-food fish house, selling stereo equipment, and rebuilding an old sailboat, was as a paralegal.

"I need every document in this case that Paul H. was a party to. I need it in triplicate for a deposition that I forgot about. It starts in forty-five minutes."

"I need the original paperwork of each cost estimate on this project as well as a memo of some sort from that time that chronicles these as the only proper estimates."

"Lose this document without destroying it."

What can I say? It was challenging. It was ugly. I removed myself from the legal aspects quickly and focused on their first computer systems instead.

Lawyers are one of the great American stereotypes and, I'm glad to say, that for the most part it is not true. A tad bit humorless perhaps but otherwise few were overtly offensive.

This day's irritating stereotype turned out to be most agreeable—the California coast.

I rolled away from the high hills and left the Avenue of the Giants behind.

I descended the long rise of the Siskiyou Mountains down to the California coast in grand sweeping runs with light traffic and smooth roads.

The headwind, which had often added hours to my day for four weeks, switched to a strong tailwind. The sun, which had shone but briefly three times in as many weeks, blazed forth drying my laundry. As the temperature rose, it forced me to strip layer after layer until I stood in just bike shorts and shirt for only the second time on the road, feeling more naked than when lost in the trees.

A few days later I camped at Half Moon Bay Beach. I'd ridden well, eaten a good meal, and done my yoga. My first sunset in far too long shimmered off the great expanse of the Pacific, stretching unbroken for ten thousand miles between here and my next destination.

Yet bliss and contentment has its price.

My next destination: Japan. By now I should have some of the language under my belt. I couldn't even say "please" or "thank you" yet. I hadn't read anything in the guidebook that I'd toted so many long, weary miles. My friends were now over a thousand miles behind me. All the worries and fears that had been kept at bay by my struggles to get in shape and survive riding day in and day out in the cold rain raised their shaggy heads from the mire in search of prey.

"Ride through it," I told myself. "Ride through it," I repeated as I crawled into my tent and listened to the roar of the generator on an RV parked too close to my tent.

"Ride through it."

Crossing the Golden Gate Bridge, California

Up One Side and Down the Other

I did cheer up as I worked my way down the California coast. Stereotype or no, it is a beautiful area washed in the sun.

The road rises and falls past headland after headland,

grinding up one side and sliding down the other in an exhilarating burst of speed. The downhill speed that is nursed and coaxed for a good punch into the next climb. Oregon is like that, but no rollercoaster ride is a patch on the ups and downs of the California coast. Coastal 101 is a continuous challenge for hundreds of miles.

Still, the beauty (and lack of rain) made it hard to be grumpy. Even fixing flat tires, punctured by smashed beer bottles along the road, was not an arduous task when my fingers were warm. Every flat but two I had on the entire trip were due to low-life, pond-scum, American dweebs smashing their beer bottles out their car windows. Foreign cyclists are shocked at the huge quantity of glass they must traverse along North American roads.

"At first I thought it was just a glittery rock you chaps set in your paving. After someone winged a bottle right at me, I figured it out. Strange customs you have here."

Strange indeed as I pulled out yet another bit of glass that had managed to evade my tire's Kevlar-banding, and patched another tube.

I arrived in a campground near San Francisco at the same time as a weekend rider. We set our tents side by side and looked at the odd juxtaposition of our bikes. He had one pair of lightly laden bags; my four bags were crammed to the gills. His bike had been state of the art twenty years ago, mine was still fairly exceptional. Five speeds versus twenty-one. Sticky side caliper brakes versus center-pull mountain brakes. Wire baskets versus waterproof panniers.

He talked about touring years before and that the best thing he did for keeping limber was this old yoga book. I delivered the coup de grace when I unearthed the same teach-yourself book with a newer printing date, *Richard Hittleman's Yoga*. We talked late into the night of traveling as discovery versus as running away.

Stopping mid-story, he turned to look me square in the eyes. His narrowed eyes would brook no evasions.

I suddenly thought back to my friend George and his question, "Why are you doing this to yourself?"

Please, I thought as loudly as possible, *not another life-changing imponderable.*

He aimed a long finger at Junior. "All those fancy fittings you have there. Don't help you climb the hills one bit better than me, do they?"

Too relieved to speak, I shook my head sadly. "Not one bit."

The Elusive Art of Not Planning

LA was to be my last stop on American soil for four years if my wildly vague and indefinite plan had any meaning at all.

I don't plan much.

Honest.

Okay, I'm lying through my bicycle chain.

A decade before, I'd taken a six-week road trip to introduce my sister to the Southwest. I'd been there a number of times and had completed an itinerary that didn't miss any of the "good bits." It took three full days before she ripped the itinerary out of my hands and tore it into a thousand little shreds. She then threw it on the campfire for good measure. Oddly enough, the side trips and detours that began the next day turned out to be great fun.

So, with that lesson firmly in mind, I did my best to keep my inner planner in line. I allowed broad strokes, but no details. Further, I didn't write it down until this moment.

Matt's Five-Continent, Forty-Country, Twenty-Language, Four-Year, Non-Plan.

(After all, every insane plan needs a comprehensive and descriptive title, right?)

- Seattle to LA for warmup / shakedown.
- Three months in Japan. I'd read both good and bad reviews of this society and was curious to see it for myself. Also, all of the cycling books I'd ever read had not included Japan. I wondered why. (I'd find out soon enough.)
- Six weeks in Vietnam. Vietnam wasn't open to the US yet in 1993, but a former GI, who used to go AWOL just to hitchhike up and down the coast because he loved the country so much, had promised to join me for a ride from Hanoi to former Saigon.
- South Sea Islands, maybe by freighter.
- Cross the Australian Outback.
- Dive the Great Barrier Reef (never been diving before).
- Hitch a sailboat ride to New Zealand for the spring, October through December.
- Catch another sailboat back to Sydney and ride across the south of Australia to Perth.
- Up through Indonesia, Thailand, Burma.
- India, from the south up into the north and finally do some trekking in Nepal. Perhaps some yoga or meditation courses while I was there.
- I hadn't planned on Africa at first but heard some fantastic things about the road from Nairobi to Zimbabwe. (I'd been told that there was a good chance the fighting in Zimbabwe would be over by the time I got there.)
- Israel, Turkey, Greece, Italy, up through Switzerland, Austria, Germany, perhaps the Nordic countries,

back down through the UK, especially Scotland and Ireland, and finally France. I planned to take a month off here and there, perhaps get an apartment and work for three months to get into some culture or other.
- Fly into Halifax and ride home across the US.
- Or, perhaps, ship the bike home and take the Trans-Siberian rail back across Russia to Japan and finally return home via more South Sea Islands.

Or something like that.

At the moment I was headed for LA, and, you can bet, I was right on my "non-existent" schedule. Type A personalities don't give in easily.

Risks on the Road

I arrived at a friend's house ignominiously.

The ground-out bottom-bracket in Oregon had only been a foretaste—I rode the last thirty miles in the back of a pickup truck with a shattered rear rim and a broken cogset (that's all those gears in the middle of the rear wheel). Four years of year-round bike commuting, and the first eighteen hundred miles of the tour were just too much for poor Junior.

Rudy, a great bike mechanic, built up new wheels, discussed spares, and taught me a few cool maintenance tricks I hadn't known. It's guys like that who take the pain out of spending $500 on bike parts.

A word about Junior. I know, it's still weird that he was named, but he was and there was nothing I could do about it. Besides, it seemed rude to not address my companion properly. When I wasn't riding him, I was either tending to him or making sure he was safe. Even when riding with large groups, you ride alone. It is very rarely safe to ride side by side due to passing cars. Sure, cyclists meet at rest stops and sit around huge piles of spaghetti or pizza in the evenings, but cycling is at heart a solo activity. Cycle-touring is far more so.

Local cyclists are moving much faster and appear like flies, sidling up just long enough to be annoying. "Where are you going? Where are you from? Isn't that bike heavy?" And then they flit off back where they came from, often before you can answer.

Riding with other touring cyclists? The ones who are strong on the hills, not me, pull ahead. You might catch up on the big descents if you're crazy, yes me, but probably not. You catch up at lunch, but they've already been there, eaten that, and cooled down for half an hour, so they roll out shortly after you arrive.

So, I sit and spin, hour after hour, alone down the roadside, watching the world and waving at the little kids who are always filled with wonder when such a bizarre creature as a fully loaded touring bike moseys by.

Sometimes I'd ask questions as I rolled along and my sole companion, Junior, would answer back. Well, not really. I wasn't that far gone. But it was nice to pretend. And my anthropomorphism had a useful side benefit. It was my job to take care of my companion. I could ignore a mere bike, but Junior would complain.

My brake is rubbing on the left rear, you know.

"Yeah, I noticed that." I'd pour my soup into a thermal mug to keep it warm and grab a spoke wrench. Little twists and tweaks in between sips of steaming hot dinner is not a bad way to spend an evening.

As to what Junior is, beyond a very well-equipped Raleigh Peak Mountain Bike, I won't burden you with the details—I put them in an appendix along with a lot of other practical tips about cycle touring for the avid cyclist.

Suffice to say that by the time I reached LA, we'd had one hell of a shakedown cruise. I was fit and Junior, after some rather expensive professional pampering, was as well. We'd traveled 1,844 miles over roads, mostly wet, with and without shoulders (Oregon generally has a foot or two outside the white line, California rarely has more than three inches). The paths we'd taken had been both choked with motorists and empty but for us. Cities, towns, rivers, and beaches had slid by, some remarkable, some not.

Some places I will always remember. I can still taste the cheese curds of the Tillamook, Oregon, cheese factory, tangy and almost bitter, yet with a sweet aftertaste. The towering majesty of the redwoods. The deep rich oak and dry grass smell of the central California hills, and the long, smooth bike trails of southern California cluttered with the ringing bells of tricycles and baby joggers.

I'd only been driven off the road once. While descending Big Sur, an RV simply had to pass me because I was only going 45 mph (72 kmph) and the traffic ahead was going perhaps 48 (77). He'd left his stairs folded out to the side and I'd spotted them only moments before they tried to remove my ankle.

I shot off the road into the deep runnels of a washed-out ditch.

The several-hundred-foot drop was close, far too close to only be protected by a knee-high rock wall. When I finally struggled to a stop only a breath from pitching down into the sea, I sat for half an hour before the shakes abated sufficiently for me to continue my descent.

Junior parked where I almost took a flying lesson off Big Sur, California

But sometimes there is justice. At the bottom of the descent, I pulled off at the first beachside turnout. There, quietly eating lunch, was the culprit.

I was kind.

I was pleasant.

I inquired, in the nicest of tones, if he would prefer I sued him for assault with a deadly weapon or for attempted homicide. I was more than happy to let him choose which.

If he hadn't been so apologetic, I might have really got going, but his chagrin convinced me that he will be more cautious in the future. If not for some cyclist's sake, then to avoid his wife's sharp disapproval at his need to pass me in the first place—an act she'd already berated him soundly for prior to my arrival and was glad to reiterate.

In addition to Big Sur, I'd climbed two and a half times the height of Everest. My cycle computer had an altimeter on it and I had ground my way up, and flown down, 72,500 feet (13.7 miles). I had just voyaged from north to south through the fourth largest country in the world and I was terrified of what lay ahead.

I phoned my friend Mac. "What am I doing out here?"

"How should I know? I just suggested you sell the house."

"Yeah! And look at what that started."

"I think you're doing the right thing, Matt, but I certainly can't know why you're doing it."

I went for a final walk along the beach. The gentle westerly breeze tore long streams of tears from my eyes. I was leaving for Japan in eight hours and I've rarely been so scared in my life; nearly dying on Big Sur was trivial by comparison.

US & Total to Date: 54 days / 1,844 miles (2,967 km)
Elevation Climbed to Date: 13.7 miles (22 km)

2

JAPAN

21 MAY 1993 – 20 JULY 1993

Japanese: *Watashi to jitensha wa sikai ryoku-sumasu.*
English: *I and my bicycle (personified) are (ever so politely) traveling around the world together.*
Translation: *OMG! I have no idea what I'm doing!*

Compression and a Crossroad

Load up the night before.
Up at 3:30 a.m.
Out the door in Malibu ever so quietly at 3:50 a.m. so as not to wake my host.

Scoot through the dark on a wide, paved bike path that runs south for mile after mile of lovely beach—and take a wild-ass guess where to turn eastward.

Somewhere on the far side of LA lies LAX airport. I hit it fairly accurately, a fair wind indeed. However, all the freeways in the entire state seem to converge on this one spot—none of which allows bicycles.

To approach the airport, I entered a labyrinth of streetlit cargo roads, rolling past emergency vehicles and airplane service hangars. Actinic lights washed over the blood-red of the No Smoking signs around the fuel truck loading station. Containers filled with FedEx packages were hurried along by crews sweating in the predawn light.

Not so long ago those might have been *my* corporate rush freight.

Never fast enough.

Overnight is too slow.

Use counter-to-counter with messenger delivery.

Rush. Rush. Rush.

Yet, as I pulled away from those containers of little white boxes and their headlong flight in a thousand directions, I missed my job. For perhaps the first time in the nine months since I'd burned out and walked away, I missed it. Briefly, but nonetheless a slight ache pulled across my shoulders.

I'd been in the thick of it. Building corporate systems for Fortune 100s. Half partner in one of those lean, mean consulting firms that were the true herald of the dot.coms by a decade. In 1986 I'd built the largest PC network in Seattle other than Microsoft (our small law firm and Weyerhaeuser were neck and neck for second—frequently in touch when we had problems). People were flying in from around the country to see it.

After a dozen years at the bleeding edge of IT, I thought nothing of committing to delivering million-dollar projects and reengineering major systems I'd never even seen before. And that was before I joined the small consulting firm.

We were important and we knew it.

We were good and we knew it.

And pride cometh before the fall.

"The fall" was just beginning in several ways. I'd left job, business, and home thousands of miles behind. Soon I'd be on another continent. The one thing I had left to face was…myself.

Little did I know *that* would be the hardest challenge of them all.

I arrived at the LAX terminal at 4:30 a.m. Oops! That had been way too easy. The counter didn't even open for two hours.

This left me time to repack different ways and play with the luggage scales, something I've always wanted to do. For the first time on my journey, I weighed everything. Junior scaled in at a svelte thirty-three pounds, a couple lighter than I thought since he had front and rear racks, three water bottle carriers, heavily modified handlebars, and a mounted bicycle tire pump. (This was also in the pre-titanium era).

The rest of my gear was over *ninety* pounds? I weighed it on three separate scales because I could scarcely credit it. I'd been pushing a hundred and twenty pounds (fifty-five kilos) up and down the steep coastal roads from Seattle to LA for six weeks and eighteen hundred miles. And that *didn't* include food and drinking water. That didn't even count the days I must have had pounds of road mud and rainwater permeating every nook and cranny of me and my gear. I suddenly felt tired just remembering all the hills I'd climbed.

I stuffed everything I could into a small backpack and a fanny pack. I was still over weight limits and could barely stand when I shouldered the load. But a pleasant smile and a bit of cajoling the check-in clerk (this was all in the pre-TSA era), and I was ready for my 8:30 departure to a new country.

Of course, the universe decided to play a joke on me as it so often does. I had a great travel agent. If there was a cheap way to travel, she could find it. So, Japan was to be via Vancouver, Canada.

LA to Vancouver.

Crap!

I'd just ridden from Seattle to LA. Sure enough, the road and the coast spun along beneath us as we retraced in hours what had taken me so many weeks of effort. I dreaded our passage over Seattle. Thankfully some shred of kindness remained in my psyche—I managed to sleep for fifteen minutes of those forty-eight hours from LA to a Japanese ferry boat...the fifteen minutes in which we passed over Seattle.

After a little switching about in Vancouver, I was on the plane to Japan.

There was another joke awaiting me, but this one I had perpetrated upon my own head. I knew nothing about the Japanese culture. I figured that the amount *Shōgun* had to teach me about modern-day Japan, or Stephen Sondheim's *Pacific Overtures,* was irrelevant at best and rude besides. Now I was on a wide-body jet over the middle of the Pacific.

As soon as the door was closed, the announcements switched to Japanese first, lightly accented Canadian-English second. Other than the Air Canada crew, I'm fairly sure that I was the only person on board who wasn't Japanese. The two businessmen in the seats next to me spoke no English and I still spoke none of their language. Well, for six weeks of intended study, I actually had managed to force three words and one phrase into my head: yes, no, please, and "*Ferī Hokkaido?*"

I was in trouble. But rather than get mad at myself, as I would have even a few months ago, I pulled out my journal and began listing all of the things I'd been doing.

- Walking away from my career.
- Finishing and selling my dream house and most of my worldly possessions.
- Trimming, a bit, those mighty hawser cables that tied me to my father's whim.
- Riding 1,800 miles on a bicycle.
- Learning all the tricks to bike camping, weeks and weeks of eating off a cookstove, bike repair, and all the rest of it.
- Getting truly fit for perhaps the first time in my life.

Okay, so I'd been busy. I inspected the odd seaweed soup they'd provided, *miso* according to my guidebook. At least that seemed a reasonable guess.

I inspected the oddly pungent and, well, rotting-low-tide-like liquid, and listened to the three or four hundred Japanese voices mingling with the aching of my heart for home.

Then the plane began to shrink.

I knew what was happening.

I had a friend tell me once of her agonizing training as she adapted herself to Seattle's ferry boats. She wanted to attend a wedding on one of the area's many islands but was terrified of water. She'd told me what it felt like, though I'd found it hard to imagine, as she'd forced herself to take more and more risks until she could make the crossing.

Now I could imagine it clearly.

As the DC-10, rigged with eleven or twelve seats across, flew higher and higher, it felt like the pressure was acting wrong and rather than bursting a seam, the fuselage was crushing down to a long thin tube. The men next to me had to move into my lap to avoid the pressure of those being shoved at them from across the aisle as the plane compressed.

My journal records the sweat dripping out of my beard and onto my soaked shirt. Cold dampness chilled my palms as I wiped them time and again on my pant legs. If there'd been room, I would have escaped to the bathroom; but we were all pressed in so close together that I couldn't move.

The pocket with the barf bag was beneath a phrase book that would burn my fingers should I attempt to extract it from where it was stowed.

A tray of sushi was somehow slid between myself and the seatback before me, crushing me from in front.

The English language soundtrack to the in-flight movie was broken.

I slept not a wink in twelve hours of flying.

I writhed in my misery for minutes.

Maybe hours.

I don't know.

I was going to land in Tokyo and walk up to the nearest ticket agent and say, "America, today, please." Bracing myself, I scorched my fingers on the searing heat of the phrase book to look up the correct words. "*America, kyō, dōzo.*" These, of all the words, I found easy to remember. I'd just ride home from wherever I landed and be done with this whole mess.

I didn't care where. I could always ride back home from wherever I landed.

America, kyō, dōzo.

It was all that mattered.

When the plane did finally return to land, I shouldered my load and trudged toward customs. At 5'7" tall, I towered over most of the crowd. I glanced past the glass wall herding us toward customs. A sign flashed on and people began to queue up with their tickets at a gate beyond the glass. "Seattle, 45 minutes." There was probably just enough time to get Junior, pass through customs and ticketing, and climb back aboard. I could be home in 13 hours.

I squared my shoulders—and turned away. I felt powerful to be able to walk away from that sign.

Me and Indiana Jones.

I was on the adventure.

I was going to see Japan now that I'd come all this way.

Walking away from that sign may well be the hardest thing I've ever done in my life.

It Takes a Village

An hour later I stood in the center of Narita Airport's main terminal. Circled up like wagons guarding the women and children, or gawkers observing the wreckage of a massively fatal accident, a large crowd had gathered with Junior at the center, lying on his side. (I'd removed the kickstand long ago to save the seven ounces of weight.)

"Can't put you on the subway with that." The helpful lady from the travel center took back the ticket she'd sold me and refunded my yen.

"You could ride," suggested the manager of the main terminal.

"I haven't slept in nearly forty hours, I think, and I'm not up to riding a hundred kilometers in the dark to Tokyo." With the aid of the travel center clerk, I'd booked a ferry to Hokkaido Island, her fluent English negating my one good phrase, "*Ferī Hokkaido?*" The last rays of the deep orange sunset slammed through the glass wall of the terminal and lit Junior in a fiery glow. He lay like a Wagnerian hero in his puddle of bloody sunlight. How to get him to the ferry?

"You could take a cab and we'd ship the bicycle along after you," offered the head of taxicab control for all Narita. "Of course, the cab fare from here would be about fourteen thousand yen." I've always been good with numbers, but I didn't trust the answer of a hundred and sixty US until I'd done the math several times.

"I can't wait for my bike to follow. The ferry goes at midnight."

"How about a bus?" The combined managers of the travel center, the taxis, the subway system, and the airport all looked at the man with the broom in surprise.

Five hundred yen (about six dollars) and three minutes later, the janitor helped me load Junior onto a bus and I was headed to the bus station in the heart of Tokyo.

The light trickled out of the sky as we shot toward one of the world's largest cities. I'd been assured that since they were so much closer to the ferry terminal, fifteen kilometers or so (about ten miles), that the travel center there could help me.

Eight thirty at night is half an hour *after* the travel center closed. Once again, I became the only English speaker, the building rapidly emptying with the end of day.

"Ferī Hokkaido?" sounded my plaintive call with an ever-increasing echo. Bus drivers, pedestrians, travelers all shrug and shake their heads and watch me lug a fully loaded Junior toward the next victim.

"Ferī Hokkaido?"

A taxi driver took pity on me. Over the next twenty minutes or so, he placed several calls and determined there were two ferry terminals, but he didn't know which I needed. I clutched in my hand the subway map provided back at Narita. The agent had circled the stop at which I was supposed to exit. The driver cried in joy and dragged me over to a massive street map on the wall. He pointed proudly at a ferry dock and then poked his finger near what must have been a subway station. I compared the three Japanese characters on the map with the ones on my crumpled guide. They matched.

There was much joy. Several people came over and joined in the general shaking of hands. With a sigh of relief, I indicated that I wanted the driver to take Junior and me there in his taxi.

He was dumbfounded.

I was dumbfounded. Apparently, he'd gone to all this trouble *merely to help*. Such kindness was such a surprise that I wonder what he made of the expression on my face. I had assumed he was doing it just so he could scalp me with a horrendous taxi fare.

Fifteen minutes and fifty dollars later (well, not a horrendous fare by Japanese standards), a massive white ship loomed out of the darkness ahead. Within moments I was ticketed and ushered aboard into the cavernous interior of the great craft.

I struggled to remain awake for the fifteen minutes it took to locate the dormitory (I couldn't read any of the signs): two dozen tatami mats along either side of an otherwise barren metal room. A few more moments in the bathroom and then I passed out for thirty hours.

I was awake for less than six hours of the two-day journey. A university student befriended me and guided me to meals and a shower. He practiced his English and aided me in my pursuit of basic Japanese.

"Why you go Hokkaido?"

"I read a book about a man who walked from Cape Sōya in the north to Cape Sata in the south."

"No. No. Why Hokkaido now? Still winter there."

It was May. But when I checked my world map, I saw that northern Japan resides as far north as the top of Nova Scotia. I checked my world weather guide...it didn't bode well.

"That why boat empty. No persons go now except poor students like me and workers."

I sighed and decided to sleep rather than vainly attempt to bolster my weak Japanese. I might have chosen differently if I'd known it was the last time I was to speak English for almost a month.

A Smizzle of Kindness

I finally landed in a scene I knew only too well. The low gray overcast released a strong mizzle (a "smizzle?"), the kind that could stay for days or even weeks. Five thirty a.m. and cold rain dripped through the air holes in my helmet. I had no idea what to do next.

I rolled into a gas station and huddled in a corner of the immaculate waiting room. The three attendants sat on the far side of the room in a small cluster, carefully not looking my way; not even speaking of me as that would probably be considered rude.

I spent that time piecing together a few key sentences from my phrasebook and carefully recording them on a piece of paper by writing in between the damp spots so my pen would work.

When I'd done what I could, I approached the group. Leaping to their feet, they bowed. I bowed back and, with a great show of smiles, they huddled around to see what I had wrought.

In short order I had a reservation at a hostel just thirty miles, er, fifty kilometers away, a cup of tea, a thousand yen phone card that one man insisted on gifting to me though I tried to pay him, and a carefully hand-drawn map showing that I should follow the coast road. I checked. The fact that it was the only road on the map I'd purchased in LA was beside the point. Their map painstakingly echoed the curves of the shore road and marked the various forests and horse pastures I'd be passing. Their kindness made me feel I was, indeed, on the right road.

As I rolled back out into the wet, they all rushed out after me and stood waving goodbye as if it were a sunny day and not smizzling at all. I tried to imagine such a scene in the US, but failed.

Go North Young Man

As I rode north along the seaboard of Japan's northernmost island in the rains of May and early June, I had my first opportunity to observe a truly foreign culture. I'd been to Austria and Germany with a high school German language class. I'd been to Sweden and England as part of a business trip, to New Zealand on a bicycle for three weeks, and traveled all over the US and Canada. But this was something else.

For my first two days, I had a blinding headache. Studying my pocket medical guide revealed nothing. That night in camp

I strained to read a book I'd picked up in LA, Dr. R.S. Argarwal's book on eyesight retraining. (I had hopes of training myself out of reading glasses. It worked...until two years later when I sat back down in front of a computer screen for eight hours a day.) He pointed out that attempts to focus on unfamiliar shapes could be incredibly tiring to the eyes.

A typically informative road sign. I ran into this problem a lot on my trip.

Hokkaido has no English tourist signs like the ones I'd seen out the bus window on my ride into Tokyo. Here everything was in Kanji, Japanese writing. My eyes throbbed from focusing on sign after sign that I couldn't read. The headaches were gone the next day when I gave up the curiously shaped characters as not interpretable and focused upon people and landscapes instead.

Road signs were of little use anyway. First, I'd look at some road sign. Then I'd find the matching characters on my map which happened to be all in Kanji—often by sheer luck, sometimes with the help of a passerby. I would then match the shape of the roads to the English-language map I'd purchased in LA. Then I'd know I was in Hiroo or Ombetsu, not that such knowledge was terribly illuminating.

Apparently, it requires a completed high school education

to read a Japanese newspaper. A Norwegian who'd taught English to Japanese students for three years told me that he could tell me that one word on the sign was "bridge," not that it wasn't obvious from the span before us, but that he was wholly unable to interpret the other part of the name after only three years of daily tutoring, study, and cultural immersion.

All this was further complicated as I began to unravel what little details I could. Kanji can be written left to right (typical on maps), top to bottom (it is the same set of ideograms the Chinese use, mostly) or right to left (typical on most road signs). Once I had solved that last bit of detective work, navigation by matching symbols became significantly easier, almost up to marginally possible.

Thankfully, many of their signs are diagrammatic, picture words. A circle with steam rising from its center is a public bath or a hot spring (*furo* or *onsen*). A very important sign indeed.

There are two entrances: men's and women's. I was never able to interpret the ideograms, so I'd simply wait for someone else to enter first.

Drop all clothes and valuables in a basket, no need to worry. Except in perhaps the largest cities, no Japanese would be so rude as to steal something. Walk naked into a room with a dozen or so strangers. Grab a little stool, a small bucket, a bar of soap, and sit down next to one of the pools of steaming water. Do not dip the soap in the water. Ladle out a bucketful, wet the soap in there, and lather yourself up.

When all set, ladle scoop after scoop of scalding water over your head and attempt to remain breathing as your skin is burned off, sluices onto the tile floor, and trickles down the drain. Soon you have seared all the soap off every crevice of your body. My Caucasian skin was now a charming shade of cherry-red despite my tan—a fact which always elicited jokes in a language I didn't understand.

Climb into the pool!

No, really. This is not some mild American hot tub that little kids may not like but adults do. This is as physically painful as entering the icy waters of home.

A kindly man looked upon me in pity. As I struggled at the treacherous moment beyond which there is no return, he exhaled a loud, sighing, "Ahhh!"

When I tentatively continued my descent, he shook his head. He rose up until he was in the same position as me and then he settled back into the water releasing his loud, "Ahhh!" once more.

"Ahhh!" I tried to keep the panic out of my tone as I entered the scalding fluid. Another "Ahhh!" as I settled in up to my neck and he smiled heartily. All around the pool, I received nods of "Job well done." The water was so hot that the "Ahhh!" was necessary even for the hardiest Japanese.

I waited until someone else got out of the pool first, some ten minutes, before attempting to exit myself. Even the heartiest *onsen'er* will sit for a while on the cool tile edge before attempting to stand. Any attempt to stand immediately is met with a very abrupt lie-down on the cool tile floor.

American hot tubs are regulated very carefully to 103.5°F (39.7°C) because above 104° (40°C), your body's enzymes start breaking down—think 104-degree fevers and sudden trips to the emergency room. Japanese *onsen* have no such limitations. You have to cool down before you're likely to function again.

Restaurants, thankfully, were easy to navigate. There is no menu. All the meals are already made and on display, in near-perfect plastic replica. Point to the seared prawns in a bowl of udon noodles and soon after they would arrive arranged in precisely the same way as the display model. Whether life was imitating plastic or vice versa, I'm not sure I wanted to know.

Another great food shock was the plethora of Circle Ks and 7-Elevens dotting the countryside. I wanted to avoid all Americana on my trip and get to know each country, but after several days of speaking no English to anyone and eating foods I didn't recognize, I broke down and headed in. I needn't have worried about spoiling my resolve.

Nothing remotely familiar existed beyond the sign over the door. The scoured shining-white store was stocked with more kinds of instant noodles than I'd known existed. These were no Ramen noodles with a flavor packet. Some had three and four little packets to be added at different stages: flavors, dried vegetables, dehydrated meats, and so on. There were odd snacks like Pocky Sticks (little chocolate-covered crunchy sticks that have since come to America). Pocari Sweat, a sports drink that tastes even worse than its name. Fresh-made sushi was available where we would buy a hot dog.

At the counter, every item was always wrapped in paper by the clerk, even the Ramen, and then slid into its own plastic bag. Multiple items were bagged separately and then placed together in a larger one. It was useless to say that I didn't want the bags, that I hated killing all those "plastic trees." At long last I understood that I was the one being rude in my attempts not to accept what it was their duty to provide.

Of course, if I wanted to avoid the bags, I only had to roll up to one of the ubiquitous vending machines. They were everywhere.

Once, in a rather remote region of northern Hokkaido, I climbed a long, winding hill. A power line followed up this tiresome road as I weaved my way toward a windswept pass. Not far from the top, the power line, which had kept me company for the last half dozen kilometers, turned aside into a carefully mown field. In the center of the field, at the terminus of the power line, was a Coke machine.

And these machines didn't sell just Coke. As I didn't enter any big cities, I only saw a limited display of what these "countryside" and "small town" machines had to offer.

Coke, of course, offered in cans and bottles, up to two liters.

They also sold blazingly hot coffee in small tin cans that looked impossible to hold without third-degree burns. Ice cream (well frozen), umbrellas, raincoats, hot and cold meals, porn videos, the latest graphic novels (Japanese adult comic books—that we would definitely also call porn), and, of course, cigarettes, beer, saké, gin, and vodka.

Children typically weren't allowed to smoke (although 80% of the men in the country do). At least not, one man told me, until they could reach the coin slots on their own.

The odd thing about Japan, which no one who's been exclusively to the cities will believe, is that Japan is the dirtiest country I've ever been to, with the possible exception of India. The roads are clean swept, but off the side are old refrigerators, computers, washing machines, hundreds of Styrofoam meal boxes with bamboo chopsticks, and tens of thousands of small plastic 7-Eleven and Circle K bags. For my entire journey, it never failed to amaze me when a Japanese family would rise and walk away from a beach picnic and simply leave all the trash behind. The nearby trash can empty except for my own bento box and wooden chopsticks.

When I descended out of the Japanese Alps, I was startled by the dense brown layer of smog. Outside the cities, everyone burns their own garbage including paper, plastic, and worse. Billowing black clouds of smoke tower like some insane Godzilla above the old flaming car tires from which he was born.

I suppose it is no wonder the Japanese Cycling Federation recommended (at least in 1993) no more than four hours per day of riding. I began to wear my green paisley bandana as a Western-cowboy-bandit kerchief. Each night it was coated in black and my goggles were so thick with the grease spumed out of the ancient diesel trucks that I could barely get them clean with soap and water.

The cars, in sharp contrast, were all very new. Ramshackle

huts in tiny fishing villages each had their own white Toyota or Nissan. A car mechanic explained it to me in sign language over dinner one night.

He showed me a copy of the Silver Book, much like the American Blue Book. Within five years, every single car, whether a cheap sedan or a $50,000 top-of-the-line model, has a listed value of $0. After year five, cars are subject to rapidly *increasing* taxes and severe mechanical testing. It rapidly becomes much cheaper to purchase a new car and keep feeding their economy than to maintain an old one. The mechanic showed me an old, immaculate 1983 Honda Civic he kept under a tarpaulin. He was clearly proud of being able to afford this ten-year-old car and its upkeep.

I reached the northernmost point of Japan. Beyond the slashing rain inundating Sōya Misaki (Cape Sōya) lay the Kuril Islans the outermost reaches of Siberia (though the Japanese also claim these islands, the Russians are in possession of them). I had reached the top of Japan, the northernmost point of my journey. From this slashain- (slashing rain) battered cape, I was turning south and beginning the road that Alan Booth had walked years before, setting my path.

Cape Sōya, northernmost point. Twenty-five mph (40 kmph) winds and 38° F (3° C) in heavy rain. So glad to be turning south.

The Mother Tongue

But all this is not what defines a country. I hadn't traveled to see the great wonders of the world, they're in the big cities—which I fear look a bit too alike. No, my journey was to meet the people. And Japan's people never ceased to startle me.

I slogged south from the inundation streaming out of the Sea of Japan to the Wakkanai Youth Hostel and settled in to rest for two nights and the day between.

Joy of joy, my dinner companion, the first Western person I'd seen in weeks, spoke a heavily French-accented English. It was an unimaginable pleasure to speak and be at least partially understood.

I slept, I ate, and I watched the rain from the dry side of the glass. Sitting on my narrow bunk, Junior dry and well-oiled against the foot of the bed, I was somehow home. Well, not home—less restless perhaps. Maybe, even for a moment, content.

The final morning, I suited up...yet couldn't cross the threshold. I stood within the safety of the swinging glass door seeking deep inside me the strength to venture once more into the cold slashain. No, it hadn't abated even once in the last three days. But I wasn't hesitating because of the weather. It was the road ahead, that vast unknown and unknowable path I had somehow, to myself and all my friends, committed to.

At long last the desk clerk, who had politely not intruded on my lengthy contemplation, could no longer restrain himself.

"*Doko desu ka?*" (Where do you go?)

On my last day in LA I had stumbled upon a travel store. They had a Tyvek windbreaker upon which was printed a map of the world. (I had no idea how many times I'd do this over the course of my journey.) I pulled this out of my pack and traced my route with my finger. I indicated my past route by pointing behind me. I then pointed out the door and traced a less sure path, punctuating my tracery with shrugs and uncertain waves of the hand.

He leapt to his feet.

"Bigga Dleam-ah!" He danced a little step around me. "Bigga Dleam-ah!"

It took me a while to realize he was speaking English.

"*Hai.* Crazy dream. *Watashi* (I) crazy."

"No! No!" he shook his head emphatically. "No clazy! Bigga Dleam-ah!" He ran behind his desk and returned with an envelope bearing the youth hostel's logo. With a very low and formal bow, he offered me the gift cradled in both his hands. I'd read that it was rude to open a gift in front of the giver—what if I didn't like it?

It is also very rude not to give something in return. All I had to offer was a traveler's business card I'd made before leaving. My name, mail drop, and the word "traveler," with a small bicycle in one corner and a globe in the other. I offered it with all the ceremony I could muster, and he was either very polite or truly very pleased. I found that this was always a success in Japan, honoring someone with the gift of a name and address.

I slid the envelope into a back pocket of my jersey, zipped up, and ventured out into the unabated storm. Once again, a kind host stood in the driving rain until I was out of sight despite his light shirt and sandals.

Two days later I had ridden out of the rain, at least for the moment, and into high winds. They howled and tore at me. Any smells that might have been gathered up as they rolled from the Arctic over Siberia and the Sea of Japan were lost in the chill hammer that slapped me sideways across the road. I took to wearing an earplug in my windward ear to block the pain. My face was rubbed raw, windburned into an ache that was matched by no sunburn I'd ever had.

During a break, I crouched in a muddy roadside ditch to gain a respite from its fury at the mad cyclist daring to claw down *its* road. I cursed my idiocy at thinking I could do this. Every part of me not rubbed raw simply ached. I dug in my back pocket for a map to check out the distance to the nearest airport. Seattle beckoned—hard.

Instead I pulled forth the envelope the clerk had given me two days before. Inside was a single slip of paper, 5,000 yen, nearly $50 US. Given to me by a man whose name I'd never heard and whose face I would never see again. This complete stranger believed in my "Bigga Dleam-ah" far more than I did.

I wanted to ride back and tell him, "Here's your gift. Take it back. You've given it to the wrong person. I am not bravely pursuing some dream; I am fighting to keep my last hopes alive."

I stood from my refuge and the wind slapped me over backward into the mud. For a moment, I'd forgotten. I could doubt myself all I wanted to, but the faith he had in me became a bolster that allowed me to ride past the turnoff to Sapporo airport.

That night, camped in the barn of a closed nursery by the kind grace of the gardener, I stowed the badly wrinkled and water-stained envelope away to be sent home safely with my journal. As I reached to the bottom of my pannier, my fingers brushed something I couldn't identify until I had brought it to the light.

A shortwave radio. My friend Barb had insisted that I would reach a time when I would be desperate for the sound of the English language. It crackled alive. Within minutes I was listening to the BBC World Service. They were reading a short story about who knows what. I didn't care. I merely drank in the words, a release from an aching thirst.

Through the night I discovered the fine jazz of Radio Moscow, the humor and rock 'n' roll of Radio Australia, and the intense propaganda but wonderful sound of Radio America. I fell asleep with a Scottish folksong singing to me quietly through my tiny headphones.

A Goodbye Wave

My first foreign mail stop.

I had all my US mail delivered to a friend's house. Then I would let her know when to FedEx everything, and to which American Express office. I rode hard and fast to this first precious word from home. I strode into the clean, bright office and, in return for showing my identification, received...two postcards. No packet at all.

One from my sister saying, "Hi."

And one from my friend Ruth saying that she was too busy grading final English papers to write more.

I stood outside in the wind and let the rain wash the postcard ink until they were blank. It was only twenty kilometers backward to reach the airport. But there is something in a cyclist that hates to backtrack and the 5,000 yen still in my pocket said to try again.

So, there I perched on a curb studying my map, blurred

more by tears than rain. There were no campgrounds ahead, so I was thinking about going to a beach some dozen kilometers farther along.

A man stopped and looked over my shoulder. "*Doko desu ka?*"

"*Iie kyanpuba.*" (No campground.) "*Watashi kyanpuba—*" (I camp—) I didn't know the word for beach. I pointed at my map.

He studied it for a moment before emphatically shaking his head and indicating I should follow him. He climbed into a car and drove slowly with his flashers on as I followed for a few kilometers.

He had a doublewide construction trailer with the center wall knocked out. It had a couple of low tables and a large stack of tatami mats. A small bathroom was off in a curtained corner. He pointed at the tatamis and then emphatically at the floor. I bowed my thanks. Another night out of the rain and wind, a true luxury.

I pulled out my maps and we pored over them. I traced my route and showed him where I had stayed each night. Then I indicated the Shakotan Peninsula as my next destination. Ryuzoh shook his head and made great hill and valley motions. I shrugged and attempted to describe the California coast, but he would have none of it. Tomorrow he would show me the Shakotan.

My plan to ride the length of Japan was getting iffy. I had a ninety-day visa, but the wind and weather had slowed me as I circumnavigated Hokkaido. Ryuzoh indicated the top third of the main island of Honshu and made vast yawning sounds. Very dull.

"*Ferī Otaru wa Niigata. Hai.*" Yes. He poked his finger at where we were in Otaru, then at the port of Niigata well down Honshu island. "*Hai,*" he repeated very pleased with his decision. He held up two fingers and made sleeping motions. Two days.

I love massive projects. My current one was to ride from Sōya to Sata, because it was...um...somehow...important? The word "ridiculous" also puttered about my brain, having a little difficulty finding a place to dock.

That was one of the things about Alan Booth's book. To many people, Japan holds a certain mystic fascination. James Clavell's *Tai-Pan* only enhances this. It was the same thing that had brought Alan Booth here to teach years before. After a decade in the cities, he felt he knew nothing of the country. So, he set out on an end-to-end walking tour.

He didn't enjoy it much. Not due to the walking, but from the strangeness of the culture. For some reason, that had only made me more committed to seeing it for myself.

I ultimately discovered many things to admire, as well as many not to. That is true of any culture I've traveled through, including my own. But in Japan there is a strangely stark purity. Perhaps it's because Japan is nearly a monoculture—over ninety-five percent Japanese, four percent Korean, and perhaps one percent something else.

When something in Japan is one way, it seems to be that way everywhere throughout the country. And while it makes sense to them, only parts of it made sense to this outsider.

One trait is that when a Japanese person chooses to give advice, they don't do so lightly. It is seriously considered and always well meant.

I looked the mad planner chittering away inside myself square in the eye—and nodded to Ryuzoh.

"*Hai. Ferī Niigata.*"

Ryuzoh beamed.

The place he had brought me to was actually a "rider-house," a very cheap place for motorcyclists to stay while traveling. Ryuzoh recruited one who arrived later that evening to help with translating and he took the next day off work.

Between them they showed me many corners of lovely Shakotan I would never have found.

Walking through a mountain village, we climbed into a cave. After a short passage we emerged high on a cliff overlooking a broad bay. The first sun I'd seen in a month sparkled on the crystalline water. A fishing boat, little larger than a canoe with a sail, appeared suspended above the bottom by little more than a sparkling shimmer as the woman cast her net upon the water.

Ryuzoh led me to the bottom of a ski area, the trails swept up the mountain in broad strokes of pinks, oranges, and reds. The flowers had been specially planted to make these brilliant paths in the summertime. Over the years since, I've often seen photos of those exact slopes in the news...and they always make me think of that day in the sun.

We ate noodles in a restaurant and I was corrected for not slurping mine. To eat noodles silently is an insult to the chef. I slurped strongly, and inhaled a dose of hot sauce deep into my lungs. My new friends, along with most of the restaurant, dissolved into gales of laughter as I attempted to catch my breath and wipe away the tears streaming down my face.

That night, Ryuzoh, one of his salarymen (employees), and a half a dozen motorcyclists sat and ate with me. The beer and cigarettes flowed. Liter after liter of beer disappeared. No one could believe I didn't smoke; I was American, after all, and time and again someone offered me a fresh pack or a different brand.

In the morning, a very bleary Ryuzoh—too drunk to go home, he'd stayed with us in his rider-house—loaded Junior into his salaryman's van because it was too far to ride to the ferry. I learned that was why an employee had also stayed with us the night before rather than return home to his family. Five short kilometers later I was unloaded at the dock and Ryuzoh guided me through purchasing a ticket and loading Junior aboard.

For an hour, Ryuzoh and his salaryman sat on the dock and waited.

When the boat finally dropped its lines and pulled away, they leapt to their feet and began waving madly. I felt like a voyager of yesteryear, off to find deepest Africa aboard some grand Victorian ocean liner rather than a weary, somewhat hungover cyclist headed for the heart of the world's most modern country.

I waved back just as madly.

Ryuzoh made me forget the rain. He made me forget the winds. He will always be a hidden sparkling bay with a lone fishing boat and someone waving goodbye from the dockside.

Not once in the two days and nights I spent in his company did Ryuzoh utter a single word of English. His kindness and our friendship were through signs and drawings and the few feeble words I'd managed to learn.

Lost in the Words

The afternoon I departed the ferry in Niigata, as I rode along in the spattering mist (yes, the story of my life), I was flagged down by a passing motorist. He shielded his eyes against the sprist.

"You speak English? Please?"

"Yes."

"American?"

I nodded.

"You must follow me. You must come to my house. It is dry there."

Becoming used to, though not comfortable with, Japanese hospitality, I shrugged my shoulders and followed along to a modern two-story house a little ways out of town.

And my estimation was right, Tatsuo had just failed his third-level English exam (whatever that meant) and wanted desperately to practice his language skills. However, the benefit was mutual and the kindness unquestionable.

In fact, I was placed in a small room, two steps above the living room. I was disturbed when I observed the Shinto altar was the room's only decoration.

I stepped back, "This room special."

He insisted I was to spend the night on the tatami before the family shrine in the place of honor. His wife's deep bow and easy smile showed that I was indeed welcome, despite arriving unannounced. Tatsuo was very proud of her as she had her own business, hairdressing in a back bedroom. His son, obviously his pride and joy, was introduced the moment he arrived, and I bowed with respect appropriate for the first-born male of the household—and like teenagers everywhere, his bow offered the smallest possible honor to an elder foreign visitor that politeness permitted. I was careful to keep my amusement to myself.

Tatsuo's cousin, with his wife and daughter, arrived in time for dinner. The niece had just passed her fifth-level English exam (I never found out quite what that implied, but she was far in advance of her uncle).

After a generous meal, the saké began to flow in the time-honored challenge of "Get the foreigner drunk." I ran into this everywhere, as did every Western traveler I asked. I don't know why, but it was very hard to avoid. Saké is served very warm and is supposed to be drunk that way, all in a swallow. The catch is that the instant you drink it, the cup is refilled and it's supposed to be drunk while it's still warm. Then...

The cousin and later the niece played the samisen for me. While it looks like an overlong banjo with three strings and a triangular head, its sound was more reminiscent of a mandolin. His cousin was an accomplished concert player of national stature and was a joy to listen to despite the rhythms and sounds as foreign to my ear as the road signs were to my eye. Perhaps I was adapting.

We gathered cross-legged once more about the low table. The son had gone off with friends, so Tatsuo, his cousin, and the niece sat around me. The two wives sat off to one side. Tatsuo and I practiced our English and Japanese with each other. He was especially fascinated by golf and other sports. I couldn't help him there, but I tried.

Often we would become stuck on a word. Finally, I would wave my hand across the surface of the table to get the niece's attention where she sat with bowed head and folded hands.

"Could you help us with this word, please?" I was never able to get her name as she wouldn't repeat it above a whisper.

She would utter the single word, and as the men cried, "Ahh!" in great revelation, she once again bowed her head. Not once did they ask for her assistance when *they* were stuck.

For one brief moment, both men were absent from the table. Instantly the two wives came to life, peppering me with questions through the niece.

"How can you travel so far from home? Have you no wife, no family, no friends?"

"What is your house like in America? Are they all as big as we hear?"

"What is the greatest difference between Japanese and American women?"

The instant Tatsuo returned, all three women folded their hands and bowed their heads in silence. Slowly and painstakingly, with no aid from his niece, he told me how proud he was of his family. He wanted to be like a modern American businessman and wanted his family to be the same. He emphasized this several times, probably embarrassed by the women questioning me, perhaps remonstrating them.

Tatsuo was unerringly kind and generous, and probably a

very forward-thinking man of his culture. But as I rode away, I wished I'd spent more time assuaging my and the women's curiosity and less being plied with saké and sports facts.

Only one time in Japan did a woman speak with me on a casual basis. She was a motorcyclist, the only female one I ever saw though I was passed by hundreds of riders. We had both stopped at the top of a pass in the Japanese Alps. For half an hour we played with our limited vocabularies and talked about our journeys and our lives.

"Only time woman free in Japan, when alone on motorcycle," she informed me sadly.

My view of the Japanese gender dynamics may be very biased, but I found this aspect of their society very hard to tolerate. Frequently, Japanese women eyed me with curiosity and unspoken questions while their husbands (or any male in the room) rattled on about the nature of America or golf, their two favorite topics.

"Of course, golf course fees are very expensive," one man finally conceded after a long dissertation on the sport. "I cannot afford to play. That is why I wear this golf glove to the beach. At least I will have the right tan in the office. It is very important for promotions."

Tatsuo's family. His wife is at my left and the unnamed niece sits beside her father with his samisen. Tatsuo is behind the camera.

Reality at 1,500 Meters

I climbed high into the Japanese Alps to Kamikochi with the hopes of doing some hiking, perhaps even scrambling up one or two of the lower peaks. The road was brutal. After three days of climbing steadily and camping along a riverbed, I reached the final stretch.

For over two kilometers I had to push Junior upward through a marginally lit one-lane tunnel, dripping with enough moisture that I had to keep my slicks on. There was no possibility of riding, it was a twenty-five percent grade. While the bursts of alternating climbing and descending traffic roared through the narrow tunnel, I couldn't even hold my loaded bike against backsliding without the brakes on as I lay against a wall. The steepest road I'd ever found in Seattle, a city built on hills, is only an eleven percent grade.

At long last I arrived at Kamikochi Park and set up my tent. The park is at 1,500 meters (almost a mile up) and the climb had left me terribly light-headed; I could barely walk down to a nearby pond and back. I was surprised—I'd climbed twice that elevation the day I rode around Mount Rainier. Of course, that had been on my ultra-light twenty-two-pound custom-built road bike, not a hundred and thirty or so of touring machine.

Through a brief sun break, I saw the circle of magnificent peaks I had come to find. I crawled into my bag to sleep off the weakness left by the three-day ascent.

I woke in the middle of the night and thrashed about seeking any comfortable position. The hundred-yard journey to the bathroom left me dizzy and weak.

"We're only at 1,500 meters," I railed at my body. "You're in the best shape of your life. What's going on here?"

After another hour of tossing about in my sweaty sleeping bag, I had an idea. So far I hadn't been plagued by a single day of sickness on my journey. I pulled out my med kit for the first time. My temperature was 101.6°F (38.6°C). Bleary-eyed, I followed the shaking beam of my flashlight through my medical reference book. Dr. Stephen Bezruchka's *The Pocket Doctor* informed me that foreign colds often strike with more force because we have no resistance to them.

This was actually a comfort as the chills slammed into me the next day so hard that my knees were black and blue for days afterward from banging together. Then the burning sweats set in...

Over the next few days it was at the limits of my endurance to hobble to the nearby *furo* for a long, hot soak each afternoon. In an intense battle of will, I forced myself to cook, eat, and drink fluids rather than just curl up and groan as I would have preferred. Firing off the stove and cooking spaghetti was so exhausting that I required a few hours' sleep before I could stay awake long enough to eat the now cold meal.

And to make it even more horrible, if possible, for that whole time there were two lines of a Monkees' song stuck in my head. It was a torture, worse than the flu, that I would not wish upon my worst enemy. It was not my last meeting with their dreaded music that, yes, I admit, I *had* enjoyed in my teens.

The second night after returning from an extra-long soak, loaded to the gills with Advil and liquids, I checked my temperature. The thermometer portended a night even worse than the last.

I pictured a park ranger finding my decaying body in my tent a week from now; they would be too polite to intrude on my privacy until I started to reek.

I thought of leaving the front flap open, so if I was unconscious, they might see me—but it was raining. I considered calling Mac and Ruth so they would at least know where I died, but there was no way I could make it to the phone by the park entrance in my weakened condition. I did try to instruct my subconscious to, just before the coma slipped over me, thrust my hand out through the slit I'd left by unzipping the corner of the bug screen. At least that way they might find me before I began to decompose.

For the second time on the trip, the first being the descent off Big Sur, I was faced with my own mortality. Apparently I was slow to learn not to doggedly plan the future at the expense of enjoying the present. Just that fast, I could have been gone. And what would my decade of hundred-hour work weeks have done for me? A sad thought as another bout of chills bruised my aching knees.

I was lying atop my sleeping bag with the sweat pouring off me when the fever finally broke—dropping nearly two degrees in minutes.

In my newly recovering state, I was able to observe the world of Kamikochi Park about me.

Around 10:00 a.m. the tour buses began to arrive. They leave Tokyo at 3:00 a.m., then after eight hours in the park they are back in Tokyo by midnight with hundreds, perhaps thousands of photos safely captured for posterity. And these were not just idle photographers with a point-and-shoot and a love of jagged snow-capped peaks. Some people wore entire backpacks of equipment. Ten- and twenty-thousand-dollar Nikon kits and Hasselblad setups dotted every trail.

One man carefully assembled his tripod camera and lens, aiming at no reasonable photo I could see. Once he was prepared, his wife took a picture of him *and* his equipment against the backdrop of the mountains with her little point-and-shoot. He then packed up and they moved along without a single shutter click.

A painter, the only one I saw, had planted his easel with the far leg well off the trail and in the midst of a wide mud puddle. I wondered if the mud and water mightn't warp or damage the wooden leg. But as I stood back, observing and resting a bit (I was still pretty shaky and had to stop every ten minutes or so to rest), I saw that he had his reasons.

People came up and saw that he was painting. They trudged in front of him—right into the center of the puddle, usually deeper than the tops of their shoes—to photograph the precise "artist's view." Slogging out of the puddle, they'd then shoot a photo of the curious man with his easel. Sometimes he would take his painting down for a few minutes to break up the crowd standing in the puddle that was wholly blocking his view.

Another man walked fifty paces—I heard him counting—set up his camera, took a photo, repacked all his gear down to the last lens, and counted out another fifty. I left him as he sought desperately for something to photograph in a particularly dull stretch of trail. At my painful ambling pace, I'd already been his subject twice and I suspect my departure added my backside to his home slide show.

In camp that night, after a long nap, I met Phil and Tako, an American / Japanese couple. I told them of my observations, and they laughed.

"You would not believe what we go through trying to avoid

yet another tedious slide show." He mimicked lifting a phone receiver.

"Tako is sick... No, she's so sick I want to stay with her... No, I don't want to hire someone to sit with her... No, I don't want your brother's wife to risk catching... No, it's just a cold... Yes, if she isn't better in the morning, I'll take her to the hospital."

"We were just starting dinner," he started again. "Oh, you'll wait for us? How...kind."

"We died. So sorry."

One-hour photo processing finally made sense to me. It wasn't so that your film could be processed while you cruised the mall. It was so that everyone in Japan could share their photos the next day. And they are all traded. A mandatory part of any group photo is an immediate exchange of business cards so that copies may be sent. The Japanese were shocked to the core when I informed them that I was sending my film home unprocessed and I wouldn't be able to send prints for several years. Sure enough, when I did at last complete my journey, a fair stack of pictures was waiting for me. I did send out copies of my own to everyone who had given me their cards.

I suggested to Tako that, perhaps for the Japanese, a moment hadn't occurred unless it had been recorded. In the distant past as a haiku, in the present a photograph.

"Yes. Yes. I see Western person wait for people to move out of way to take scenery photograph. Japanese person will find someone, even stranger, to help make photograph into event."

I can just imagine my appearance in dozens, perhaps hundreds of slide shows. "See, I was there, and my wife, and this crazy, bearded *gaijin* who is bicycling around the world."

I helped make it real. If only they'd known how unreal all those moments were for me, especially in my Kamikochi delirium.

I never did get to climb a single one of those peaks.

Finding the Right Focal Length

I'd run out of food, despite the extra five or so kilograms (fifteenish pounds) I'd hauled up those vertiginous roads. It was time to drop down out of the Alps. It felt good to be back on the bike after five days, even if three of them were spent mostly unconscious. Feet spinning, music starting back up, and even a day without rain.

Because of the high spin rate I mentioned before, combined with the fact that it made for a fairly steady rhythm, there was pretty much always some music going on in my head while I rode. Back when I skied a lot (mostly as a kid), I became a much better skier when I found an internal soundtrack. I once went downhill skiing after nearly a decade off the slopes, and by the third run, that same nonsense humming tune I'd created came back into my head and suddenly I was riding my edges and carving around moguls with a pleasant ease.

Bicycling is like that, provided I'm not grinding up a steep slope in a desperately low gear. The music was back and I was doing fine. It wouldn't become a mortal curse to my sanity until I hit the Australian Outback.

I descended through the brutal tunnel in a matter of minutes. I felt surprisingly strong as I climbed over the next pass and began the long descent through Takayama and south toward the Inland Sea.

Religion has always piqued my curiosity. This is odd when I consider that now. I was raised in a marginally Jewish household. When I was four, Dad had asked if I'd rather go to Hebrew school twice a week or go outside and play. Easy answer.

My sister, four years older, made the opposite choice. So I went back and forth in the car with her, and while I didn't get to play outside, I did get to interfere with Mom's grocery shopping twice a week. My prize if I was good? Dipping a kosher dill pickle out of the great wooden barrel at the end of aisle four. My sister tried to quit six months later but my parents held her to her commitment for two more years until we moved. Thirty years later, I hadn't been in synagogue since.

My first real exposure to religion began when I took over the operation of the college planetarium my freshman year. The constellations are peopled, at least for most of Western society, by the heroes and villains of Greek mythology. And the stories overlapped and integrated with other cultures. I took several classes in Greek mythology and culture, which began to alter my world: gods and beliefs and daily living intermingled. Stumbling on a course entitled "Comparative Eastern Religions" exposed me to Confucius, the Tao Te Ching, and the Buddha's life among others. By then I was reading the Bible, the Koran, and the Book of Mormon for fun. Yes, we all get our kicks in curious ways.

The thing I liked best about my wandering studies was the revelation that they all teach essentially similar lessons about how to live life. I liked that.

In Japan, Shinto shrines pepper the landscape, even more so than Coca-Cola vending machines. Huge Buddhist temples swell from the cities that were formed around them in central Honshu.

Before crossing over the Japanese Alps, I had visited the Zenkō-Ji Buddhist temple in Nagano, a vast and glittering complex. During the morning service, there were perhaps fifty people huddled before the altar. A half dozen spectators and myself were grouped along the back wall, farther from the clouds and sharp smell of incense that has always made me sneeze. The massive structure soared above us, emphasized by the (literally) gold chandeliers.

"Did you notice their robes?"

I looked over at the silver-haired man who'd left the same hostel I had this morning, definitely American by accent,

Midwest perhaps. He was pointing off to the side. In a back room, screened from the altar but not from our remote spectators' position, were a group of monks having their morning tea and cigarettes. They were apparently having quite a time telling jokes and stories.

"Their robes?"

"Silk and gilt. And the begging bag?"

I'd missed the traditional begging bag reimagined in all of its glory and golden stitching.

"And the Audis all parked along the main road?"

I had noticed the preponderance of Audi Quattros. Hard to miss that many gleaming, yes, gold-colored, luxury cars all in a row.

"All belong to the monastery. All given to the monks."

"Where do they get all the money?"

"They own much of the country about here, since the 800s."

"1800s?"

"800s."

"I forget how young America is."

"The other place they get their money is..."

I followed his gaze toward the sudden swell of noise. A group of some fifty Japanese came in being herded by someone with a megaphone and waving a number on a little placard.

Three more tour bus groups piled in and those attending the service were rapidly outnumbered by the camera-clicking crowds. The monks' chants lost except for brief snatches between the megaphones bellowing out point of interest.

"Every morning?"

My companion nodded. It was a very popular tourist site.

I had done a lot of thinking about the cultural habits I'd observed in my brief time so far in Japan. Why had the gas station attendants left me alone for so long when I first arrived on Hokkaido and sat puzzling over my phrase book? I had not looked at them. I recalled a snippet of information from *Shōgun*, perhaps not so useless in modern Japan, after all.

"A Japanese person must be private in their head, as there is no privacy in their crowded world."

I had learned early on that it was rude to speak to someone who was looking away. It was okay to stand for a moment and see if they'd look at you, but if not, you turned away. This lesson was driven home by the morning service at Zenkō-Ji. The devout attended the service by attending temple yet not seeing or hearing what went on around them. Or perhaps, not allowing it to interfere with their world.

In the West, I had let everyone's opinion shape my own. In fact, I was so skilled at reading into the tiny nuances of others' reactions to me that I was notorious for missing the obvious. My sister is the opposite, she sees people quickly and clearly.

Just as George had at the beginning of this trip, my sister had asked near the end of my high school years, "Whatever happened to the girl who was chasing you so hard?"

"Which girl?"

She proceeded to describe this amazing girl who I had liked sooo much. The problem, I finally figured out while leaning against the back wall of the Zenkō-Ji temple two decades later? She had been too obvious. She had gone to some trouble to show me that she liked me, whereas I had been too carefully observing the minutiae of her reactions and completely missed the bigger picture. Besides, there was this other boy who liked her, and I didn't want to impose, just in case she liked him more than me.

It took the Japanese specifically ignoring the bigger picture in order to focus on the present for me to understand that I had focused on all of the distractions and missed so much that was important.

In my "bumblebee" Lycra outfit at the 400-year-old Matsumoto Castle. (I also had a purple set. In the tropics, I just wore a light shirt because the Lycra was way too warm.) Most Japanese simply stared in wonder as I rolled by. But one young boy understood what I was at first glance and gave me a very Sylvester Stallone-like "Yo!" complete with a high-raised fist pump. I offered the same back as I rode by his radiant smile.

The Sacred Cows

After descending from the Alps, I came upon the city of Nara. Japan was ruled from here in the 700s, and Buddhist shrines and temples grew thicker than office buildings in the city's core. The *largest* wooden building in the world contains a massive Buddha. The flow of tourists, myself included, completely washed away any religious observance or feeling beyond, "What an amazing structure."

A dozen temples later, I was southeast of Nara at the *oldest* wooden building in the world. This amazing five-tier pagoda has survived since the era the Vikings first began raiding Scotland and the British Isles, and Charlemagne was yet to build his kingdom. Inside this ancient temple, behind rusted screens, rested the greatest works of religious carving from 1300 years ago. As I squinted to see them by the light of the sole remaining bulb, a woman with a thick Texas accent leaned over to me.

"I wish they'd dust off their Buddhas."

I couldn't have said it better. All of the various temples I'd been to felt like museums that weren't quite cared for.

"And India should wash their sacred cows."

I seriously considered that for this book's title: *Dust off your Buddhas and wash your sacred cows.* What can I say, I have a low sense of humor.

Over the Top

The unending rain finally broke on July 5th.

On my little shortwave radio, the BBC had a minor news item that much of the Japanese rice crop had been destroyed by the severe monsoon, the worst in recent recorded history (*oy vey!*).

The destruction of the rice crop was so bad that, for the first time in their history, Japan had to import foreign rice. A great blind taste test was held.

As a man explained it to me, "Can you imagine? We trying do better than America at all thing. Big tasting. Everybody taste. What rice wins? No Australia. No Thai. No even Japanese premium, special brand. *California* rice win. How can this be? You do everything better than we."

Japan is definitely a land of turmoil, of conflict—the past with the present. Service to others is given to a point of disservicing self, and women are not allowed to speak. Yet their technology, education, and low crime rates are the envy of the world. The inordinate neatness of every home and shop I entered versus the horrid pollution of the air and the common land.

The reason I remember the rain stopped on July 5th was that is the day I arrived in Hiroshima. I delayed an extra day to avoid arriving there on American Independence Day. It had poured that day as I sat in a youth hostel and discussed bread with a Swedish traveler.

In Japan, every baked good is white bread. There are no loaves except white bread. Rolls are soft, white bread. Near the end of my time in Japan, at a Fukuoka train station, I passed a bakery with these lovely, lovely croissants in the display case. Beyond joy, I purchased one, which was appropriately wrapped in paper, then plastic, then put in a plastic bag. I hurried to the front steps of the station, unwrapped my treasure, and bit down on the perfectly formed dainty. White bread.

So, we had spent that long rainy day of July 4th making both of ourselves crazy talking about French croissants, good Swedish rolls served with breakfast sausage, American cinnamon rolls, and all the other bready delicacies we had each consumed in the past. Even telling each other to please stop didn't help—we were both eating the homesick roll, so to speak.

On July 5th, I arrived at Hiroshima Peace Memorial Park in the brilliant sunlight. The gray clouds were shattered into jagged leftover pieces on a field of impossibly bright blue. I had been to a wide variety of intricate Japanese gardens with bridges, pools, and hidden cul-de-sacs for contemplation. I had visited a manicured garden of rocks made by a poet a half-millennium before to emulate the mountain ranges of China.

The Peace Memorial Park had wide manicured lawns divided into geometric grids by concrete strips from which a small airplane could be launched. Shockingly, jarringly Western. It must have been a hundred times more jarring to the Japanese.

There were many artifacts of what had happened there.

A cenotaph's flame burned beyond a stone coffer. A placard noted that the coffer contained the names of the seventy-five thousand people known to have died in the initial blast.

Another noted that the flame was not an eternal memorial flame, but rather one of protest that would be extinguished only when the *last* nuclear weapon had been destroyed.

A great grassy mound off to one side had a simple sign, "Here lie the ashes of uncounted tens of thousands."

A tall statue rises above a colorful pile of flowers. Except on closer inspection, the flowers were revealed to be tens of thousands, *hundreds* of thousands of small, origami cranes. Sadako Sasaki, a young schoolgirl, believed that she could survive the radiation sickness if she folded a thousand cranes, the Japanese symbol of longevity and happiness. She died after folding six hundred and forty-four. Her surviving schoolmates folded the rest and she was buried here with the thousand cranes. Each day, bags of these arrive from around the world. On August 6th each year, the anniversary of the bombing, the piles of these tiny bits of paper rise many meters deep. On July 5th the blessings rose past my knees.

I toured the Peace Memorial Hall. Half the displays were unrecognizable until the placards identified them as common household items. A stone from a building emblazoned with the perfect outline of a person burned upon it; no body was found. A wrecked bicycle twisted into a pretzel-like shape was found eight hundred meters from the blast site. A force that could destroy Junior from over a kilometer away was inconceivable, yet it had happened.

I forced myself to inspect every item, read every sign. I mustn't forget. I mustn't. The sunlight at the exit door was so disorienting I was nearly ill. Only by laying my face against the cool glass did I manage to get my breathing under control.

Once more outside, I finally halted at a bench overlooking a small depression. It looked like a fountain with no water running. A simple sculpture rose in the center, drawing the eye ever upward toward the shining steel-blue sky. I focused on the placard before the bench, but I already knew where I had come. It didn't require the words written there to force my gaze upward once more to the place a hundred meters above. The place where the world had been changed forever in just a few milliseconds. I was at the epicenter.

I stood dazed, unable to make my feet work to drag me from this place. A woman approached and handed me a card. I struggled to focus my eyes, but was unable to do so and returned it to her with a shrug. She nodded and spoke briefly in Japanese. I bowed and that seemed sufficient to the moment as she did the same and departed.

Able once more to move a little, I wandered clear of that place and collapsed upon a low stone wall. A young man in his teens came and offered me a similar card. This time I was able to make out the English lettering.

"I ask permission to offer a brief prayer to cleanse your soul and bring you peace of mind. There is no charge."

I nodded. His chant, similar to the woman's, though whether longer or shorter or the same I'll never know, was a Shinto prayer. He explained in very broken English that it was a service, a duty done of their own free will after seeing how the park affected some people. They were offering the best hope they knew how to give. A hope for peace.

I sat in Hiroshima Peace Memorial Park and knew that the three months from home had been worth it to arrive here in this place, at this time. All the leave-taking, hardship, rain, and isolation were made worthwhile in this moment. In this understanding that you could rise from horror and seek peace.

A friend who had traveled around the world for four years once told me, "If you want to come home in the first three months, that is because it is hard. If you want to come home after three months, perhaps you were not meant to travel."

I'd been homesick every day of my journey, so much so that it was an aching emptiness I could curl around at night. Yet he was right. I wanted to see what was to come more than I wanted to return. I wanted to learn the true importance of being at peace, have it become a part of my soul, become a part of the unconscious living I do day-to-day.

But I couldn't continue in this Japanese world of density. I needed some time and space to not have to think in Japanese, to not avoid questions by looking at the ground.

I arranged for tickets out of Japan and onward to Australia —the best price was a week away. I found a closed campground on Kyushu, the southernmost main island—my original plan of reaching its southern tip, Cape Sata, never crossed my mind. I stamped down a circle in the high weeds and spent my last week in Japan staring out at the southern reaches of the Sea of Japan.

Japan had been both an incredible challenge and an amazing education. My Western sensibilities had been challenged at every turn. So many things that I took for granted…weren't. Road signs, such high standards of politeness, the treatment of women so different from the Western standards I'd become accustomed to, and so many other things that I would never look at the same way again.

Also, and perhaps most importantly, I had survived. I don't mean coming out alive—though I do count that as a plus. I had tackled an incredibly hard road and surmounted the challenge. Over the crest of that high pass, it wasn't all easy coasting.

There were hard roads ahead, but never again was I to hit such fear as I'd found so often in Japan. Having climbed over the top has made everything that has followed—both on the trip and since—if not easy, at least more manageable.

Beyond Okinawa, far down the curve of the Earth, Australia beckoned.

Hope as a Default Position

I had to slide into one last city. My final Japanese mail stop awaited me in Fukuoka. The American Express office handed me a thin envelope that contained a dozen letters from home. I found a park and chose a bench in a shady nook and reveled. Chatty letters from my sister and several friends occupied me happily for a long while.

At long last I faced the final one, a letter from my father. It was the response to the letter I'd scribed in the dark rain of the Avenue of the Giants two months before. I opened it cautiously and peeked within. A short note. I could deal with a short note.

He was shocked that I had ever thought he'd try to stop me. He didn't agree with, or even pretend to understand what I was doing. But other than destroying my life and disappointing him so deeply, he didn't question my right to do it.

I answered his letter first. The pen flew across the paper. I apologized for the misunderstanding and told him of the people and experiences. I told him how it felt to not be under the burden of a hundred-hour-per-week job and an unmanageable mortgage.

I wrote of my hopes for Australia and the future.

How my need to do massive projects was, if not abating, at least better understood.

I didn't think it was all fluff and roses, but I told him that I hoped our relationship was on the mend now that we were communicating about our beliefs and desires. I couldn't stop smiling as I sent it off. Perhaps I could perform that most magic of things, make a parent into a friend.

Cocooned in Mystery

On my last night in Japan, I splurged on a capsule hotel. This uniquely Japanese facility is intended for salarymen who live too far out in the country to afford the train ride home each night. I locked Junior to the front gate and dropped everything in a locker, including my clothes.

First stop is the *furo*. All the new arrivals enter in a slow, naked stream. Set aside any movie fantasies. A very matronly, fully-clothed Japanese woman issues a washcloth, bucket, soap, and stool. Though it is the first time I've seen a woman in the *furo*, I barely noticed it. For an extra fee, she will offer you a shave. She eyed my full beard in a slightly worried fashion, but I declined having it removed.

Once clean, she issued each of us a set of baby-blue pajamas. Everyone wears them. They'll even wear them out into the local neighborhood or restaurants, each capsule hotel having its own trademark color.

As I was getting dressed, I fell to talking with an older Japanese gentleman, born in 1925, who spent his teens in the midst of WWII.

"Older Japanese, we feel very inferior to Americans. First the four Black Dragons (Admiral Perry's fleet of four black warships, which forced open Japan to trade in 1853 and still stand out in the race's collective memory), losing World War II, and the feeling that we are copying everything we do from you."

"But we are amazed and a little afraid of Japan," I countered. "Your ability to manufacture so much, so fast amazes us. I've owned more Japanese cars than American ones, and my favorite American one, the Ford Taurus, was built using Japanese methods."

"Yes, but an American brought those ideas to us."

"But we wouldn't listen to Dr. Deming and sent him away."

I was unable to convince him that America wasn't the magical, misty land of golden opportunity peopled solely by brilliant, rich, world leaders. It is the image I experienced throughout my travels and was never to be gainsaid, not even by personal experience of those who had traveled to see my country.

No one would believe that a third of our children live below the poverty level.

"But you are so rich."

"But they go to bed hungry."

"Why are you lying to me? You make so much food that you export millions of tons of wheat. I hear you even pay farmers *not* to farm."

They are also universally convinced that we are an incredibly violent people, always at war with ourselves.

"All those television shows are just that, shows. Do you think we live in a land of constant robbery, murder, lust, and..." My argument always dribbles out ineffectively. The United States apparently is a land of gold, long-legged blondes, and gun-toting...well, everybody has one, of course. And they use it frequently to fight over the gold and the long-legged blondes. SIGH!

I watched TV in the capsule hotel lounge for a while, which makes the Japanese just as unreal to me. There were seven big screens and rows of deep armchairs. Small controls set the speakers in the chair sides to the appropriate channel, all in Japanese so it didn't help much. The government who had run Japan for thirty years was losing the election that night and most were following that closely. The other two appeared to be sitcoms involving scantily or wholly unclad women broken up by commercials targeted for men by more unclothed women. The men were, of course, always fully clothed whether talking, fornicating, or striking the unruly women.

Perhaps I misinterpret it.

I know I don't understand it.

I went to the lower floor of the hotel. Row upon row of capsules lined the darkened hall. Each was a meter high—you can't quite sit up; a meter wide—you can touch both walls at once with your elbows, easily; and two meters long—your toes don't touch the back curtain. Mounted in the ceiling were a tiny TV, a radio, a light, and a little air jet—like those on airplanes. I slid down the cloth curtain by my feet and slept far into the next morning with nothing to wake me from that dim, warm cocoon.

Japan: 60 days / 3,221 km (2,002 mi)
Elevation Climbed: 12.7 km (7.9 mi)
Total Distance to Date: 6,190 km (3,846 mi)
Elevation Climbed to Date: 34.8 km (21.6 mi)
(1 / 3 of the way to space. Fingers crossed that they give me my astronaut badge when I cross the Kármán line.)

3

SOUTH KOREA, SINGAPORE

20 JULY 1993 – 23 JULY 1993

English: *I'm trying to get to Australia.*
Translation (in Korean, Hebrew, Russian, Thai, and six other languages in 90-plus hours of transit): *Shrug.*

Silence is Golden

Originally I was to meet a friend in Vietnam. When he dropped out at the last minute, I wasn't quite brave enough to go it alone. Vietnam wasn't technically open to American travel yet, which definitely raised the barrier even higher.

Entry involved flying into Bangkok, with its wild reputation, on the chance that I could get a visa and air travel to that still-closed country and survive the rigors of traveling alone there.

I just wasn't up for it after Japan.

The reports I later heard from other travelers about their welcome and adventures there made me truly regret that cautious decision.

"Cautious?" I can hear you exclaim as so many of my

friends since have. "You're riding alone around the world on a bicycle!"

Okay, I concede it. There are degrees of caution, just as there are degrees of vegetarianism. Vegans won't eat eggs or cheese, meat-asaurs want steak at every meal. Most of the rest of us fall somewhere within that broad spectrum. I fall in the realm of "cautious traveler." Overly timid to most of the long-term travelers; madly adventurous to those who stay home.

Anyway, I needed a new route.

Well, after Vietnam I'd planned to go to Australia. I'd planned to go in the spring (September to November) and it was still dead winter in the Southern Hemisphere.

Ah! Perhaps August *was* the right time to be crossing the Outback.

I checked on plane tickets. Short notice out of Japan to the Land Down Under was $1,900 US! I finagled around, and with the help of my US travel agent, I figured out a route for $700 US. It involved a ferry crossing to Korea, twenty-two hours there, then fly to Pusan (Busan Metropolitan City), Seoul, Bangkok, Singapore, and finally Darwin, Australia, in just under twenty-six hours.

I had no preparation for Korea beyond a bunch of old *M*A*S*H* episodes—filmed entirely in southern California. I didn't know anything about the culture, the language, the belief system, any of it. At that last mail stop I picked up my tickets and a guide to Australia that my friend Ruth had forwarded from home.

While waiting for the ferry, I began to browse the book.

"Visa required for entry."

I leapt to the nearest phone and dialed the phone number for the Australian embassy in Tokyo.

"Do I have to get the visa before I enter the country?"

"Aye, mate, that you do."

"I'm hundreds of kilometers away and I'm leaving the country in a few hours."

We discussed my itinerary.

"Well, Seoul, Bangkok, and Singapore all have embassies. Just hop off the plane for a day and then you're in. No worries."

I called Korean Air about stopping in Seoul. "Forfeit ticket if get off."

I explained my dilemma.

"Forfeit ticket if get off. We no stop baggage, it will go to Australia and be impounded."

I called Qantas, they were the Bangkok, Singapore, Darwin portion of my journey.

"Never been to Bangkok, ooh, I'd try Singapore, mate, much friendlier, especially what with having a pushie and all."

"Pushie?"

"Pushbike. Yeah, we'll just bump you out at Singapore for twenty-four hours. You want your baggage and pushie to meet you in Darwin, or bump 'em out with you in Singapore?"

"Bump 'em."

"No worries, mate. All booked, no fees what with you not knowin' 'bout the visa and all. Thanks for flying Qantas."

If I have a choice, you can be certain that Qantas will be my first choice—anywhere, *ever*.

So, I boarded the Fukuoka-Pusan ferry twenty minutes later and went off for my twenty-two hours in another new land. On the ferry I picked up a few brochures and decided I'd visit an old temple north of the city of Pusan before riding over near the airport and finding a hotel.

The thing that surprised me most on my arrival in South Korea was not the noise (blaring horns had been totally absent in Japan).

It was not the driving. Two Japanese enter an uncontrolled intersection at the same time and both cars slow to a halt. One bows over the steering wheel, the other bows lower, at long last one decides they are lower socially and bows their head to the steering wheel and remains there. The other bows perfunctorily now that they know they are of higher station and zips on through. Easy as can be. Two Korean drivers enter an intersection in a burst of loud horns and wild veering to slalom around each other. Even a New York cabbie would have to be on their toes.

It wasn't the poor. Japanese poor are hidden behind carefully swept roads and new cars. I never entered a big city in either country, but neither did I ever see a beggar. But I grew up in the US; poor didn't surprise me no matter what non-US folks believed.

The air smelled...livelier than Japan. It is the only word I have for it. It wasn't any scent that I hadn't encountered in Chinatown, New York City, or on the wrong side of the Zone in Boston. It was just livelier.

What really shocked me was the side of the road they drove on.

I rolled down the ferry ramp and tried to veer left into the congested traffic and found myself head-on with a large, US army truck. I swung right, found the curb, and hugged it for the rest of my time in South Korea. Japan drives on the opposite side of the road from the US, but it had snuck up on me. Starting in the quiet back roads of Hokkaido had given me time to adapt. I'd had time until right-hand driving seemed natural, made sense. Korea was a shock as the ferry disembarked into a major intersection of a country in a hurry. Adapt or perish appeared to be the theme here.

I decided to stash Junior and try the subway system. I made friends with a parking garage attendant and locked Junior opposite his booth. The subway dropped me right near the Pomosa (Beomeosa) Temple that I had chosen to go see. I was set. Everything is posted in English and Korean and the natives are fairly fluent in English. Our long military presence has made it easy for a weary traveler, no matter what other good or bad it has done.

I climbed the narrow footpath to the temple. The dirt path was arched over by a mild-looking god or beast, I was unsure which, a story tall. His paint was bright and perfect. No flecks, no wear, no dust; bright colors danced about his torso and framed his calm, perhaps smiling face.

I passed beneath and entered the main compound.

It had none of the majesty of the Japanese temples. No towering pagodas guarded by huge parking lots filled with buses. No "largest wooden building" mobbed by thousands. Pomosa was half a dozen structures nestled together in the woods. And they were beautiful. These buildings were clearly cared for with love. Even garden borders gleamed as if freshly polished. Doorways were framed in spring greens and sunset pinks and apricot roses.

I spoke at some length with a monk who had lived, studied, and taught there for the fifteen years since entering on his seventeenth birthday.

"There is one monk. He is a painter. His personal worship takes a year and a half. When he finishes painting the temple, he starts over at the beginning." He'd been doing this for decades.

Pomosa, like the mighty Zenkō-Ji, was a Buddhist temple. But here the prayers were not lost among the blaring of tour bus groups, but rather filtered out into the courtyard and mixed with the singing of the birds. The monks wore simple robes and spoke in whispers. I was one of the few tourists on the grounds. The gentle hush was unlike anything I'd ever experienced. Now when someone says they feel closer to God in a particular setting, I know what they mean. Pomosa is closer, much closer than most. No revelations. Just a calmness that was as much within me as around me.

Pomosa held one other surprise. Video cameras. Rather

than taking a thousand still images of everything like the Japanese, Koreans record things very slowly with video cameras. I don't recall a single video camera in Japan. I carried the only still camera at the temple that day. (Looking through my slides a year later, there wasn't a single image of Pomosa. I had never even thought to pull out my camera in that wonderful peace. I would never have captured the important essence.)

Hours later, I boarded the subway to return to Pusan and retrieve Junior. I wanted to find the airport and a hotel before dark. I fell easily into a discussion with a Korean about my observations.

"Yes, very true. Pomosa is a special place. I had never noticed the cameras, but you are right. Perhaps we wish to show the place to our friends and share the wonder of it as well as we can. Video does this well. How long are you in our country?"

"Just a day. I'm in transit to Australia." It was only when he turned abruptly away that I understood what I had just said. "I'm taking up to four years to travel around the world, and I'm visiting your country for twenty-two hours because I have to catch a plane." I attempted to explain that I was here by accident, but now that I had seen a little of their country and met some of their people, I would definitely come back. He barely nodded before turning away again. Someday, I will learn to think before I speak.

However, being socially awkward has always been one of my gifts that would continue to serve me poorly for, well, pretty much ever since. My friends have learned that's just part of me. I'm no Sheldon Cooper of notorious *The Big Bang Theory* awkwardness. But in groups of more than two, I tend to go silent. And, as I'd just proven, sometimes I should keep my trap shut in groups of two as well.

Smuggler's Blues

The next morning I rode out to the airport and proved why it is good to arrive three to four hours before a flight when traveling with something as odd as a touring bike.

They wanted to X-ray the bike. I pointed out that it was made of metal and that wouldn't work. Junior and I ended up in an office behind the check-in counter.

The official started out like a television police detective, the "bad cop" one.

"We will have to cut the tubes open to test the bike for drugs."

"It would be of little use to me afterwards."

"That is not our problem."

I tried to catch my breath. Picturing Junior on the floor in little pieces was not a happy image.

"There are other ways to inspect it. Like removing the seat. Then you could inspect that tube."

He pointed sharply, "How about that one?"

"Well, I have a tool that can remove the pedals, I would just need to borrow a two-foot adjustable wrench. I'm sure your plane mechanics would have such a thing."

He eyed me carefully and pointed again. For well over an hour I had a captive audience for one of my favorite topics, bicycles. We discussed how to inspect bicycles, debated the pros and cons of stowing different types of drugs in different places. He would tell me how they were usually packaged, and often how they were smuggled(!), and I showed him the likely places on my life-sized model. Junior was only too happy to take center stage in his efforts to remain intact.

My approaching gate time had little relevance to the man. Minutes before the final boarding call, he returned me to the check-in station. With a flick of his wrist, he deleted any overweight charges and waived any need to box or disassemble Junior.

It was with a very solid and sincere handshake that I left at least one airport official more kindly disposed toward cyclists. And I still had just enough time to buy a breakfast snack before my flight.

Make 'em Laugh

A quick hop through Bangkok and I arrived in Singapore near midnight. I had twenty-one hours to obtain an Australian visa from the embassy before I had to return to the airport. A quick nap at a youth hostel and I was at the embassy minutes after they opened.

As I waited, I noted a rising tone of ire at one of the windows. A very pretty American woman, mid-twenties perhaps, and by her clothes, traveling pretty low-budget as I was, demanded that the rules were ridiculous. Why did she need to purchase a ticket back out of Australia before she arrived, especially when she didn't know where she was going next? Finally, she insisted that she be allowed to talk with a supervisor.

She stepped aside and it was my turn. I approached the agent and asked for exactly the same thing the woman had been demanding, a visa to visit the agent's country.

I tried smiling. I tried pleasant jokes. I tried asking if Singapore's sweltering heat was all year round, or just brought in for my benefit. The woman didn't crack a single smile. Though by the end she did unwind enough to suggest that I purchase a more expensive, refundable ticket. Then I wouldn't have to throw it away if I decided to depart by a different route.

I purchased my ticket at a nearby agency, had a pleasant lunch, and returned to the embassy that afternoon. The young woman had returned first. She huffed away from the window clenching a crumpled ticket as yet another problem was found with her paperwork. Once again, I followed immediately after her with the same agent.

"Are we having fun yet?"

Finally, the agent almost laughed aloud, unable to resist a glance at the seated woman. We had a bit of a chat; she was actually second-generation Singaporean and had acquired her Australian accent along with three decades at her job.

As I departed, visa in hand, the young woman stopped me.

"How did you do that so easily?"

I looked at her, a trim, showstopper in any circle, and a lack of awareness that would take years to outgrow. I looked at her crumpled ticket and wondered if it was the cheapest thing she could find, and she'd just have to throw it away as a cost of travel? What could I offer that might help?

"I made her laugh."

First Words

I still had a couple hours to kill before my flight to the Land Down Under. I strolled the shopping malls that litter downtown Singapore; that *are* downtown Singapore. They're full-city-block square and five to seven stories high, each floor packed with a hundred tiny shops. Along the way I purchased a little handheld computer that weighed one pound and ran for forty hours on three AA batteries.

I know. I know. Here I am traveling close to the land. Trying to leave technology behind. Struggling to forget my failed IT career (which was still called "Automation Systems" back then) as I continue court battles with my ex-business partner via long distance phone conferences.

And I buy a computer.

But on the flight from South Korea, I'd attempted to write a story.

Inside those last few words is a statement of such huge impact upon my life that it is still unfolding a quarter of a century later.

Other than a terrible little piece of science fiction at the age of twelve and the one obligatory weekend-workshop short story in my twenties (seems like everyone has done one of those), I'd never written fiction. I'd hadn't intended to start now either. I'd written computer manuals, technical articles for magazines and professional publications, and a grand total of four months of journal entries.

I love to read fiction, but to write it? No interest at all.

My mom was the aspiring author. After she finally shed herself of Dad in my twenties, she decided it was time to settle in and write the murder mystery she'd been talking about since before I came along. Sadly, like most writers, her efforts resulted in little more than a pair of severely noir, autobiographical short vignettes.

Any scraps of her murder mystery regrettably died with her well before my burnout and this trip.

My grand plan was to write a book about my trip, which was why I was keeping a thorough journal and recording every photo I took.

I did *not* set out to write any fiction.

However, on the plane flight from South Korea to Singapore, I'd started a story about a freshman college roommate who killed alarm clocks—literally. When they went off, he'd slap out at them. They'd hit the end of the power cord, arc into the wall above my bunk, and the smashed bits would trickle down to the floor. Every few weeks, he'd dig out all of the shattered alarm clock parts and spend an afternoon reassembling as many as he could. (On the days I had to wake him up myself—when he was between alarm clock piles—I learned to shake his bunk. From the foot end.)

Writing that little vignette was an amusing way to pass the

time (so different than the flop-sweat panic attack provided by the US-Japanese leg of my trip not so long ago). What I wasn't ready for was what happened when I got to the point where he slapped the clock.

The story turned.

Finding no clock, his violent motion flips him out of bed... and into a seat at a conference table. The other person who is sitting there? St. Peter! And it turns out that he needs help because someone (I'd eventually discovered that it was a Buddhist Hungry Ghost) had stolen the Software That Runs the Universe.

I stared at that in quite some shock.

Where the hell had that come from? (I would soon discover that was *precisely* the right question, as the true heroine of the story turned out to be the Devil Incarnate, a rather pleasant woman named Michelle.)

This would eventually go on to be my first-ever novel, my first-ever fiction sale, the #1 novel of the year for the tiny press that released it, and—most importantly—an outlet for my insatiable love of fiction that has since bloomed to sixty novels and over a hundred short stories by the time of this writing.

So, curiously enough, I know the exact day I became a writer because it's in my journal on the flight between South Korea and Singapore: July 22nd, 1993.

There was another problem. I'd worked with computers for over a dozen years and was far too used to having cut-and-paste available in my writing process. By the third page of the story in my journal, I had to give it up as a lost cause because of all the circles, arrows, and cross-outs. I couldn't read what I'd just written.

So, departing Singapore with my visa tucked safely in my passport, I wrapped my new toy in a cloth and two Ziplocs and slid it in next to my journal. Ultimately I would write the first draft of my first novel over the next nine months and six countries.

As I moseyed out to the airport to face whatever rigors awaited me there, I wondered how the lovely woman had fared in the Australian embassy's visa office. Maybe she's there still.

South Korea / Singapore: 3 days / 41.8 km (26 mi)
Elevation Climbed: 0.1 km (0.06 mi)
Total Distance to Date: 6,231 km (3,872 mi)
Elevation Climbed to Date: 35 km (21.7 mi)

4

AUSTRALIA

24 JULY 1993 – 9 OCTOBER 1993

Strine: *Fugingudonyamate!*
English: *Fucking good on ya', mate!*
Translation: *No! Really? That's great! Well done, you!*

A Word of Advice

I landed in Darwin after four days, five countries, four planes, a ferry, and one embassy. I'd struggled with communication in Japanese, German, Russian, Hebrew, Singapore English, and a half-dozen other linguistic snafus in the ninety hours I'd been in transit.

A customs official inspected my passport, "Ridin' a pushie. Good on ya'. Welcome to Australia."

I almost kissed him for speaking in some way that didn't require pictograms.

I pedaled the half dozen kilometers into town. It was a cool morning as the sun rose. The plane had landed at first light. Long before the midwinter heat rolled in, I was sitting on a park bench looking across the Beagle Gulf toward the Timor Sea.

Waves of jet lag washed over me as muscles twitched and released from so many hours and kilometers. I wallowed in the sun and the scent of the sea. There was a little sharpness, a dryness on the air that somehow permeated the salt with an arid tint. A mother parked a stroller at the next bench over and talked to her little girl. I could understand it. I wanted to go over and kiss her, too, but figured that wouldn't be advisable. Besides, I probably smelled like I'd been in transit for four days. Instead, I just sat in the sun and let the cool aqua-blue wash the thousand colors of five countries from my retinas. It was hours before I could find the energy to traverse the three blocks to the hostel.

"I'm riding down the Stuart Highway to Alice Springs on a bicycle." I spoke tentatively to the youth hostel clerk: half statement, half question. Seventeen hundred kilometers (over a thousand miles) of desert and bush separated me from my next goal.

He brightened up. "Down the Alice on a pushie? No worries." It turns out that "the Alice" is both the highway and the town in Australia's center.

"No worries," I was to learn, was the Australian answer to almost everything.

"I'm sorry. I don't have the right change."

"No worries."

Someone slows down to make sure I'm okay when resting beside the road a hundred kilometers from anywhere.

"No worries," I call. And with each repetition it becomes a little more true. As each day passed in Australia, "no worries" worked its way into my attitude.

"I don't know if I can do this," I tell myself. "I mean, it's seventeen hundred kilometers of Outback." A little voice crops up from somewhere, "No worries." And I roll down the road. (Twenty-five years on, it is still a common response for me; a key element of how I try to approach any situation.)

Before I left town, I wallowed in Darwin for about a week. I bought a poncho and shipped home the heavy rain gear (an act of great faith that I was finally free of the worst of the rains—which thankfully turned out to be true). I picked up some extra tires and tubes.

The roads in the Outback are sealed, not really what an American would think of as paved. The existing surface is sprayed with a thick slurry of tar, then covered with one-inch angular gravel that gets squished into the tar by a road roller. I actually passed a sealing operation at one point. A steady stream of tar and gravel trucks feeding a monstrous paving machine, followed by a small fleet of rollers. They were able to lay fresh pavement at about two kilometers per hour without ever stopping.

I'd been warned by other cyclists: This surface chews up tires something fierce. They were right, but I was ready.

Most travelers stay in hostels, called "backpackers" in Australia. The majority are fresh out of college, and they're also called "backpackers." They're twenty-two and taking a year off to "like, travel and party, man." The conversations became tedious when they tried to relate to this crazy cyclist in his mid-thirties busy having an, albeit early, mid-life crisis.

The night before I moved on, I was sitting at a small table outside my Darwin backpacker, writing postcards and enjoying the cool evening air. The cards were peppered with pithy comments about watching for thunderstorms, despite it being the middle of the dry season. Most of Australia only has two seasons, the Dry and the Wet. I wrote and let the wonders of the English language flow around me without joining in much. Sometimes the Strine was a tad thick, but sometimes it was Californian Valley Speak.

A coed stopped near my table in a tight, blue miniskirt. She didn't sit down, she just sort of posed a few times, perhaps gauging my reaction to her long legs and deep cleavage, and jumped into the middle of a conversation.

"I'm like going to Cairns real soon, you know. But I just like haven't left yet. I'm sort of still here after two weeks."

"Can be a problem."

"Don't you just know." She tried another pose, then flounced off to practice her poses elsewhere.

Inertia is a force to be contended with when traveling. And Darwin has a strong draw despite being a small town isolated at the Top End of Australia. (Top End is the common reference to the north-central state named the Northern Territory.) There's a splendid little museum, a huge number of pubs, and very friendly locals.

"Nice skirt. Think there's a brain in that body anywhere?"

A man, a little older than me perhaps, was the only other occupant of my table. His Strine was thick enough to require a foghorn.

I shrugged. Maybe just impossibly young.

"Where you headed?"

"Down the Alice on a pushie. In the morning. Has me a little worried."

"On a pushie? *Fugingudonyamate!*" My first encounter with this monosyllabic praise. "Too many folks travel too fast. Don't take their time. It's beautiful out there, nowhere else I'd rather be."

Ian introduced himself, cracked open a second can of beer, and slid it across the table.

"Alice is easy. Be careful, but no worries. Now doin' a cross of the Simpson or the Victoria, that's harsh. Gorgeous, but harsh."

Ian was the first man I'd met at the hostel who didn't speak primarily of bungee jumping and seeing a saltie at the zoo. A saltie is a really nasty breed of crocodile.

The Californian cruised through again, and yes, I'm sorry to say because of my thing about stereotypes, she was blonde, her long hair now up in a ponytail. She'd changed into pink shorts that were at least a size too small (they looked actively painful) and a very skimpy halter top. She paraded by, clearly trying to assess reactions from us and the couple dozen others lounging outside the backpacker as the evening settled in.

Ian waited until she was out of earshot once again. "Miniskirt was better. Left more to the imagination."

No argument from me. "You travel much?"

"Most Aussies get a fair bit about, but not many can live in the Outback. I had to learn. There's a warrant out on me in all five states. I'm headed back out tomorrow myself. Couple months in the bush and any recent trail will be a bit cold."

I eyed my companion. Was I being treated to a whopper, Australian-style? Or was he really some criminal? I prefer to think the latter. He was well-traveled, and an interesting and widely-read conversationalist.

He didn't offer details.

I didn't ask.

"I've heard that it isn't safe to free camp out there alone." I nodded toward the bush. "Is the Land Down Under so dangerous?"

"Don't say that. The Down Under bit. That's not us. You're in Oz—Australia, Aussie, Ozzie, Oz. And, yeah, it can be bloody dangerous. Not on some track like the Alice, mind. Though, I'd sleep in my tent if you don't know the critters' ways. The worst snakes are west of you and the red spiders are over east, but you should still be careful. Ozzies, on the other hand, there are some bad ones. Wait 'til no one's around and just duck off the track and into the bush. You'll be good."

I tried to imagine what a hardened criminal would consider a "bad one" and I'd be careful.

"So, it's possible to camp out there?" The bush still loomed before me as some great unknown beast that just might want to eat me alive. I've never been very good about hiding my emotions, so I'm sure it showed, but Ian (if that was his real name), was awesome about it.

"Now most Ozzies can't make it in the deep bush, but I love it out there. I've done it so much I can live near as well as an aborigine."

We glanced up at blue Lycra shorts and a braless, wet T-shirt working its way through the crowd. The blonde hair now in a braid over the shoulder. After Ian barked out a laugh, she gave our table a wide berth for the rest of the evening.

"Trolling for a free ride, that one." All the twenty-year-old males were dying, their tongues dragging in the dust. She'd find someone glad to pay her way plenty soon.

"In the 1960s I rode a pushie across the southern Victoria. Ran dry and lived under a bush for two days before a car came by. I was in such sad shape, I could barely flag them down for help. Too many people now." He nodded toward the crowd of backpackers around us. "Only place you could be that alone now is in the middle of the Simpson, and you don't want to go there."

We talked long after our free floor show had given up, or perhaps succeeded without our notice, and most had departed for their beds or another round at the pubs.

His last bit of advice saved me from a bad spot of trouble in a few weeks.

"There's these water tanks they put about every hundred kilometers, but don't count on 'em; sometimes they tap dry when you need 'em most."

Many Welcomes to the Alice

I crawled out of Darwin much later than I planned the next day and it was in the mid-90°s F (35°C) already. At lunchtime I crouched in the shade of a tree and chewed on a marmite sandwich. Marmite is the peanut butter of Australia. Vegemite, its much stronger cousin, was too much for my palate, but Marmite's sharp tang made sure I was awake and ready to continue. I batted at the flies trying to clean the salt from my face.

There's an old Ozzie joke about the Queen coming to visit. She descended from her plane and instantly began batting at the flies buzzing about her face. All the Ozzies in the crowd thought she was waving hello and remarked at how friendly the Old Girl was.

I hadn't noticed the problem at first. I hadn't ridden in a week and was riding strong. But farther down the road, as I slowed, I learned that anything under fifteen kilometers an hour (9 mph, which is pretty typical for a touring bike) and the flies could attack my sweat-soaked face. I inhaled them so frequently that I lost the grim desire to be ill each time it happened. Anything over that speed, and they'd take a free ride on my back, waiting for me to slow. I displaced whole colonies of flies many kilometers down the Alice each day as they freeloaded a ride in my wind shadow.

But during the midday break, I sat by the side of the empty highway and batted flies away from my face for several hours.

Once the midday heat dropped enough, two to three hours later, I'd remount and ride on until near sunset. It was July, their midwinter, and the days only had eleven hours of light. I frequently rode from sunup until just before sundown with a three- or four-hour break during the heat of the "winter's" day —summer was much hotter.

That first night into the Outback, I stayed in Tumbling Waters Caravan Park.

Campgrounds vary hugely from country to country but vary little within a country. Oh, there are fancier ones and simpler, but the nature of them stays the same in any particular country.

American campgrounds are for sleeping or being with a group of friends.

In New Zealand, there is always a central kitchen, even in the smallest and most remote place. Everyone gathers there to cook their evening meal and socialize. During my three weeks there, I came to really appreciate the communal fun. I'd sometimes stake out my place at the end of a table and spend the whole evening chatting with whoever was passing through to cook and eat.

Japanese campgrounds are terribly expensive, $25 US a night and up, with minimal facilities, and no one would think of being so rude as to talk with you. Very lonely places to be.

Tumbling Waters Caravan (i.e. small RVs) Park was a hoot. There's no other word for it. They served grilled barramundi (a fantastic fish somewhere between swordfish, salmon, and cod) for such a reasonable price even I could afford it. I was joined by half a dozen locals at my picnic table. They were excited about what I was doing and were filled with suggestions on neat things I shouldn't miss farther down the track.

Our conversations were interrupted by singing. This wasn't karaoke or some performer. Someone simply burst into song and everyone that wasn't busy chewing joined in. They were a group of Ozzies singing together for the fun of it. By the time the fourth song or so was going around, my table was spending more time laughing than singing. My attempts to pick up their songs on the fly and adding raucous solos where I expected a chorus was too much for them.

A few nights later, I chatted with two college professors who were taking a month-long road trip without their wives. Two old friends rolling through the Northern Territories (NT) together doing a little fishing and a lot of relaxing. They invited me to tea, and I accepted with great trepidation.

The Japanese need to give a gift no matter how inappropriate had made me gun-shy. I had once attempted to refuse a gift of sausages by telling a man that I didn't eat meat. I know I had the sentence correct; I'd used the phrase many times by that point. Because I wouldn't take them, they ended up set carefully beside my bike, and I was the one being rude for not accepting them. They were the only gift he had to give in that moment to a foreigner visiting his country.

Another man insisted I take his lunch, though the leavings of my own were spread about me and we were far into the country. He went hungry yet left his food for me against my protestations. I even tried asking him to join me in this second repast to no avail.

Not how Australia worked. Lee and Colin were simply a joy. I finally explained my initial hesitancy.

"Not in Oz, my friend. We find people to be interesting, fun things. Sure, scenery is beautiful, but it doesn't make you laugh."

The NT is perhaps the friendliest place I've ever traveled. One day—deep in a scorching afternoon as I rolled down the track—a car pulled up right alongside me. A window rolled down and a hand held out a juice box. I couldn't see the driver, just the arm and box. I took it without really thinking. The shock rippled up my fingers and I stared at it in disbelief as the window rolled up and the car pulled away.

It was cold.

It was frozen solid.

I was riding in hundred-plus degree (38°C+) heat holding a

large block of ice. I shook myself free of amazement and waved my arm over my head. He flashed his brake lights twice and disappeared into the heat haze shimmering off the sealed road. It took a whole hour to melt as I rubbed it across my forehead and around my neck time after time. Before it got too warm, I stuck in the little straw and sipped ice-cold nectar down my parched throat. Heaven.

A few years back, while riding through New Zealand on holiday, I learned that Kiwis have an innate kindness that seems appropriate to an American 1950s sitcom—they're so polite that it's almost surreal.

There'd been a time on the South Island—even more polite than the North Islanders—when I'd been climbing a blind curve. The road was newly paved with a deep ditch close by the side. Nowhere to even stop, despite knowing that cars were lining up behind me as I labored upward. No view for them to safely pass.

Ten minutes later I finally reached the top of the hill and the curve, pulling off into the first dirt driveway. I turned back to look. There hadn't been a single horn honk or shout for the entire climb, but I wasn't ready for what I saw. As each of the twenty or more cars drove by, each driver waved hello before driving away.

Now, I'd hit Australia. Here they might well have cursed me or called out a ribald, teasing cheer. But there was no question that some of them would be waiting to buy me a brew and wish me well at the next roadhouse—which did happen several times.

The Kiwis' kindness is very British—reserved and thoughtful, just like the people—Ozzie kindness is a hard slap on the back and a *Fugingudonyamate!* shouted in your ear.

Stay on Track—or Bust

Farther down the road, I had gotten off the main track on a side road to see a wildlife preserve. A thin line on the map called me toward my next recommended destination. Rather than backtracking from the preserve for thirty kilometers to the Alice, going south a ways, and turning back in for another thirty, I *could* just go down this back road.

The spirit of adventure took hold—at least I prefer to think of it that way in retrospect.

Ten kilometers farther from the main track, I made the turn onto the Wangi Road, marked as gravel on my map. Three rough kilometers later, I was thrown aside and almost fell as the surface changed abruptly to deep sand. I've ridden through gravel, snow, hail, and mud, but sand is the worst to ride on a bike. It just sucks. Nor was this nicely compacted beach sand; it was dry, deep, and shifting.

That didn't stop me, however.

I'm too Type A to be so simply turned aside.

If I just put my head down, I can bull my way through anything.

Five kilometers farther down the Wangi, I was thrown from Junior for perhaps the tenth time in an hour-long struggle to remain upright. The fine red sand had filled my nostrils and lungs and my sweat was gritty where it ran down into my eyes. I was so strained that I didn't even notice if there were flies or not. I looked down the shimmering sand "road" hoping for a sign of gravel, knowing there was none to see. My trail behind looked little different except for the long, snaking slice of my tires that was already filling in with the slow rolling of the little grains in the breathless air.

There are so few residents in the NT that individual homes are marked on the state map that spans an area the length of

California and three times the width. The next habitation of any kind was sixty kilometers ahead. Scrub trees spotted the landscape among the low, gray brush that covered this region of the Outback. No water on the Wangi Road.

While turning around was the obvious choice, according to my journals it was anything but, despite Ian's words about the hazards of the Outback still clear in my mind.

I backtracked five kilometers of sand and fifty kilometers of sealed road to the Alice. I just kept repeating, "I don't have to prove anything to anyone. Including myself." I didn't have to survive a ride from hell just to prove I could manage a dirt track. A year ago, I would have ridden the dirt, even at the risk of dying in the desert, because... I don't know why.

- 29 July 1993, Caravillage Caravan Park, Batchelor, NT

How many things had I done in order to "prove" I was good enough, strong enough, skilled enough? It was perhaps the first time in my life that I wondered what I was doing to please others rather than myself. Much of my computer career had been at Dad's prompting. I'd set out to prove to him that I was indeed "good enough," that I did deserve respect.

It would take me years to understand that was never going to happen, despite having proven it many times.

We used to sail together in a little twelve-foot fiberglass boat called a Sunfish—my favorite part of every summer was our family's two weeks out on Cape Cod, most of which I spent on that boat. Nearing retirement, he had finally purchased a twenty-four-foot boat and we'd sailed it together several times when I returned to the East Coast for a visit.

Well, I mentioned in "The On Ramp" introduction that I had once bought and rebuilt an old fifty-foot wooden ketch (a two-masted sailboat). I'd learned how to really sail it by the next time Dad visited me in Seattle from his home in Connecticut.

We'd sailed hours out across Puget Sound one evening. On our return the next morning, the wind had kicked up to twenty knots (about twenty-five miles an hour). A big boat like the *Lady Amalthea* just lives for those kinds of winds, so I started hauling up every bit of sail.

"Shouldn't we be taking in a reef? Maybe turn on the engine and douse all the sail?"

I'd never heard doubt in my dad's voice before and couldn't identify it at first. He was a man who was always completely sure of what he was doing, whether taking a wrong turn against directions or tackling some untried project.

In that instant a flash of joy slammed through me. And a wave of guilt once I understood the reason for that joy.

For the first time in my life, I was *measurably* better at something than my father. It was a victory in a race I hadn't ever imagined we were running. (That night at dinner with a couple friends of mine, he completely changed the story. He literally made up a scenario in which he was the triumphant one. While I sat their speechlessly aghast in silence, a friend consoled me, "Don't say a thing. Whatever the story is, you know the truth.")

Still, here I was, halfway around the world, and might well have killed myself if I had continued down the Wangi Road. Over a decade later and I was *still* making some vain attempt to appease my father.

I'd gone to Japan for much the same reason. I went because of *The Roads to Sata* in which Alan Booth said he didn't much like Japan despite having lived there for years. I didn't either.

I'd remodeled a house for a family I never got around to starting, making it larger and more spacious, never acknowledging my own preferences for small and cozy. How strange was that? My wife and I now live very happily in a small, cozy house.

And deep in the heart of Australia, I rode the extra kilometers of that sealed road, so rough before and so wonderfully luxurious after the Wangi Road.

I hoped that I'd learn someday.

A harsh lesson on the Wangi Road. All the footprints were me trying not to fall and break something thirty kilometers from the nearest help of any kind.

Along the Alice, I passed through kilometer after kilometer of low trees, sparse bushes and scrub, and open patches of red dirt. Ian was right, it was by no means unchanging. Near Darwin there were more frequent trees, here they were fewer and the grasses were slowly replaced by scatterings of scrub, mostly brown and dark green in the middle of the Dry. I found the variations subtle and soothing; I was moving slowly enough through the world to notice the little changes.

The Outback was like choosing a single hue from the vast palette of the rainbow to make a quilt, perhaps blue. But within "blue" there are such variations and textures that a whole world can be painted and brought to life, even more so by not being lost in the panoply of other colors.

One day, as I rounded one of those long sweeping curves that occasionally broke the unending straightness of the track (Oz for "road" in the Outback), I came upon an acre of wildflowers. I drifted to a halt. The terrain was no different in form than the dry land of the last fifty kilometers or probably the next fifty to come. It was simply lush with greens, blues, reds, yellows, tiny purples, and bursting whites. The Outback had offered me a gift to remind me to move slowly and keep my eyes open.

I continued down the track paying less attention to the arduous riding and more to the land shifting around me. In three days, I had ridden two hundred kilometers yet climbed under a thousand meters. It was the second flattest stretch of my entire journey. The flattest was from that point on south to Alice Springs.

I turned aside into Litchfield National Park. It is one of those impossible places that spring up in the Outback. Out of nowhere, trees began to soar upward. Most of the Outback was peppered with one-story trees, sparsely struggling upward against the lack of water. In Litchfield they soared five stories above. They were all clustered together in a small copse set in the middle of the arid landscape.

In the midst of the wood, at the south end of the Wangi Road that had defeated me three days before, lie the Wangi Falls. A ten-story waterfall careens down the face of a towering cliff and splashes into a wide pool. I stepped off the bike and threw myself into the lower pool: bike shoes, helmet, and all. My skin soaked up water like a sponge that has dried into a curl in the back of the cleaning closet. I wanted to just sink to the bottom and wallow like some old water buffalo.

Later, I settled into a pool about halfway up the waterfall with an Ozzie teenager. Level with the treetops, we looked down upon the whole park spread out clearly below our eagle's aerie.

"It's a lot quieter than our American parks. No generators, stereos, TVs. You have these little caravans; we have fleets of these large modern RVs."

"No pets either."

I looked over the edge of the pool at the little world below us surrounded by the unending bush. I'd missed that.

"No animals allowed in any NT parks. The salties and freshies aren't stupid. They learned a simple lesson; dogs will bark at them rather than run away. Pretty dumb when you realize that a full-grown croc can run at twenty klicks and eat a dog in a single chomp. They generally like to be left alone but come from far and wide when a dog barks. Nothing like a loud invitation to a free lunch."

I looked at the pool I'd plunged into so freely just a few hours before.

"No worries. The park rangers keep the pools clear. Catch 'em and take 'em for a little ride. I remember once when me and my da..."

I could feel an Ozzie tall tale coming on.

"We were camped along this billabong (a sharp river bend) cooking our day's fishing over a campfire. This croc comes up out of the water, eats our fish, cooking sticks and all. He continues right through the coals and dives back into the water on the other side."

Okay, I wasn't going to buy that one. People don't camp next to croc swamps. Well, Ozzies do have a certain stronger-than-the-world attitude. Maybe... The sad truth is I have a huge gullible streak for a straight line that is far wider than that tiny pool in the middle of the Outback. Pitiful but true.

Truth and Tall Truth

The line between reality and tall tale is always blurred in this vast country. On my ride from Litchfield to Katherine, I passed some very strange road signs. On a perfectly flat piece of road, stretching unvaryingly from horizon to horizon, I came across a series of posts. They were a bit taller than I was with a large "1" in the middle and a "2" at the top. Two or three of these posts were spaced out over a kilometer or so.

I halted at the last one and pulled out my monocular (half a binocular, saves weight, a constant concern when you have to haul everything with you for over ten thousand miles). Sure enough, there was a definite dip in the road behind, perhaps two meters in three kilometers. I asked someone about them later that day when we were both stopped at a water tank.

"During the Wet," (their summer) "there be these rainstorms and flash floods. Those posts tell the motorist how much water is over the road."

"But they're kilometers apart."

"Aye, and the whole area will be covered a meter or so deep after one of the storms. No worries, it'll drain down in a few hours or a day at most. If anyone is dumb enough to drive the Outback without a few days of food and water, they get what they deserve."

This was hard to imagine. But that afternoon I rode on a bridge across a half-kilometer-wide, dry arroyo. Sure enough, when I looked over the side, it was marked like a ship's waterline to a depth of eighteen meters (nearly sixty feet). Water five stories tall and several city blocks wide was impossible to imagine in the parched wash below with its occasional spotting of desperate scrub. A local insisted that the bridge had been covered up to the road deck four times and washed out once in her lifetime.

Everything is somehow bigger in Oz.

There isn't a Texan tall-tale story that some Ozzie couldn't outdo or wouldn't at least die trying.

Eight of the ten most poisonous snakes in the world live here. Six-foot-tall, four-hundred-and-fifty-pound kangaroos. The northern beaches are closed for three months, literally no swimming, during the Wet due to the deadly jellyfish. Great white sharks in the southeast. Salties and freshies well into the interior. Bloodworms, I don't even want to know what those are. An area the size of the continental US and almost entirely desert. Deadly dangerous expanses of sand that have taken many lives.

The list seemed unending—and these are all the verifiable and true bits *before* the tales even get born, never mind grow tall.

The locals, of course, play it for all it's worth. But I did see a sixteen-foot croc, I stopped and measured it, as roadkill along with all the roos and emus. On some stretches of the Alice it was hard to breathe due to all the roos rotting in the midday sun; I'd barely finish holding my breath from one corpse before arriving in the windage of the next.

Once I was trying to determine the nature of a large lump in the heat haze. As I neared, it began to move. At the last moment two enormous vultures took off from a dead roo. With a wingspan greater than my reach, one enormous bird struggled aloft directly toward me. I had to duck to my handlebars to avoid being struck by his pumping wings. Their stench nearly knocked me off my pushie anyway.

In the Outback, most people don't drive at night. Those few that do have enormous bull bars mounted across the front of their vehicles. It is the only thing that offers any chance of survival from hitting one of Australia's nighttime fauna. The emus and kangaroos are attracted to the roads by the relatively lush growth along either side. Moisture that condenses on the fast-cooling road, as well as runoff from the occasional rain, feeds the roadside flora and attracts the nighttime foragers.

I visited one other Top End park before I rode back out into the bush and pointed Junior firmly south. Just outside the town of Katherine, my last town but one with a population over ten in the next twelve hundred kilometers, lies Katherine Gorge.

The gorge twists its way through the Outback, apparently starting nowhere and leading nowhere. A company rents small kayaks at the head of the first gorge for individual journeys through the canyons. The walls tower up to fifty meters on either side. I paddled across the placid, crystalline water and struggled across the various rock falls between the long stretches of river trapped and isolated by the Dry. They might be waterfalls during the Wet but they were a hard portage now. I camped with a few other adventurous folks who had made it to the seventh gorge.

I spent the evening talking with a twenty-three-year-old Finnish woman.

"I came to Australia with a boyfriend from here who nearly convinced me I was stupid and not really worth looking at."

It took me a moment to recover. Her svelte, fit frame clad in only a bikini, never mind the intense blue eyes and white-blonde hair, had been trying to curdle my hormones for the last few hours.

"He said I was so immature that he'd take care of me. I think he just wanted to control me."

"Not to judge someone I don't know, but he sounds like a complete asshole."

"No. Well, perhaps some, but it's okay. Before I go home, I decided that I'd best straighten my head out and see some of Australia."

Later, lying in sleeping bags a meter apart, I could see her profile against the vast night sky. The nearest light not from the heavens was some ten kilometers away at the kayak launch, yet the stars of the Southern Hemisphere are so much brighter than our Northern counterparts, I could see her clearly. There was no sign of invitation and I hadn't the nerve to ask.

"So, you're saying that all those stars in the Milky Way, it's like we're looking at a plate edge on?" We'd been talking about the stars and the shape of the galaxy.

"Yup."

"Then what holds it together?" And we were off on the topic of gravitation and galactic spin.

We spoke on and off the next day as we paddled up to the farthest canyon, far past where most people gave up, and paddled back.

"I've spent four weeks traveling alone now. I liked him, but you're right, he was a jerk. Men in my country are not so cruel. I almost believed him."

I finally found my voice at our last rest stop, back in canyon Number Two, before returning to the launch and the bus waiting to whisk her off to Darwin and home.

"I think that you are not only quite intelligent, and funny, but also astonishingly pretty. I think that you are the most adult and thoughtful woman I've met in some time. I am sorry that our paths are traveling in opposite directions. Truly sorry."

She squinted her eyes and tilted her head to one side. "Really?"

I nodded though I couldn't speak, for quite different reasons. How many times had I avoided saying what I felt to a woman for fear of appearing stupid or perhaps offending? I've had any number of female friends over the years, and some wonderful women who have consented to date me for a time.

But floating in Katherine Gorge was perhaps the first time I had spoken my feelings to an attractive woman rather than folding up into my usual tongue-tied self. Wherever she is, I hope that she is with someone who appreciates her and who listens. I guess that is what I'd wish for anyone, but it is definitely her turn.

That night, I slept on the green lawn at the park entrance in just my sleeping bag—my tent was too heavy to drag over all those rockfalls and I'd left it back at a youth hostel in Katherine.

In the middle of the night I was awakened by a tearing sound. It wasn't loud as it moved slowly around my sleeping bag. Finally, able to stand it no longer, I sat upright, ready to run, and aimed my flashlight at the sound.

A couple of small roos, wallabies barely a meter tall, were happily cropping the irrigated grass around the trees. No need for lawnmowers here. They blinked at me with large, dark eyes before returning to their task. I went to sleep to the gentle sound of roos munching their way around my sleeping bag.

Kayaking Katherine Gorge with a young Finnish lady, seeking her own way home.

Spinning Along, Just Singing a Song

Spinning down The Alice is kind of monotonous, but is also a level of training I had never done before. Open stretches of road, no goal, just spin until too tired to continue. A hundred kilometers, two hundred, and the unchanging Outback shifted and shimmered around me like a kaleidoscope seen from the corner of the eye. Looked at straight on, nothing had altered, the same browns and grays against the sharp, desert-blue sky. Trees, bushes, grass, sand.

Yet glanced at sidelong, it shifts.

The road ends at the top of the world, a two-meter rise just sufficient to block my view ahead. On the crest, the next rise ends at the top of the world once again—perhaps three, perhaps twenty kilometers down a perfectly straight track.

And I keep on spinning.

Every twenty kilometers I stop for five minutes or so, wave away the flies for a bit, and climb back aboard. On the move again, in moments the no stop never existed, just spinning as the kaleidoscopic Outback shifts again.

Sometimes I'd tap my fingers to counterpoint the beat of that spin. It starts at the very end of my right index finger and slowly coaxes the others into play. My left hand, not used to strumming from my many attempts to learn to play guitar, starts making little chord progression-type movements, slightly compressing the cork tape wrapped about my handlebars. Soon there is music moving on its own. The sound has my hands moving back to the hard beats of playing percussion in high school band. Jazz riffs ripple back and forth, and I start singing to the beat of my knees swinging up and down and up and down.

There's a problem here.

It isn't Junior. He provides the nice little taps of joints in a concrete road or random crunches of gravel as we cross an Australian sealed road. The occasional odd squeak and whirr slide into the music just fine.

No, the problem is that I can only remember the first two lines of any song.

Ever.

I sing out:

"Early one morning, the sun was shining, I was laying in bed

Wondering if she'd changed at all, if her hair was still red. Hmm hmm hmm hm hm hmmm. Da da di da di dum. Tangled up in Blue."

It didn't matter who I mangled; the third line was always a major roadblock. Being so anal retentive, it was thousands of kilometers before I let myself start making up words to fill in the gaps. Sad, I know. But Junior put up with it all adding to any chorus as needed.

Squeak squeak. Crunch-a-rumble, crunch.

On a typical day, I would pass two or three turnoffs to distant cattle stations, a gravel pit, or a town of a combined gas station, caravan park, and three houses. Sometimes I paralleled an old dirt runway left over from the World War II defense of The Alice against the incursions of the Japanese.

A hundred kilometers later, stopped?

It is just the unchanging bush. My tent easily hidden by a cluster of scrub fifty meters toward the nothing. The nearest human being is perhaps sixty kilometers away. Because of the roos on the road, the night is truly silent except for the occasional night bus. Even the road trains don't dare run after the sun completes her daily task.

The Mighty Beasts of The Alice

Road trains.

My first encounter with one was shortly after leaving Darwin. On an empty stretch of road I heard a distant truck horn. I checked my mirror. He was well back and I was surprised at such a decent forewarning. I glanced again and he was right on top of me. I shot off the road onto the sandy shoulder and was nearly pitched over the handlebars as Junior jerked to a standstill. The truck roared by at well over a hundred and fifty kilometers an hour (~100 mph). The wind actually did knock me over as not one or two, but five full-length trailers shot along in the semi tractor's wake.

There are no curves in The Alice and fewer towns. They crank it up as fast as they can, and everyone, especially lousy little cyclists, needs to stay clear. Most will pop their horn as they approach but I learned to keep my ears open and check my mirrors often. One driver regaled me at a roadhouse with tales of "killer trains" whose drivers hated pushies. And more stories of pushies getting sucked under the rear wheels by the backdraft and the driver never knowing. Then I saw a double-wide house flying Down the Alice at 150+ kmph (100 mph). It drove down the centerline and was as wide as the pavement. I never saw what happened when a double-wide met a road train.

Ozzie tall tales or not, I dove for the sand whenever a road train approached.

At night, a deep tranquility sets in. As the sun sets, the temperature drops twenty or thirty degrees (10-15°C) and the flies retire for the night. I'd cook up a pot of rice and throw the veggies right on top to steam. A little spice and soy sauce and it was time to watch the stars come out.

My "home" lies just behind me. A small tent with one stake driven between Junior's spokes so that he can't go walkabout without me. He still wears all his panniers. Sometimes I turn on the Russian shortwave jazz station, but more often I listen to the crystalline silence of the stars coming out.

Japan's moist air, thick with pollution, is a distant memory. The ozone here is so thin that most Ozzies wear sunblock, even to go for a casual walk—I hate sunscreen but slather on the SPF 30—and come out as brown as a chestnut. I write in my journal by the shining of the stars and can read a book without candle or flashlight if there is even a sliver of a moon above the horizon to augment the starlight.

Mid-Life Crisis on Wheels

I sleep in my tent each night, contemplating the possible reality of Ian's spiders and snakes. I felt cut off from the stars, but help is a long way off.

– journal entry somewhere south of Tennant Creek, Australia

My routine as I traversed the Outback was comfortable, safe, quiet.

At least until "That Night."

I was woken by a tear and a crunch. Teeth ground nearby and, I swear, the patter of dripping saliva. Heavy thuds actually vibrated the ground beneath my tent. Way less than a millimeter of ripstop nylon would provide no defense against such a foe as I knew approached me in the dark.

I need to preface this moment.

Over the past six months, I had suffered from a severe marketing inundation. The hype and media blitz for *Jurassic Park* was perhaps the biggest-to-date for Hollywood. After months and months of ads, promos, merchandise, and trailers, *Jurassic Park* was released in the US three days *after* I flew out to Japan.

A postcard from my sister had raved about it. "All of those dinosaur dioramas at the Museum of Natural History that we always loved so much?" (My second favorite part of visiting New York after the Hayden Planetarium.) "They make sense now. They brought them to life!"

JP opened the last week I was in Japan (after another nine weeks of marketing inundation). For $25 US, in dubbed Japanese (not even English subtitles). More marketing in Singapore and in Darwin... I wouldn't actually see the movie for another two months, but at least those last months of marketing were in English. However, I'd seen plenty of the trailer with the mighty, ground-pounding footstep thud and the ripples in the glass of water that's sitting on the dashboard.

That, *THAT* was the sound I was hearing outside my tent. The ear-shattering roar would soon follow. My survival would be decided in the next few moments. Fight or flight?

There are those who face fears, those who run from them, and those who just plain freeze.

Years later, I took a two-day course in the Las Vegas desert called *Firearms and Fiction* that demonstrated this particularly clearly.

A group called the Second Amendment Foundation was sick of how guns were mis-portrayed in fiction and decided to do something about it. For five years they sponsored a free-of-charge seminar to educate writers. The first day was all classroom: forensics and real-world CSI taught by the head of the Las Vegas Police Department's forensic team, hand-to-hand, hand-to-knife, and hand-to-gun combat demonstrations by ex-soldiers and fifth-degree black belts, ballistics samples, and far more.

The second day had two parts, both at a desert gun range under the scorching sun. The first part included a long line of twenty-odd weapons. Each of the fifteen authors was walked through loading and firing everything from a palm-sized midnight special to an Uzi, an M16, and even a .50 cal Barrett sniper rifle that could kill a person over a mile away. An Olympic gold medalist let us attempt skeet shooting with her $10,000 custom-made shotgun.

Mid-Life Crisis on Wheels

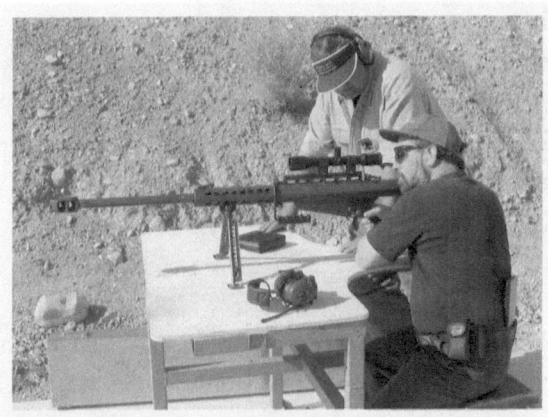

Learning the feel of firing at .50 cal Barret sniper rifle; a weapon model responsible for five of the fifteen longest sniper kills in history. Little did I know at that time that five years later I would end up launching a successful career writing military romances and thrillers. – photo by Karen Abrahamson (2007)

The other part of the day was a room-clearing exercise in a plywood shoot-house. Wrapped in full protective gear—bulletproof vests, gloves, neck guards, full face masks and helmets—we were sent in with simulated munitions (think paintball on steroids as this was the stuff that the US military trains with) to free a hostage.

Some broke down in tears when not allowed to run away from the exercise. Most simply froze in place, though some of these were coaxed to try the challenge.

A few of us, a very few, didn't ask. We went in to win the situation.

The fact that it was a rigged, no-win scenario was something we didn't learn until afterward, but one thing I did learn—I'm a runner-inner. If there is true danger, I may shake with fear later, but in the moment I will go on the offensive (a surprising revelation for a computer nerd).

Another ground-shaking thud outside my tent in the middle of the Australian Outback halfway between Darwin and Alice Springs. Would anyone ever know what happened to me if I failed? Who would ever stumble on the shreds of a tent and a rusted-out bicycle carefully hidden from any possible view of the endless road?

No one.

Time to succeed.

I took my only two weapons in hand: a flashlight and a Swiss Army knife with the three-inch blade folded out. As a bonus, I'd opened the corkscrew so that the sharp point stuck out between my knuckles in case I had a chance for a back swipe.

Not daring to risk the time or noise of putting on clothes, I silently slid on my sandals—I didn't want to die from stepping on a scorpion *if* I survived the upcoming battle.

I gently unzipped my tent's screen and eased it aside.

Holding my breath until the next deep thud shook the ground beneath me, I leapt forth with a loud yell. I held the knife low in one hand and the flashlight high to the other side to distract my adversary for that crucial second I needed to slash at a jugular vein—assuming the beast had one.

From a meter away, just the other side of a rusty barbed-wire fence I'd barely noticed when setting up camp, a huge head raised itself from the sparse grass. Two large brown eyes blinked at me twice before I began to laugh in shaky relief. My giant, rampaging, man-eating T-Rex—chewed its cud for a moment before returning to her grass. I grew up around cows and should have recognized the sounds, but nothing could have been more unexpected. I was fifty klicks from the nearest living soul, human soul anyway, but Australian cattle stations are truly immense.

I fed her some lush roadside grasses I harvested with my

mighty Swiss Army weapon. She seemed very pleased as I scratched her nose between her eyes, a favorite spot for cows, and didn't seem to mind my birthday suit in the slightest. She had wandered off a long way before the adrenalin jitters settled enough for me to sleep again.

Silence

In Daly Waters, one of the original Outback post offices, I made a dangerous mistake.

I had a beer with dinner.

Henry's idle comment back in Oregon came back to haunt me.

The Outback is so flat that it was easy to gauge my riding strength. There were no hills to take the blame and thankfully little wind. That one beer took thirty percent (*thirty percent!*) off my distance the next day. It made me too slow to reach my water stop. The tank I'd passed that day was dry. I'd remembered Ian's warning and had packed extra water for this multi-day dry stretch, but the beer had slowed me too much. Maybe he *had* told me fewer tall tales and more facts.

I stopped and camped twenty kilometers, normally an hour's ride, short of the next roadhouse when darkness hit. In my parched, post-one-beer condition, it would have taken two hours, possibly more to reach it. I'd planned to be the same distance again beyond the roadhouse and out in the bush by this time.

Exhausted by the long, slow day, I dropped to sleep with only a few pieces of bread for dinner. I couldn't waste my last half bottle of water on soup or pasta. I crawled into the roadhouse the next morning with one carefully conserved swallow of water still in my bottle. There was never any true danger, I'd been passed by two cars already that morning, but I learned my lesson well as I sat for a couple of hours rehydrating and playing with the roadhouse dog. That's after I'd refilled my ten quarts of water carriers—ten kilos (twenty-two pounds)—nearly twenty percent of my weight load and I'd never again begrudge a single ounce of it.

While I was sitting on the front porch, a tour bus rolled up and a pile of tourists dribbled out into the morning heat and gasped their way to the soda fountain. That particular roadhouse was a nice old place, filled with bit and pieces of gear from the old donkey and camel teams that had worked the area before the sealed road was built to accommodate the WWII road trains for getting supplies up to a Japanese-devastated Darwin.

That was good for perhaps two minutes. Then they returned to the front porch. Suddenly I was a display.

"How did you get out here on a bicycle?"

"I rode." Mind you I was eight hundred kilometers from both Darwin and Alice Springs at that rest stop. The true middle of nowhere to their way of thinking.

"Wow. Where are you going?"

"Around the world." A much more evocative answer than the name of the next town.

"How long did it take you from Darwin?" They'd probably been aboard the bus for some fifteen hours.

"Two weeks." (I had stopped at several nice parks but didn't see any point in mentioning them.)

Once again, I was busy becoming a participant in home slide shows. "There was this crazy American cyclist..."

They could barely tolerate the bus ride and there I was in my honeybee yellow, black, and white Lycra, green goggles, and white helmet sitting on the porch of a roadhouse in the middle of the Outback as if it was the most normal thing in the world.

I ended up with the entire busload circled around,

interviewing me. It was too much for the dog and he retreated under the porch until a long while after they departed. I longed to join him.

It was hard to imagine a sharper contrast, the busload and the bicycle tourer. I'd been spinning my pedals, so to speak, for four and a half months and five thousand miles (eight thousand kilometers). Do enough of anything and it may start to feel normal, no matter how bizarre it may be. Despite their questions about the hardships, I never thought to tell them about my bicycle seat.

I'd replaced the uncomfortable one back on the Oregon coast. It had broken in Japan and I had a terrible time finding a new one. Japan may build some of the best bicycle components in the world, but they export them all. The Japanese (at least the ones of 1993) primarily ride old three-speed clunkers. I rode for two weeks with a seat held together by straps and a very damp copy of Albert Einstein's *The World as I See It*, a nice sturdy paperback.

I finally found an acceptable bicycle seat, though not a great one.

I called my Seattle bike connection, Derek at R+E Cycles, and he'd shipped me the seat I asked for—a nice, narrow racing seat that I knew well from my commuting days. As I rode down the Outback, it sought to gore me. While chatting with the bus tourists, I had moleskin carefully applied around my butt blisters and my small chamois towel was folded and stuffed down the back of my shorts for padding. By the end of each day, I could only ride three or four kilometers between breaks. Then I'd get off to let the pain subside to a tolerable level and ride again.

My mileage (kilometerage?) began to drop even more as I neared Alice Springs. At first, I thought my conditioning and my butt were failing me. Until I passed one of the old WWII airstrips. Its half-century-old, orangey-gray windsock pointed straight back the way I'd come. It takes a thirty kilometer-per-hour (20 mph) wind to make one of those go horizontal like that. I hadn't even noticed the wind as it had built up so slowly, taking days to come to life.

That wasn't the worst of it. Fighting the headwind had shifted the rhythm of my spin rate ever so slightly—until it perfectly matched another Monkees' song than the one that had abused me while "dying" of the common cold in the Japanese Alps. At least this time I knew all the words to the song, except my rhythm only matched the chorus. For the entire last part of the haul down the Alice, I had the two-line refrain burned into my brain. Ahhh!

Leaving Tennant Creek, heading for Alice Springs.
A whole lot of kilometers from anywhere.

I reached Alice Springs after two extra days grinding into the brutal headwinds. I could barely walk. I waddled around town for two or three days while my blisters healed before people stopped asking me what was wrong. It also took several days to climb back out of my isolated shell enough to talk to the people around me. Being alone constantly, except brief moments of three weeks, had made silence a habit—a surprisingly comfortable one.

My whole life I'd always been pretty much surrounded by people. I ran the high school theater for years, then the college planetarium, before becoming the computer geek for theaters, law firms, and a Fortune 100. I wasn't the background nerd; I was typically the lead project manager. Building a high-functioning team is a learned skill for me, but it's a pretty second nature one now. In all those years, my time alone had never been comfortable—like sitting in that house without the family I'd imagined in it.

Three weeks in the Outback had been a revelation. I enjoyed the solitude of being alone. Free from the judgment of family, coworkers, and even friends. It had been me, some roos, and a demon cow.

And I'd loved it.

Parked in Alice Springs, I missed getting rolling as the sun cracked the horizon. There is a fantastic feeling of lightness to have everything in its place, strapped on just right, and feel the power surge into my legs as the sun's first rays wash over the landscape in a symphony of reds and golds. Greeting the day, alone.

After three weeks in the bush, a hundred-bed backpacker filled with discussions about bungee jumping was more than a tad surreal—it was an offense to the spirit.

A Bloody Big Red Rock

There are many ways to get around a country as big as Australia. I'd just ridden the same distance as Seattle to San Francisco in three weeks including numerous rest days and side trips to parks. Over wetter and hillier roads, it had taken me four weeks of brutal nonstop riding with only two days off the bike.

I still wanted to see Uluru (Ayers Rock) out in the Red Centre, nearly eight hundred kilometers further into the desert. My butt still hadn't healed enough to ride (and I wasn't to find a new seat until Cairns), and I was beginning to be a little more rational. My need to "ride the whole way" was amended when I saw a sign on the hostel bulletin board:

"Extra seat to Ayers and back. One quarter of gas."

A person can travel by bus, but then when and, more importantly, where you go becomes limited, and costs add up quickly. Thankfully there is a whole economy in Oz based on the resale of old cars from one traveler to the next, which are beaten around the country for six months or so, then sold again. I hooked up with two male Austrian chefs and a female Israeli army intelligence officer fresh from mandatory service; all twenty-three. At thirty-five I was once again the "old man" as I had been in almost every hostel I'd stayed in. Yet another reason I camped most of the way.

We bombed out to "The Rock," as it is commonly known, in an ancient Ford station wagon with the fake wooden side panels. It was the first time I'd moved faster than a bicycle since my sedate car trip across the winding roads of Japan's Shakotan Peninsula with Ryuzoh. These guys pegged the speedometer around 110 (the car was old enough to still be marked in miles) and let the frame shake and rattle as it would. We covered a week and a half of riding in four hours and fifteen minutes.

I finally caught my breath only a few kilometers before The Rock.

We set up camp (the two chefs figured they were two-to-one and challenged me to a tent-raising competition—I was stretched out on my bag and air pad before they had theirs fully raised). After a camp stove dinner, we went to the best sunset viewpoint.

As the sun dropped behind us, it shaded through orange, red, and at long last faded into black. Uluru is a huge lump of sandstone that sticks up into the sky as high as the Empire State Building Observation Deck and is about three kilometers long.

That's it.

There are no other hills, mountains, anything over a story tall, not even trees, for fifty kilometers in any direction. In the distance, The Olgas, an equally anomalous structure, hide farther west, and a high plateau graces the distant southern horizon, but Uluru stands alone.

So we watched the sunset, which was pretty enough, and set our alarms for the middle of the night.

At 3:00 a.m., ten or so hardy souls gathered at the base in the pitch dark. After a bit of flailing around, we found the marker chain for the only route to the top. We ascended quickly through the chilly air. The sky was still starlit when we reached the broad top.

Eventually, the limitless flat horizon lit with a directionless orange glow, broken only by the distant Olgas like some leftover potter's clay thrown from the wheel to the outer rim. The world went on forever. To think that I had the audacity to go and "see" that limitless expanse. The landscape here had been old 100 million years before the aborigines. If I ignored the campground, motels, and four-star hotel behind me, I could be the first creature to ascend to this place and see just how wide the world was once I poked my head above the day-to-day living down in the bush.

It made me feel small…yet large at the same time.

The world was so vast, but I was there to see it. To witness the beauty of the moment in time.

I wanted to call my father from the top of Uluru and tell him that it was worth it, because without my being there, this moment wouldn't have happened. The sun would have risen.

People would have watched. But it would not be me watching the sun rise as if on the first day of creation filling a vast empty world with life and hope. We hung out for an hour or two watching the light do its dance across the sky.

| Sunrise atop The Rock.

As we descended, we were horrified to see what we'd done. At one point, only a few steps to the side of the chain that we had more or less followed (but not always too closely), was a vertical drop of over a dozen stories. At the trailhead, hidden by the darkness of our nighttime start, were grave markers for the various tourists who had fallen from Uluru or died of heat stroke before the ever-present helicopter could be summoned.

Long lines now ascended the burning rock. Fifteen tour buses and nearly a hundred cars were clustered about the base. To get away, we ventured out on the trail around the base. Very few people circumnavigate The Rock, and now I know why. It took us several hours to slog through the baking sands. As we walked, we debated the big draw.

"It's a bloody big rock."

"No, it's a bloody big red rock."

"The guidebook says it gets black on the rare occasions when it rains." The Red Centre is far drier than the arid Alice.

"Or at night. It's black then, too."

"So, it's a nice, unusual, bloody big, red rock –except when it's black—in the middle of the nothing."

"Right."

"So what's the big deal?"

Yet when we returned, people were still climbing the face of Uluru to be fried like emu eggs on its now-baking surface.

I kept my sunrise thoughts to myself. Partly because sunrises always do that to me. I'm a night owl by years of practice—how can I go to bed when there are so many things to see, do, and learn. But while "living wild" had forced me from the road at sunset, it had also taught me a love of the sunrise. Of that moment when the world awakens and shrugs off the dark of night.

We drove on to the Olgas. They were more interesting and much less traveled for being the extra fifty kilometers into the nothing, but we were far too near heatstroke by then to spend much time wandering there. They soared aloft and leaned into odd junctures creating canyons and passageways, as well as amazing vistas of rock and bush.

Along the dirt track to Kings Canyon, the brakes stopped working. We quickly traced it to a severed line busily spitting hydraulic fluid into the sand. While we debated the intelligence of hiking the twenty kilometers into Kings Canyon through the midday heat on the chance of finding a service station, an Aussie pulled up. In minutes he replaced the hose, patched the old one just in case, and refilled the hydraulic fluid.

"Need to carry spares if you're coming out this far."

"We do," one of the chefs protested. "We have oil, gas, two tires, radiator hoses and clamps, and water."

"Nice start. You also want brake fluid, steering and

transmission fluid, small hoses, at least one master brake drum, and the tools to replace it all. Three days food and five of water..." The list kept going.

I hadn't even thought to look at what was stacked in the back of the wagon beyond our tents.

"That's the basics unless you're headed into the Simpson." He looked over the car and the motley crew we made. "You aren't going there are you?" The chefs shook their heads in unison.

He nodded his relief. "*Goodonya!*" was his cheery parting call. He drove off refusing payment.

A country where you can break down eight hundred kilometers up a road in the Simpson Desert that is only traveled once or twice a year is hard to imagine, but that's Australia. Ninety percent or more of the population (which is about the same as Beijing, now at 24 million) lives within a few dozen kilometers of the coast, and that's mainly in the south and east. The rest is the size of the continental US with the population of New York City. A *lot* of wide-open space.

Once back in Alice Springs, not called "The Alice" once you're in it, I looked at the map of what I'd done and where I wanted to go. I'd hoped to ride out to Cairns on the east coast, half again the distance I'd ridden down the Alice, and the towns were much farther apart. There was one gap I'd need ten days of food and water to cross. How to even carry that much was a whole separate problem. That'd be a hundred kilos (220 lbs.) of water alone.

I found a pair of twenty-year-old German surfers who spoke no English but were headed on a straight-through drive to Cairns and they agreed to tie Junior to the roof. They had no interest in a thirty-five-year-old fuddy-duddy and his high school German beyond his $100 AU donation toward gas. It was a painfully dull ride.

One Type or Another

Sitting in a car for almost fifty straight hours does strange things to your body and I staggered around Cairns (pronounced Cans) much as I had in The Alice. Over a month in arid climes didn't prepare me for the subtropical lushness of coconut palms waving in cool breezes over a boat-filled harbor.

Rather than being the only town for eight hundred kilometers around like The Alice, Cairns was one of a string of shore towns. Cars were so thick that road trains weren't even allowed. They had to be broken up back in the Outback lurking beyond a ridge just ten kilometers inland. Offshore is the Great Barrier Reef. The brutal temperatures of the Red Centre and the clouds of flies faded rapidly into forgotten memories and journal entries.

I was in heaven; at least I thought so at first.

I began to watch the travelers. There was a wider variety in Cairns than anywhere else on my journey. There are the Fodor / car rental / hotel / package-tour types. Other than the few times I became the unintentional feature of one of their tours, I didn't see them much.

The second type is the most common, "the backpacker." They're on what's called the "Crowded Planet Tour." This road-phrase comes from the immensely popular Lonely Planet Travel Guide series. It is great for the budget traveler, but so many people treat it as a bible that its recommended stops have become a mayhem of twenty-somethings who'd rather lose their cameras and money belts than their precious LP guide.

They hop hostel to hostel. Most are fresh out of college and always seem to be seeking the best pub or, and I'm really not making up how often this came up, the best place to bungee jump. Busloads left Cairns on the hour headed for the best bungee spots.

I was sitting in a food court along the shore enjoying a gyro. Over my tiny portable, I'd heard an Australian radio story about the large number of Greek immigrants arriving in Australia over the last few decades. Sure enough, the gyro was delicious, and, as I was to discover when I arrived in Greece most of a year later, quite authentic.

A dozen cuisines were represented in this little food court by the sea. I heard one backpacker ask another where they should eat. They ended up at McDonald's for "the taste of home," of all things.

Backpackers talk about what they've done, where they've been, and only rarely about who they met—in that order. I found it consistently difficult to communicate with this group.

The third and rarest type are what I call "the travelers." They are easily identified because they talk about people first, places second, and what they've done third.

Someone in Indonesia (still down the road a bit from here) suggested that there were two subtypes of travelers. One, traveling to meet, see, and do; the other traveling for the journey going on between the ears, with the journey as just the catalyst. External and internal travelers if you will. I was of the internal sort...uh, yeah, kinda obvious.

Back to the backpackers.

I thought of having a T-shirt made that said, "I'm not one of them." Any "traveler" would get it, but on the back I'd put, "If you have to ask, you are." I sought out the travelers with relative success, because they were also out searching for me. Another test. The travelers loved my three-tiered theory; backpackers would protest loudly that they weren't like that.

I rode out of there as fast as I could. Well, I slowed down enough to see a movie, *Sleepless in Seattle*. I was glad of the dark as I frequently had to wipe my eyes to see the screen. If I'd stayed home, maybe Meg Ryan would have fallen in love with me instead. Okay, maybe not Meg, but some nice lady. It was sure nice to see home anyway, which is what really made me cry.

Dad's next letter caught up with me in Cairns. The tempered, considerate tone of his first letter was gone. An irate diatribe flowed from the pages about my misplaced decision to travel. I could have learned the same lessons by staying home and reading a book or getting therapy and not worrying those I'd left behind.

Half a world away from my father, I struggled to explain that I would never have learned much about myself if I'd stayed in the career trap I'd built. I might not have even survived; my ex-business partner was being treated to prevent her second heart attack when I left. She was thirty.

Perhaps if Dad had been a little less concerned with work and a little more with family, we wouldn't have become estranged. And maybe, just maybe, he and my sister would have spoken even once over the prior decade.

Only now as I write this in 2019 do I see the parallel of the two sections above. My father, a backpacker through life, was concerned first and foremost with what a person achieved.

For him, there was *no* other measure.

I've struggled desperately over the years to understand him and I'm slowly coming to accept that I never will.

Perhaps it was one of those letters I should have burned rather than sent, but I didn't. I mailed it off and burned his instead over my camp stove so that I wouldn't have to carry such an evil thing with me. Typically, I kept my letters in a bundle and sent them home to add to my trip file. Not this one. I couldn't get rid of it fast enough.

Desperately Seeking Perfection

As I traveled north along the coast to see the remoter parts of Far North Queensland, I stopped at various marina bulletin boards looking for a sailboat ride to New Zealand. I wanted to spend the spring there, October to December, and then return to Australia to ride across the south from Sydney to Perth in the warmth of the summer.

It became harder and harder to write in my journal. Partly because I often had already written my thoughts once, or four or five times, to my friends in separate letters. But there was a sameness to it all: how much I miss home, how much I miss my friends, yet another day riding along the coast, yet more backpackers and tourists and crowds.

It was the same problem I'd had along the California coast.

I didn't write then because I was deep in survival mode, training alone in the cold rains.

In FNQ—Far North Queensland—the survival mode of traveling wasn't about kilometers and bad knees and rain; it was about my doubts and fears. It wasn't just Junior's wheels that were spinning.

At the Trinity Beach campground north of Cairns, a friendly local named James suggested I ride up to Noah's Beach if the crowds were making me crazy. No buses stop there.

While resting after a long struggle atop an isolated two-hundred-meter hill, I noted in my journal: "When I read this in the future, what will make this one particular gravel and mud-covered hill stand out from the hundreds behind me and the hundreds to come?"

Little did I know.

I crossed over it like so many others and arrived at Noah's Beach, three kilometers of white sand and palm trees. The sum total of facilities was a freshwater spigot and a toilet. There were seven of us spread out on that three-kilometer-long stretch of sand for the first week I spent there: a couple from Colorado, as sick of the backpackers as I, an Ozzie-Swedish couple, a lesbian couple who occasionally joined me bodysurfing but usually passed on the communal evening campfires.

And there was singleton me.

But it was a paradise in many ways. The primeval Australian forest rolls down from the hills beyond Noah's Beach and is stopped from reaching the sea only by a thin stretch of achingly white sand. We were living in a setting right out of *Jurassic Park*. The trees here were truly ancient. Due to Australia's geologically stable position on the planet, many species of trees had survived unaltered from the time of the dinosaurs.

I spent ten days on that magnificent, prehistoric strip of sand. It was the longest I'd stopped since leaving home. Most of the time I sat alone, swam alone, and ate alone. I had plenty of books to read and letters to write, but they were hard to focus on.

My trip wasn't turning out as I'd expected.

I'd thought there'd be so much free time. Five to eight hours a day on a bike puts a hole in the day. Breakfast, packing my gear, and checking over Junior took an hour most mornings. Setting up camp was half an hour and dinner took an hour by the time I cut, heated, cooked, ate, scrubbed the plates with sand, and put away the stove. I have no idea how I used to find time to work fifteen to twenty hours a day.

I was also so much more alone. How much of my life had I spent alone by choice? If being alone was optional, I was sick of my own choices. I had a number of friends in Seattle, despite my workaholic episodes—perhaps that was why I was so homesick.

For six months of this trip I'd constantly been perched on the verge of going home. Just to see a familiar face for even a day. As I sat outside my tent beneath the swaying palms, there was a gnawing in my gut. These folks at Noah's Beach were sharing their trip. Not me.

Was my dad right?

Was I not adding to society?

Was I performing the ultimate act of selfishness by not adding my energy and hard work to the good of society?

I certainly wasn't being selfish.

I was festering in the vast silence of that primitive, uncaring beach. He was right. I was going to die alone and in poverty. The worst of my fears were coming true.

Another three and a half years on the road and I'd be truly certifiable.

Maybe *that* would make him happy.

I could skip New Zealand. And I hadn't been that excited about Africa when I'd set out, maybe drop that as well. That would drop half a year. Maybe I could drop....

"Sell the house," Mac's voice came up from somewhere down deep. Really deep.

George dropped in to ask his question, "Why are you doing this to yourself?"

I could be in Cairns in four days, three if I pushed, and home twenty-four to thirty-six hours later.

No, that didn't feel right either. But one thing became clear: I was going home sooner rather than later.

"Wait! What about the perfect trip?" A part of me clung on. "There's five continents, forty countries, and all that impressive *noise* you made before you left."

What would my friends think? I wanted to call Mac and Ruth and ask, but the nearest phone was a day's ride back over that gravel-and-mud hill. Everyone I knew on the beach had left in the previous two days; I couldn't even ask them. There was one new couple, very neat and fit with their brand-new jeep parked in the lot. They had no use for the wild-eyed, bearded vagabond with a worn-out tent and a bicycle. Once again I was alone with a decision that could completely alter the vast scope of my life.

For two days I sat there, truly alone. Traveler's inertia had set in but it forced me to think.

Where had the need for "perfect" come into my life? I didn't think it was ego. I set much higher standards for myself than I expect of those around me. I don't try to impose my actions on others, I just beat myself up for failure to meet my own standards. Constantly!

I'd once automated a law firm at night to cover the caseload I was already struggling under during normal working hours. At another firm I installed a million-dollar system with three over-hires instead of six by working twenty-hour days for three years. I didn't work that hard for money, I was salaried. I did it out of some need for "perfect."

By being perfect, my father might finally respect me! (This revelation of so-not-gonna-happen would take me years more to realize.)

Now I was thirty-five and in the best shape of my life. I was camped in paradise. If this wasn't good enough, how could anything else be?

"Good enough" was a new phrase to my vocabulary.

What if I was just—good enough?

I tasted it.

"Perfect" wasn't required? How about "good enough" for a change?

I tried it again.

"Perfection isn't required, good is triumph enough."

It was like the proverbial thunderbolt. It felt as if I'd been chewing on it for six months and finally managed to spit it out whole. I could breath for the first time.

I didn't need to complete four years abroad to have the journey be worthwhile. With that single, deep-rooted realization, it actually already was.

I dove into the pounding surf one last time and, still wet, I loaded Junior.

I didn't know about the timing yet, or even where I was going next, I just knew that it was all downhill from here. I was headed home, maybe the long way around the world, maybe the short way, but homeward.

I didn't even realize that I'd climbed that harsh mud-and-gravel hill until I was winging down the far side.

Turning for Home – Long Way 'Round

I ran into James once again at Trinity Beach campground where I'd been two weeks before.

"I'm cutting my trip short, but I can't decide how to do it."

He raised an eyebrow in surprise. "Big change."

"Yeah. Noah's Beach. Did a lot of thinking there. Thanks."

"It's a good spot for that. So you've been to the Centre and snorkeled out on the Reef. Tassie's (Tasmania) just a nice island and NZ's just another English-speaking country. Asia and India, I was there in the merchant marine. Now those are totally different. And, no, the rest of Asia is nothing like Japan."

"Had me worried." I'd told him how little I'd liked the country.

He grinned, "Yeah, I've been there too."

We watched the waves sparkling with gold tips as the sun set behind us.

"You could turn for home, but I wouldn't if it were me. You've only been to the First World. The Third World is like a whole other planet. Be a shame to come so far and not go. Indonesia is incredible."

"What, fly into Jakarta?"

"No, don't do that. Big, ugly city. Go into the outer islands. There's a little hopper flight from Darwin into Kupang. Take ferries through the islands. That's the way to go."

The next day I found a response to one of my ads: free passage to NZ in exchange for working as crew. Three weeks at sea. I'd always wanted to do a deep-sea crossing.

I called Mac and Ruth. "I've been thinking. If I go to NZ and southern Australia, I might wear out and head home before I've seen a place like Indonesia or Thailand."

Besides, other than the crossing from Alice Springs to Cairns, my entire trip had been heading west. New Zealand was a turn back toward Seattle, a dangerous direction.

"Are you coming home sooner?"

Home was the word that did it for me. "I've been wrestling with that question for days (months), but I guess I already know the answer. Classic me to fight it so." I took a deep breath and let it out slowly.

"Good is triumph enough," I repeated my new mantra under my breath.

"I'll be home within a year." With that simple statement I cut two and a half years off my journey. It had taken me six months after quitting my career and another six on the road to reach this simple conclusion.

Perfect is not required.

I was able to pass the sailboat ride to New Zealand on to the Coloradoan couple from Noah's Beach whom I'd re-met in Cairns.

How many opportunities, jobs, friends, and lovers had I struggled to "do" perfectly? I didn't expect *them* to be perfect, I'm generally told that I'm supportive and forgiving, but that was never good enough for me.

It's a wonder I survived to thirty-five at all.

I teetered on a precipice as I stared out at the Coral Sea. Directly ahead, kitty-corner across the Pacific with no land between, was my home. I knew that now for certain. That's where I belonged, so why continue?

The sailboat was long since out of sight when I unraveled why I must continue. It had taken all this time to realize, down to the very core of my being, how that need for perfection had driven me ahead and, at the same stroke, driven my true goals further away.

If I could learn one more thing, one more old tape that I could somehow shred and discard, even a small one, I mustn't stop.

Four years before, I had fallen for a wonderful woman. I thought that maybe, just maybe I'd found the person to share my future with. I thought that until the day she said goodbye.

It wasn't until months later that she confessed she was afraid of becoming another "Matthew project." Too close to that fearful cannon of my drive to "do" perfectly. When I heard that she'd married happily just a few weeks before I started this trip, I was devastated. And here I finally stood on this Australian dock, ten thousand miles away, with the absolute knowledge of how I had scared her off. And the further truth that I would have run away from myself as well.

I turned my back on my home lying ten thousand miles to the northeast. Instead, I turned west and faced it across fifteen thousand miles.

Time to continue my journey.

Hole in the Wall

To "mark" Oz in my trip, I splurged on a dive course on the Great Barrier Reef. Four days and a dozen dives was a highlight

I won't even attempt to describe—just go. I was with a great international group and, other than being at least a decade older than everyone including the instructor, we had a blast. And that first internal lesson, so long in coming, soon had a whole fleet of company. I'd opened the sluice gates and it was time to hang on for the ride.

I had a sharp reminder that perfectionism has its place. A hundred feet (thirty meters) of water has to be respected. I was also proud to be the only one not aching from all the swimming. I didn't brag. I didn't even mention it. Why was it always so hard for me to allow myself to feel good?

-24 September 1993

Nights afloat on the dive boat, I've started having dreams of the past. It's like a parade of long-lost friends, old jobs, and ex-girlfriends in an unending array. I wonder whether it was a new form of self-abuse or was it some sort of unconscious review to purge old feelings and worries so that I can get on with new ones. I decided that even if it wasn't the latter, I'd assume it was anyway. I finally get it:

I'm tired of wasting energy on the past.
I'd rather waste it on the present.

-26 September 1993

This particular run of insights was to peak in a nightmare involving my ex-business partner on my last night on the boat. I was busily fixing a problem. She came in and stopped me from doing what I knew had to be done. I stood with hands poised above something that was half bicycle and half computer programming. I *did* know what I was doing. Just before I woke, I plunged back to work—over her protests.

Trust myself. I am good at what I do.
   -27 September 1993

My daily (nightly) lessons from the subconscious.

I've never had such clear insights in my life, certainly not three in four nights. Not even during personal growth workshops from a half decade before. Maybe I'd finally cleared enough garbage and old tapes and blocked feelings to acknowledge lessons I really had learned over the last thirty-five years.

Oh my God!

Progress!

How shocking!

I was so deeply involved in sorting through my memories and rethinking them that I spent another week just sitting in a campground outside Cairns. No journal writing. No communication with anyone beyond the confines of my brainpan. I was certainly in the thick of it.

One lesson I've always embraced: *Never do anything by halves.*

I never do. My wife often comments on the Matt-shaped hole in the wall—and her surprise at how often it succeeds.

A Fresh Road

At long last I replaced thoughts with action and wrote an itinerary for the first time in my journal:

- Indonesia – Oct 10
- Singapore – Dec 10
- Madras, India – Xmas
- Nepal –birthday (March)
- Athens – May Day
- Loire Valley, France – September

- Boston, Maine, New York – October
- Fly or drive home by Thanksgiving

I'd just cut thirty months off my "perfect" trip and it felt great!

The next afternoon I was on a bus for the forty-two-hour ride back across the Barkly Tableland and up the long road to Darwin, a place I'd left ten weeks before. I could have flown but I wanted to see another sunrise and sunset in the Outback.

It was worth it.

At the end of the long haul, our driver, the fourth of the journey, offered us this uniquely Aussie advice: "If you enjoyed the trip, tell your friends. If you didn't, don't suffer in silence, tell your enemies."

I was definitely back in the Northern Territory.

One problem: Junior wasn't.

It was the first time we'd been separated, and I was quite panicked. Apparently the driver hadn't noticed him leaning against the wall in Townsville, way back on the coast. A few frantic radio calls and Junior was on his way, forty-eight hours and fifteen hundred kilometers behind me.

I was a mess until we were together again.

Leaving Oz

I kicked around Darwin, but with no sign of Ian, it was much less fun. Less alive. I'd sent a postcard to the general delivery address he'd given me, but there was just me and hundreds of backpacker college kids.

I dropped by the Merpati Air office the same day Junior arrived safely. Swinging through the glass door, I entered another world. In order to make a reservation, I first had to have tea. Then the agent and I talked about politics, travelers, and anything else that came to mind over the next hour or so.

There was no hurrying him, nor did I try. It was very pleasant to just sit and chat over tea.

Someone else came in, refused tea, and fussed so much that the agent took their money just to make them go away.

We maundered on through the slow afternoon until at long last he pulled out a binder and wrote my name on a list. There were no tickets. When the list was full, the plane was full. Indonesia, I decided, was going to be fun.

In the long idle hours waiting for Junior and then for the next plane, I began writing as I looked toward my destination across the Beagle Gulf and the Timor Sea. I'd carried my little handheld computer as I rode back and forth across the Outback and, as I wrestled with Life on a remote Australian beach, I'd done little with it. I kept my journal by hand.

Now, at long last, scenes began to sneak back into my thoughts. The little vignette I'd created on the plane from Korea to Singapore began to grow and expand. I worked out the first meeting of a computer nerd named St. Peter and the Devil Incarnate, named Michelle. I didn't know where it was leading, but it helped pass the time.

For my last few days in Oz, I had a German roommate, the only other "traveler" in the otherwise "backpacker-ridden" hostel. He'd been out nearly four years. Franz's ties to home were so tenuous, I could feel them wearing thinner by the minute. We spoke a great deal of travel and home.

"Maybe I go to home next year."

The next day he was less sure. "Yes, there are five, six countries I still will see."

And the next, "Maybe I start looking for ticket next month."

As I packed to leave, he was heading to a travel agency, homeward bound. I hoped it wasn't my passionate descriptions of Seattle and friends that cut short his travels. Even to this day I feel a bit guilty. A little further down the road I was to learn a new definition of home, as well as an explanation of what had happened to poor Franz—though I wouldn't understand it for years.

Sunrise in the Outback. My favorite memory of Australia.

Australia: 77 days / 2,194 km (1,363 mi)
Elevation Climbed: 5.5 km (3.4 mi)
Total Distance to Date: 8,425 km (5,235 mi)
Elevation Climbed to Date: 40.5 km (25.1 mi)

5
INDONESIA
9 OCTOBER 1993 – 7 DECEMBER 1993

Bahasa: *Sepeda bumi jalan-jalan.*
English: *Bicycle world travel-travel.*
Translation: *My bicycle and I are traveling for the heck of it. (The "I" is understood. Jalan is "to travel." Jalan-jalan is "to travel with no particular purpose other than traveling.")*

A Whole 'Nother World

Merpati Air didn't open their counter until a half hour before the flight despite my arrival two hours earlier. The handwritten list resurfaced; the agent was the same one I'd shared a cup of tea with a few days before. I slid my passport across the worn, blue Formica counter. He placed a checkmark on the list, wrote "19-D" on a slip of paper, and returned it with my passport. The formalities were over. Junior was waved toward the baggage hold with no more concerns than a backpack.

The sixty-seat jet had two interesting features. The first: there were no seats over the wings. Instead, two giant inflatable rafts were strapped to the floor in their place. The fact that these brilliantly yellow objects were far too large to fit through the nearby emergency exits, and that the only way to open those hatches was to stand on the rafts, was apparently of little concern.

The other feature was that they hadn't bothered to pay the extra fee for dried air. They apparently had just compressed some air in some tanks and called it good. As we flew, condensation began to drip from the vents. Like any decent rainfall, that was only the slightest hint that presaged the storm. Most of us completed the flight in our foul weather gear, rain pattering off our hoods and our plastic snack boxes with a bright pinging sound.

The flight was otherwise uneventful, and we were soon winging our way into Kupang, Timor, the easternmost island of this vast nation. There are 17,508 islands (+ / - 1,000) that make up Indonesia (it was 13,700 when I was there). Visit one island a day and you'd cover the country in just forty-eight years with one two-week vacation.

Even having ridden around it, I'm constantly shocked at how big the world is. I traveled with a map of the world. On it, I traced my route with a standard Sharpie (dashed line for flights and bus rides). That single, thin wavering line in the vast expanse of the 2' by 3' map completely covers everything I could see—obliterating a path perhaps five miles to either side of my route. All the rest of that vast expanse? I didn't see at all.

My first surprise on landing in Indonesia was that the wheels remained attached to the plane. I wouldn't want to try riding Junior across the rough surface they called a runway. My second was looking out the window as we jolted over the taxiway. A large drainage ditch was under construction and the only piece of machinery was a dump truck delivering large rocks. The ditch was clearly hand-dug and a crew of twenty or so were trying to shift a particularly large rock into place. Machines are expensive here, labor is not.

Welcome to the Third World.

Due to fetching Junior, I was the last one through customs. I received my stamp and a man rushed up and asked if I wanted something called a *"losmen."* He indicated a minivan filled with some of my fellow passengers. Ah, a rooming house. I touched my chest followed by a bicycling motion. He waved and was gone.

Within a minute the airport was empty. Officials, tourists, taxis, and pilots were all gone. There was me, Junior, and four little boys watching me avidly. Their Bahasa, the language of Indonesia, and my sign language did little to clarify whether or not their curiosity might extend to muggings and theft. I slapped Junior together in record time and, with the thankfully benign interest of my watchers, I glided away with only one knuckle bleeding, about average.

The low afternoon sunlight turned the sand a deep gold. The swaying palm trees glowed a rich green above the cobalt-blue ocean. I swept down to the shore and followed the only road as it curved along the beach. There was a primitive feel similar to Noah's Beach in FNQ. The ancient taste of the air belonged to a world having nothing to do with the hustle and noise of the US. Rows of fishing boats were pulled up high on the sand. Their colorful prows sported eyes on either side of the bow to watch for danger.

At the end of the beach, the road turned uphill.

Way uphill.

The late afternoon tropical warmth somehow became a sweltering heat as I ground up the slope. Scattered grass huts grew closer together, a few stone and stucco buildings sprinkled in and among. Finally I reached the center of town.

An occasional *bemo* flashed by, literally. A *bemo* is either a minivan or a pickup with two bench seats in the bed. These are the universal solution for motorized transport in the outer islands. There is by foot, by bicycle, or by *bemo*.

In Kupang, they are painted brilliant greens and shocking pinks. Windows are filled with different-colored Christmas tree lights, some even chasing around in little flashing patterns or strobing on and off. Each van had a name and a look: Elvis (green with sequins), Marilyn (hot pink with lace around the windows), and Arnold (painted a fierce puce and black). The *bemo's* owners live in the van, it is their only possession. They pay rent to whoever financed the rig and, if they pick up enough people during the day, they get to eat that night. The less lucky ones go hungry and work on decorating their *bemos*.

In the midst of swirling *bemos* and garish signs, a shout sounded out. Ondine waved at me. She was an Irish traveler and we'd exchanged a dozen words on the plane. Glad of any familiar face in a storm, I let her lead me to the *losmen's* owner. I was shown to a room that would have made the fussiest traveler collapse with delight. The cool mosaic floor of burgundy and cream ran partway up the walls and was offset by the bedspread in a dozen shades of white.

Ondine and her friends were headed out to dinner and had agreed to wait for me, so I rushed into the bathroom. Okay, the hole-in-the-floor squat toilet might not have thrilled most, but it was clean and didn't smell.

I stared at the large tank of water, not quite big enough to crawl into, but definitely something to do with cleaning. A small pitcher and a bar of soap rested on the ledge. Taking a lesson from the Japanese *furo*, I stripped down and dumped a load of the fantastically cool water over my head. A quick soap and a few more pitchers and I was set. The water trickled across the tile floor and down the toilet hole while I dressed, and we were off.

She and her two companions were definitely travelers. No backpackers make it to Kupang; there is no bungee jumping and zero discos. I was in heaven. Ondine and friends were catching a ferry the next afternoon to Larantuka on Flores Island, the next major island toward the heart of the country. It sounded great and I looked forward to my first traveling companions since the Austrian chefs at Uluru two months before.

Bright Ping Ahead

The next morning I rode to the Kupang market to buy some food before riding the twenty kilometers to the ferry. Perhaps ten street vendors had their wares spread out on blankets on the cracked sidewalks down the shady side of the street in the lower town.

I rolled to a stop.

A dozen people gathered close around the bike. I could have touched most of them without dismounting. They were too close, and I couldn't catch my breath. Perhaps they were so close they were using all the air.

I rode away.

Several deep breaths over the next few minutes and then I circled back.

This time I could feel the body heat of the closest ones as they pressed in about me pointing at features of Junior. They weren't touching anything. I tried to be discreet as I checked to make sure they hadn't whisked away my money belt. Nope, still there. Their whispers cluttered the air about me with strange and foreign sounds. Okay, granted, almost everyone on the planet with the possible exception of the British have a smaller personal space than Americans, but this was creepy.

The crowd grew to twenty.

I rode away again.

I stopped a half kilometer off on an empty street of gravel to catch my breath and let my heart slow down. I flopped Junior against a stone wall and sat down.

This was how I discovered the "transporter effect." It exists in every Third World country I entered.

Within moments, five or six people appeared out of nowhere to inspect me and my bizarre form of transportation. I admit we were an unusual pair. I wore my bumblebee Lycra, dark green wrap-around Oakley shades, and a bicycle helmet. Junior had oval-curved handlebars; clips rather than pedals, which mated with the bottom of my black-and-silver shoes; and panniers covered with enough straps to impress a mountain climber.

I looked toward the large crowd at the market and glanced back at Junior. In the moment I hadn't been watching, Scotty had beamed in another crew from the starship *Enterprise* and fifteen people were now gathered around us.

I swung Junior up and took a few quick breaths, as you would if hyperventilating before submerging into icy water. I'd take one more shot at the market. If I couldn't deal with it, then I'd just go hungry for the next few days. I rolled back and saw that Ondine had joined the crowd and I was rescued by her cheerful grin (a moment she caught in the cover photo).

The moment before I was mobbed again.

"Help," I managed to squeak as the pack closed about me, now fascinated by my bicycle bell. "I need to buy some food."

A tentative finger reached out and tapped the striker. A bright ring burst forth, silencing the crowd for a moment.

Jonathan, one of last night's dinner companions, flipped his long blond hair out of the way and grabbed my shoulder. "Come on."

"What about Junior?"

"He'll be fine."

So I laid him over in the midst of that teeming mob. Every now and then another cheerful ring sounded forth above the crowd, assuring me of his continued presence.

Jonathon pulled me down into a squat, facing a woman

with a large bunch of bright, yellow bananas laid out on an electric-blue cloth. She named a price and Jonathon laughed. The dickering that went back and forth amazed me. I knew Jonathon had no more words than I did; we'd all spent much of the previous evening practicing our first words of Bahasa. But with little more than the counting numbers and a few politenesses, he bartered her down to a third of her asking price. I could see several of the locals nodding, he'd done well for a foreigner.

I rushed back to Junior's rescue. He had attracted everyone not watching our bartering session. All his parts appeared to be present and accounted for. I swung him upright with a grunt. Several people were impressed and some of the men asked with gestures if they could hold Junior. After much rocking back and forth, each would release Junior to the next one with a wondering shake of his head.

Now that he was upright, his bell was more accessible and all the people who hadn't had a chance before came over to make the high ping themselves. I finally had to step back again and wait while they crowded around Junior once more to check his weight and ring the bell until I thought I would go mad.

When I rolled away at long last, it was no longer in abject fear of this country and her people. They were just people. Oddly enough, at no time in that first experience did I wish I hadn't come to Indonesia, a surprising change from Japan. I was now fully immersed and there was only one direction to go: forward.

Extreme Karaoke

I rode out to the ferry, crossing over the hilly spine of the island and dropping down the far side. While the bay at Kupang had struck me as primeval, this one was right out of a travel brochure. The wide half-moon of sand shimmered in the sunlight enclosing a crystalline bay the color of the sky. I swept down the hill in a fine mood. The only blemish along the entire shore was the rusting superstructure of a partially sunken ship. Some freighter had found its final resting place and would never leave again.

A *bemo* passed me. Jonathon waved at me from the open door. They pulled up to the old hulk and I could finally see that it wasn't sunken after all.

It was our ferry.

I stopped next to Ondine as she spoke my own thoughts aloud, "It can't be."

I pointed toward a small sign, which had the fares posted to Larantuka. I spotted a half dozen vendors at the dockside. After a quick barter, I trundled aboard the rusted hulk, the proud owner of a box of cookies to go with my bananas. I could do this.

The long afternoon that began our sixteen-hour crossing was spent practicing our Bahasa on anyone willing to speak with us, which mainly ended up being one another. At long last I bedded down for the night, curled up on the rusted metal decking with my jacket and camera for a pillow. A rice bag made a nice prop for my back and a couple of chickens cowered under the chair a foot or so from my face and watched me…plotting my demise if I even blinked. I closed my eyes and laughed as another Kodak moment went by unrecorded.

A blast shot in my ears and echoed around my skull looking for an escape. I jerked upright to see Jonathon looking around.

"Are we sinking?" I mouthed over the horrendous screech that shot out moments later. He shrugged.

With a loud thump that shook the metal plating, rock 'n' roll music pounded against us from overhead speakers. Horribly distorted by the overdriven amplifier, I thought I recognized a pop rock song. Stones perhaps, or maybe Abba, hard to tell. A round-faced Indonesian man grabbed a microphone and began the worst karaoke it has ever been my displeasure to actually survive.

The key of his unintelligible Bahasa song lines swung up and down the scale in no relation to the music, nor the calm sea about us. Perhaps this was the punishment for not paying the first-class price, which added stifling windows to seal in the otherwise identical rusting fixtures. He sang from eleven at night until three in the morning. I had to give him points for stamina if nothing else. Passengers occasionally threw fruit or bags of belongings at him, but he was undaunted. Even earplugs wouldn't let me sleep and that was more than most people had. We were a very sorry crew that dragged ourselves off the boat at sunrise the next day.

Karaoke: noun, a crime that should be punishable by being thrown overboard into the Savu Sea.

Bravery and a Snorkel

After a few days in Larantuka, my new friends hopped a bus and were gone. They wanted to reach Sumatra, a couple thousand kilometers away, before their standard-issue, sixty-day visa expired.

While we were there I befriended Toby, a bright and terribly hyper-active twenty-two-year-old Englishman, his wife, and their three-year-old daughter. Toby had the amazing ability to pack four years of college metaphysics into every conversation. His current favorite was quoting Nietzsche, at length. Each night we sat up long past everyone else, wrestling with the nature of our brief mortal treads upon this coil of existence.

But after four days in a town less than a block long, it was wearing a bit thin. Each time we went out, a band of children would gather and shout, "Hallo, Mistah!" at the top of their lungs. Continuously. At least until some elder came along and shooed them away. Everyone in town was always well warned when one of the foreigners was out and about.

I swam each day along the reef, ate *gado-gado* (cooked vegetables in peanut sauce) or *nasi campur* (rice with a selection of fish or chicken), and learned a great deal of Bahasa. Unlike Japanese, I found it easy to remember the sounds and syntax of the far simpler language.

I set off in the early morning of the fifth day. There is only one road on Flores Island, and it winds for a couple hundred kilometers down the middle of the island. The next town of any size, i.e. bigger than two huts in the same place, was Maumere. It was a hundred kilometers down the road. A good day's ride, but nothing out of the ordinary.

At 8:00 a.m. this didn't appear to be a problem.

By 10:00 I was starting to worry.

By 11:30 I'd covered just half the distance and drunk eight of my eleven quarts of water. The temperature was using 100°F (38°C) as a springboard to see just how high it could get. The humidity...I won't even mention the humidity. I'd foolishly believed that 100% humidity was somehow an upper limit before rain simply materialized in the thick air. Boy, was I wrong.

Why had I thought Indonesia had to be cooler than the Outback? It was 15 degrees closer to the equator, for one thing. For a second, it was October, coming up spring; the Southern winter was over for what little difference it makes near the equator.

I was starting to scout for someplace to spend the peak of the afternoon, if not the night. I had a bit of food, but I needed water and the achingly dry hills of the last fifty kilometers weren't inspiring me with hope. I had to keep riding.

I dragged myself and Junior up the sliding gravel of the road (nothing was paved out here) and rounded the curve into a welcome bit of shade.

A shout sounded off to my right. I blinked to focus through my sweat and dust-clogged eyes. In the distance, a large thatch building was tucked beneath the trees.

Another shout.

School kids. A large crowd of school kids. Fifty or more small children came pounding across the schoolyard away from their calling teachers—and directly toward me.

For a moment, I thought of the potential for adventure before me. I could go and speak to their class with the aid of my phrasebook. I could promote World Understanding. I could also get some water. Perhaps stay with some villagers. I could...begin to resolve the rising roar of voices into words.

"Hallo, Mistah!" rolled against me like a tidal wave might hit a low-lying salt marsh. Without thought I downshifted three gears and leaped upon my pedals. I waved back as I shot over the crest of a nearby hill, barely ahead of the teeming horde.

When I tell people about this trip, I get a lot of mixed reactions.

One common response is, "You're so brave to do that."

And it's *so* wrong!

I'm not a *brave* traveler. I'm not a brave person, at least about people. I'm something of a quiet introvert. I'm not so bad that I'd rather not meet people but, as I'd learned in many places on this trip, crowds rapidly overwhelm me.

Adding to this natural tendency of mine, I had now spent seven months alone on a bicycle—mostly in silence. The remote emptiness of the Outback was a far better fit for me than the rider houses of Japan, the backpackers of Australia, or a storm of children currently yelling, "Hallo, Mistah!" at the top of their lungs.

Yes, I traveled solo around the world.

Yes, it was an amazing adventure to some fantastically exotic places (at least from the reference point of an American who had only ridden once for three weeks in New Zealand).

But I'm *not* brave.

To this day, I wonder about that reaction and how my trip might have been different had I stopped. As their shouts were lost in my roaring descent, down which I did not coast but continued to churn my pedals in increasingly higher gears, I knew I was riding away from a unique opportunity. Given the chance to do it again, I expect I would repeat my actions and pound just as hard over that hilltop.

Early afternoon found me flogging up yet another hill with only one liter (a quart plus a swallow) of water left. I pulled over and ground to a halt, finally spent. A bus, the only vehicle to pass me that day, went by and then jerked to a halt.

Toby jumped out, ran back to me, and unzipped his pants. He started peeing in the middle of the road right next to Junior. I was exhausted beyond doing more than raising an eyebrow in his direction.

"Pretend you're agreeing with me. Nod your head."

I nodded dutifully.

"They wouldn't stop for me to pee and I thought I was going to bust a bladder. I saw you and said I might be able to convince you to get on the bus. It's not very full and I bet they need the money. Even if you don't want to, nod your head again."

I did so. I only had until Toby's water ran out to make up my mind. I hoped he had a large bladder. Was I a dedicated bike traveler who was going to ride wherever he goes? Did it make me less of a traveler if I put Junior on a bus? I looked at the bus and its conductor, who was now walking back toward us. I pictured trying to find a quiet stream in an isolated valley where I wouldn't be mobbed by a hundred kids—where there was some kind of shield against the omnipresent transporter effect.

I pictured a bus ride ending at a nice *losmen* with a cool *mandi* (bath), and a meal of *gado-gado* in the night market.

The conductor arrived, ready to haggle. He asked full price.

I pointed out that I'd already ridden halfway. He offered half price for me and another half price for Junior. I eyed the mostly empty bus and offered him a tenth for Junior, about thirty cents if I recall, and I'd only pay if he dropped me at the *losmen* rather than the edge of town. He looked at me as Toby finished peeing...wow, he'd really had to go. The conductor then looked up at his bus and waved me aboard.

From inside the dusty, pounding bus, I could see how rough the road was. It became steeper as we moved westward and crossed over the high crest of this island's mountainous central ridge. We crossed only one stream. Good choice. Riding a bus didn't invalidate my being a traveler. I had used motorized transport to cross a dangerous expanse of the Outback, both to Uluru and over to Cairns. It was like flying a plane to get from one country to the next.

One of the funniest reactions I get from First Worlders when I talk about riding my bicycle around the world is, "How did you get across the oceans?"

I found out saying that I took a plane always seemed to disappoint them or sound condescending. So I began making up answers, which gets a much better reaction. "I have a special paddlewheel rig that I fold out." "Tiny jet engines that I keep in the bottom of the panniers." "A really long snorkel." (That last is the most popular one.)

I decided I *was* comfortable with taking a bus over the roughest road yet.

He dropped us in town and leaned Junior against a large pile of rubble.

I shook my head. "At *losmen*."

He pointed over the pile and drove away.

The only water I saw on a hundred kilometers of the main (and only) highway across Flores Island.

Over the Rubble

Toby and I ventured over the rubble as his wife watched our gear and their girl. Sure enough, there was a beautiful little row of rooms and we quickly took the two that were open. After a nice *mandi,* as cool and refreshing as I'd imagined, we went for a walk about the town.

Maumere was a wreck. Almost every building was in some stage of collapse. The central square, usually the heart of any small town, was an empty expanse of broken concrete and a small, ill-constructed hut. Each block of the town had a couple of nice buildings, but that was all.

The rest were a disaster.

The dry riverbed was filled with garbage and human waste that wouldn't be washed out to sea until the monsoon began next month. The Christian church at one end of the town had an entire wall caved in. Every stone in the graveyard lay flat on the ground. Impossibly, a brand-new, fifteen-foot statue of Jesus stood at the center of the yard, perfectly erect in white-washed concrete.

We each had gathered a different part of the tale on our

travels, but it took us some time to piece the whole tale together.

Ten months earlier, a massive earthquake had shattered every concrete building.

The tsunami that swept through a few minutes later was said to be over seven stories high—in a town where the tallest building was two stories.

The destruction went several kilometers inland.

Every wall parallel to the coast was gone.

Every empty concrete square we'd seen was once the foundation of a thatched building, but now scrubbed clean of all signs that people had lived there.

The government claimed five thousand souls were lost along all of Flores Island.

The people of Maumere said that one in three had died, nearly ten thousand in their region alone.

I realized that the town was not a wreck, once I looked past the surface. The whole scene shifted as we returned through the streets. The collapsed buildings were no longer "typical," rather the new buildings were a sign of strength and hope for the future. Nowhere else in Indonesia did I see anyone working through the midday heat.

In Maumere, they worked from sun to sun. Men swung hammers at the remnants of old walls. The women moved the broken concrete away piece by piece. Children erected palm frond shades and played with broken bits of rebar. The owners of our *losmen,* the surviving parts of four families, lived in two rooms at the end.

They pointed to the huge pile of rubble we had to climb over to reach them from the road. "That was our restaurant."

Comments on the casualties? "Many died. It was very sad." But they didn't talk about it much.

The next day Toby and I were debating the proper pronunciation of *sepeda* and *bumi,* bicycle and world. A man stopped to straighten us out before introducing himself as Antonio. He'd come to visit his widowed sister, Suri, who lived with their grandfather and her two children in the end room. Antonio was fluent in English and I learned the majority of my Bahasa from him that afternoon as we discussed the quake.

"I was in the hills visiting my mother. After the quake and the wave, I hurried back. I lost a brother, a brother-in-law, and two nieces. But we are still alive. We go on."

"Do your people talk about it among themselves? They certainly don't with us."

"No. That is partly our language," he settled into Toby's chair, who had departed in keeping with his restless nature. "Bahasa, as we speak it out here in the islands, has no past or future tense. It makes it very hard for us to learn your language. We only have *sudah* and *akan* to give us any sense of time that isn't the present. They mean before and after. 'The bus is come *akan*' means it's coming. In a minute, an hour, a year, it doesn't matter; it will come.

"To us the quake is *sudah*. The deaths are *sudah*. We are sorrowed, but today is where we live by the force of our very words."

We chatted long into the afternoon before I thought to ask him how he kept his positive attitude—for his pleasant cheeriness seemed inborn, though I don't believe there is such a thing.

He pointed at my chest. "You make life much too difficult. It is very easy."

He pointed at his own chest, "Good heart." His head, "Good thoughts." He pointed past me as if indicating a road before us, "Automatic good actions. See, very simple."

I could only smile at him. It couldn't be that easy...could it?

I spent several days there, helping now and then to move their unending supply of rubble. I played with Antonio's surviving niece and nephew and received a shy smile from his widowed sister as a reward.

I'd never been comfortable around little kids, mostly because I'd had so little exposure to them. These two (perhaps four and five years old) opened up to me with an unconscious heart that I wouldn't understand until the night I met my stepdaughter-to-be.

In that four-year-distant future, it was time for the make-or-break meeting. I really, really, really liked this woman but it was time to pass the kindergarten-age-kid test. I avoided sheer panic by focusing on *simple* fright when I first visited for dinner.

"I taught her sign language for the fun of it." My future wife was a librarian who had taught herself ASL in order to provide sign language assistance in public libraries.

It turned out that her daughter now knew some signs (cat, dog, bear, man, woman, house...) and how to form the alphabet...but didn't know how to spell most of the words. We sat on the floor together for two hours as she taught me the signs and alphabet and I taught her how to spell them. I went on to be the first one to read her a bedtime story other than her mom—ever.

At the end of our evening, she asked her mom to tell me I couldn't leave. And we've been that close ever since. To say that was a moment that utterly changed all three of our lives would be a crass understatement.

How had I been lucky enough to connect so thoroughly—in both directions—with this one little girl who unknowingly held the key to so many of the best things that ever happened to me in her small hands?

Or maybe it hadn't been so unusual.

I remembered my adventures in Maumere and my easy connection with Suri's children. Somehow, somewhere, despite my long hair and beard at that time (I barely trimmed them between Seattle and Europe), they knew me and liked me. And they did it at a time when I was less than confident about my likeability.

To this day, I am still awed by the gift of children who greet me with such trust.

With my true family still four years in the unknown future, I imagined what it would be like to stay here in Maumere. To help in something as immediate and important as rebuilding a wall. It was so far removed from the remote world of complex computer systems integration and information engineering. Those so-familiar words now sounded alien even in my thoughts.

I live as healthy a fantasy life as the next man. I imagined what it would be like to stay, and perhaps, if all went well, fill some of the aching void left by the death of Suri's husband. What it would be like if this child riding on my bicycle rack around the square, her little hand holding on to my waist, were to become mine? If evenings were spent discussing life with Antonio and chatting with the occasional traveler; would they be more or less full than my life in Seattle had been?

If this wasn't just some passing moment, would I be content living in a remote village with no electricity? With none of my friends? No movies and only a few books?

No more content than this family would be if whisked ten thousand miles from everyone they knew and loved into my world of Seattle. Maumere was not my home. Any more than Seattle would be home to the shy widow with the shining black hair to her waist and her two wonderful kids with their bright and easy smiles despite the loss of their father. In my memory now, she and her children are standing together, and wave goodbye a little sadly. Is it circumstance, wishful thinking, or accurate memory that she is still one of the most beautiful women I've ever seen in my life?

It was hard to leave a place where a simple question of pronunciation could lead to a beginning of friendship.

Before I left, I asked Antonio what, if anything, he had learned from this awful experience.

"Family and friends. They can be gone. Not next year, not tomorrow, but in the next instant. A third of our town died in less than three minutes. This is where I was born, where I grew up. The few I didn't know, I at least recognized. So you tell me, which is more important: that I go to order supplies for my business, or that I sit with you and we teach one another about our countries that we each love so much? You must cherish them now. Right now."

I wrote many letters home in the next few days, thanking my friends for being just that, my friends.

I wanted to thank them, now, while I still had the chance.

The *losmen* over the rubble. Their shattered restaurant is on the left.

Jam Karet

It was in the town of Moni that I first encountered the volcano sickness. It is a disease that only appears to attack Western travelers. The manifestation of this particular bug drives Westerners to flock to the top of volcanoes in the middle of night to witness the sunrise.

I had heard of this malady farther up the track, but in Moni it ran to a near fever pitch. *Bemo* drivers offered special 4:00 a.m. rides to the top of a nearby triple-coned volcanic peak for the outrageous sum of 4,000 Rupiah (about $2 US). Where a room costs 1,500 Rp and a good meal 500 Rp, I didn't care to participate in such a rip-off. Worst of all, the drivers appeared immune to any attempts to haggle. Very un-Indonesian of them.

Rainer, a German, and Lorna, a Brit, were going to hike to the top in the dark. I was less than excited as this would require a 1:00 a.m. departure. But I was missing Toby, Jonathon, and Ondine—all now gone ahead—and decided to join in just for the company.

We departed in the depths of the moonless night and they quickly outdistanced me. Even breaking into an occasional light jog was insufficient to keep up with them. Twice they stopped and waited. Finally, Lorna asked if they should slow down. I said that would be really nice.

It was the last I saw of them.

For fifteen kilometers, three hours, and almost a thousand meters up, I chewed on this one. I struggled to change my expectation of a friendly walk together and the resulting anger at their "betrayal" as I trudged upward alone in the night. I recalled a book on relationships from long ago. "Change an expectation to a preference and then reconsider." (*A Conscious Person's Guide to Relationships* by Ken Keyes, Jr.)

"I would have preferred to hike together," I told the vast darkness. "But it is beautiful. And they wanted to hike with a flashlight, and I wanted to go by the stars. The southern stars are so bright, why would anyone wish otherwise? It is more than bright enough to see the road."

By the time I reached the top, I'd done it. I'd thoroughly enjoyed the cool night and the slow building of the breeze as I climbed. The sky had wheeled a quarter turn around a blank spot in the southern sky as I'd walked; no South Star marked the axis as Polaris did in the north, but the mighty Southern Cross scribes a very stately circle.

I found them huddled in the lee of a peak marker.

"Did you enjoy your race?"

"No," they replied in unison. We unraveled what had happened. Lorna used to be a racewalker, Rainer had very long legs. He realized he'd matched the rate of his stride to Lorna's thus covering more ground. She'd accelerate her pace to keep up with him. And so on. They'd covered the time to the top in a third less time than my steady pace. We had a good laugh, huddled out of the wind, and shared our biscuits while we waited for the sun.

Note to self: *preferences beat the hell out of expectations.*

Our chatting and laughter awaiting the sun was certainly better than the blistering tirade I'd initially wished to heap upon these strangers.

My account of the attack of the screaming school children amused Rainer no end. He admitted that he had been equally cautious on his first trip to the Third World. We decided to travel to the next town together. We ultimately spent the next two weeks exploring the islands; it was the longest I traveled with anyone in the first year of my journey and we stayed in touch for years afterward. All for a choice of preference over expectation.

The ride from Moni to Ende was a short but brutal hour and a half ride, climbing five hundred meters of slippery gravel starting at the *losmen* door. It was a bad day for Junior. The rear rack snapped in two places on the rough descent and a sidewall blew out of one of the tires. I gave the ruined tire to the group of five kids who had beamed in to watch me change it. They were thrilled and whooped away across the yard, rolling it back and forth.

Along with an hour-long construction delay, for work on one of the many bridges that the killer-quake had knocked off its foundations, I should have been miserable.

I had a blast.

"You've switched to *jam karet*," Rainer told me that night, "Rubber time. It is how the Indonesians describe their approach to life. 'We'll get there when we do'."

"Waiting is," I replied as we strolled the night market in search of minor delicacies to round out a dinner of *nasi campur*.

Rainer looked at me askance.

"Waiting is. That's all. It simply is. 'When does the bus leave?' *Akan*. When it is full or the yard master won't let it hang around any longer. What can you do in the meantime? Get upset? Why? No, the answer is simple: wait."

"A state of grace," he tested the thought. "No matter how much you wish life to hurry, it will go at its own pace. Simply accept it."

"*Jam karet*," I confirmed. "Waiting is."

Waiting for Chickens

Ende, and the towns after it, had none of the charm of shattered Maumere. There was less damage, but they were just as dirty and run-down, perhaps more so without the galvanizing impact of total destruction as a wake-up call. The *losmen* in Maumere had been immaculate, even construction dust was swept away quickly. The few operating restaurants had served hot food with a smile and perhaps a joke.

In Ende, the toilet reeked, and none of the locals wanted conversation with us. The crowded night market had none of the vitality of the carts pulled up around Maumere's central square each night. The food was good and the people pleasant, but that was all.

Perhaps my attitude was colored by contracting a fierce case of diarrhea in the Ende night market. I relaxed my guard and drank some local water without filtering it first. After throwing up the fried peanut butter roll and anything else I might have eaten over the previous year or so, I spent the whole night squatting in a dismal, mosquito-filled toilet. I was a complete wreck the next day.

Without a second thought, I put Junior on a bus and crawled aboard. We stopped at a small town a few hours out and I went seeking a toilet. There was quite a stir as I walked over to the village toilet. There was only the one in a village of a few dozen families.

Three bamboo walls, and a fourth made of burlap surrounded the concrete hole. Little kids ran back and forth to peek through the burlap weave and gape at the white man squatting to empty his entire guts in a mighty liquid blast.

Just as I finished, I heard the bus start. I rinsed the hole with a bucket of water, washed my hands, and stepped forth.

The entire village, forty or fifty men, women, and children had gathered in a huge arc outside the facility. A large cheer burst forth as I came into view. I raised my right hand and waved. It would have been an insult to raise my left as that is the "foul" hand, the one used to wipe one's butt after defecating. I trotted toward the bus feeling ever so much like a marathon runner jogging on his victory lap.

Me and Sylvester Stallone as *Rocky*—a moment of personal triumph. *Yo, buddy!* I would have laughed at the memory of the Japanese boy who'd given me the cheering *Yo!*, except I didn't dare laugh or do anything else that might impact my aching guts.

At a restaurant stop hours later, I walked into the room late and asked where their toilet might be. A wave of laughter, including the owner and kitchen staff who'd obviously just been told the amazing tale, guided me to the proper location.

Upon my return, signaling that I didn't dare eat anything yet, the owner offered a large mug of tea and refused payment.

There was no lack of sympathy, but they also liked a good story.

"You're a hero and I'm jealous," Rainer informed me as we reboarded.

"Don't be," I gasped as I settled carefully onto the hard seat to have my fragile innards pounded for another several hours.

Toward the end of the day, I was recovering from my high fever and felt nearly human. An old woman came aboard. The seats were filled with people. The aisles were jammed with rice, coconuts, and a live hog, all being carried to market. People's bundles were everywhere, and several goats were tied to the top of the bus. I tried to rise to offer her my seat.

The young conductor pushed me back down. "It is not your problem. Don't make it your problem." He found a fine place for her, perched atop a bag of rice.

I dropped back into my seat stunned beyond words. How many times in my life had I done precisely that? Thousands, perhaps more.

In the early 1980s I was working in theater, designing and installing a sound system. The slide designer was not very good with computers, and the controller for the six projectors that ran the eight hundred slides was beyond him. I was already working insane hours, yet I took over all the slide programming while I was at it. I then helped the lighting designer with the Microstar interface and...

That was how I'd lived my life.

I remember an assistant at my first law firm. I was a paralegal (a glorified document clerk) and their in-house computer geek. An attorney would step into our shared office, ignore my overwhelming workload, and ask me to do something. Behind the attorney, Gail would look at me and mouth, "No! Just say no!" "Yes," I would cave every time, now making it *my* problem. Even her lectures afterward wouldn't bolster my resistance for the next time.

It is not your problem. Don't make it your problem.

I barely noticed the harsh jolts and pounding body slams

the bus offered up over the next several hours. I was lost in the world of "what if?" What if I'd lived that way all along? Sure, I'm always glad to help out, but there was no need to make every single burden that came along my own personal divinely-mandated trial. Which, of course, I had to do perfectly. Totally nuts. I vowed to be more balanced henceforth. Honest.

At long last we entered Bajawa. I'd again arranged to be dropped at a *losmen*. Normally the buses deliver you to the edge of town and then you had to pay a taxi service for the last kilometer or so. I could ride, but I wanted to save Rainer the fee. I assume there were kickbacks involved as the bus drivers were always lined up at the night market in the center of town by the time evening fell anyway.

The conductor said they had to go to the far side of town before they could drop me off. Neither Rainer nor I could quite straighten out why, something about chickens and bicycles.

"*Jam karet*," we shrugged. We were in no hurry.

"*Bagus*," he replied. Literally "good," but it also covered the range of fine, you bet, grand, nice, and half a dozen other words based on intonation. It can easily extend to *"losmen bagus,"* a nice place to stay. I was fast growing to love this language and the people who lived within its curious scope.

When we finally stopped, a *long* way across town, I climbed out to see what was up. That morning they'd tied Junior to the back of the bus. At some point along the way, they had tied a hundred or so live chickens to, over, and around him. That's how they're transported when there is no refrigeration. Tie a rope to a chicken's legs and hang it upside down. The blood rushes to its tiny brain and they go stupid. Well, they're already stupid; they go calm.

After the numerous layers of chickens were removed, we were taken back toward town. We were deeply settled in the arms of Rubber Time. "Waiting for chickens" became my definitive definition of *jam karet*.

Waiting for chickens (with enough removed to actually see Junior).

Dressed for Success

Rainer was very good at bartering for meal-sized amounts.

To my own surprise, I developed strong skills on the larger-ticket items like rooms and buses. In Labuhan Lombok I needed a sarong. The piece of Australian cloth I'd been using to wrap around my waist in this hot and humid climate just wasn't holding up to daily wear.

In a big city like this, of twenty thousand or so, the market runs all day instead of just at night. To avoid everyone baking into a hardtack-like substance or simply liquifying in the steamy heat, the market is in a building. Think of it as an open-sided three-story parking garage with no one insane enough to go on the roof. Airy, shaded, and huge. Neither of us had ventured into such a large market before.

To bolster our nerve, we ate some *gado-gado* from a bright red stall with actual sit-down tables. It was strange not to be squatting, which is the native pose of relaxation.

A local kid, maybe twelve or fourteen, tried to hustle.

"Show you the sights. Real cheap. I Number One good guide." Once he determined we were immune to that, he sat with us while we ate to practice his English. When he realized that Rainer was German, he was ecstatic, and they were off way past my high school German for a while before they came back to English.

"German tourists pay Number One good. Japanese must say everything just right to them, but if I do, they never know real price, so pay anything." We fooled around a bit, but his Japanese was far better than mine. This...kid spoke three foreign languages quite fluently, each with proper accents. He had three more he was working on hard.

Sated, and a little humbled, we plunged into the cool shade of the big market.

It was huge but we had little luck finding sarongs. Batiks, trinkets, rice, produce, food, goats, and more we found aplenty, but not the elusive clothing I sought.

Rainer noticed the stairway to the second floor. Here were all the practical items of everyday living that couldn't stand the markup of downstairs rent. Here were spices, rice seed, hundreds of terribly cute baby chickens, furniture, and at long last a sarong stall next to a massive collection of coconuts and mangos that must have taken hours to drag up there.

"Fifty thousand rupiah."

That was, um, $25 US. I laughed. "I am not so rich."

"That is the price." He was totally inflexible. Rainer had paid 8,000 Rp for his, a month before on a different island.

We moved on and eventually found three women in a small

stall. There were two tables and a couple of nice hangings behind to make a cozy and colorful space. They only had two sarongs, one of which wasn't *too* garish.

"How much for that sarong?"

"Twenty thousand Rupiah." About $10 US, still totally outrageous.

"What? Oh no, I am not some rich tourist, I am only a poor traveler." One of my most useful phrases in Bahasa. "How about two thousand?"

And I sat down.

Sitting down meant that I was serious and would probably remain until a bargain was struck. My ridiculous offer meant that I knew just how much too high they were. I asked about different colors. They disappeared through a back curtain and returned with a wider selection. They offered me tea, I declined as that would put me in their debt. I allowed that the brick-red one with green stripes wasn't too awful. As I drove the price down, they once more disappeared through the back curtain before returning with a counteroffer. It was a merry game that caused much laughter and giggles before we finally struck our deal at 10,500 Rp.

The women insisted on seeing how it looked and they gave me a lesson in how to tie it properly. As we left, I realized that we'd fully circled the upper story and that behind that curtain wasn't their storage, but rather the stall of the inflexible merchant. He was very sad to see me wearing one of his sarongs. Not only hadn't he gotten the sale, but he'd had to give up some of his usual profit margin to the ladies as I pushed on their price.

When I got to the next island about a week later, I was accosted by a very serious gentleman.

"Are you a woman?"

I scratched my beard for a moment and said no.

"Then why do you wear your sarong like one?"

He showed me the proper, masculine way to tie it. I finally knew who won that round of bartering. The women had sent me out into the world—dressed like a girl.

Looking Behind to Look Ahead

It was on Lombok that I bid goodbye to Rainer. His visa expired in a few days and he had to get out of the country; I still had a month left on mine.

It was time to stop. I'd slowed way down in Cairns but had been moving fairly steadily for the couple months since Noah's Beach. I rode up to the beach opposite Gili Air (Water Island), and hopped on a ferry—actually it was little more than a fishing skiff—for the kilometer crossing. Gili Air is perhaps two kilometers across and is covered with palm trees and pleasant thatched huts. (I looked it up recently, and it is now covered in high-end hotels and fancy resorts. Sigh.)

Teaching a village leader (in the light plaid to my right) to get a satisfying "honk" out of my Australian bamboo digeridoo. Everyone was on edge as I tried to teach him how to get a sound and there was a collective sigh of relief followed by heartfelt applause when he succeeded. I often found it was the less obvious communications that mattered the most. – photo by Rainer

After a bit of wheeling and dealing, I settled into a private bungalow beneath the palms just fifty yards from a snorkeling beach. Three meals a day were included for 10,000 Rp ($5 US) per night. I negotiated a twenty percent discount if I stayed a week. I stayed two.

For a fortnight, I reveled at the Nusa Tiga Bungalows, a grouping of a dozen huts. I played chess for the first time since my teens. I'm not good, but I do enjoy the game. I chatted for hours with natives of at least a dozen countries. I shocked the owner by trying to describe what a building permit was—he was raising a new bungalow.

"You build good, it stays up. You build bad, it falls down. Then have to build again. Why do work twice? And why pay for piece of paper to build own house? Ridiculous."

I proved just how small a world it was while talking with an English tour guide. Her mentor had led my high-school German class trip through Austria and Germany two decades earlier.

In the evenings, a dozen of us would often skinny-dip off the beach among the phosphorescent algae, great streaks of greens and blues illuminating the water in response to our slightest movements.

There was leisure here to spend hours exploring a topic. Kali, an Aussie psychotherapist, was on two weeks holiday to celebrate getting rid of her husband. "He tried to control my every breath. I've met a man who likes me but isn't trying to control me. I feel as if I finally have a second chance at life."

I certainly agreed. I now had a second chance too. After years of being lost in the rat race, I could now step back and choose my path through the maze far more carefully.

"Perhaps it isn't so important to know which turns to take, but rather which ones to not fall for again."

It struck a chord with some of my readings. I was presently immersed in Tomlin's *Philosophers of East and West*, a splendid academic tome about the world's various belief systems.

"Most religions have tales of waters into which you must be immersed after death before you can be reborn. This is done to wash away your memories before you move on to your new life. The stories are rife with tales of some special person who finds a boat, or rides on the back of a turtle, and returns with their memories intact. Maybe this is our second chance and we were lucky enough to bring our old lessons forward with us."

Kali liked this.

"Rather than casting aside our past as a job poorly done, we can just hold it close and accept that it was part of our path. And now, we can choose a new path."

We raised a glass of fresh coconut milk in solemn treaty that we would both remember this.

In the long, hot days I found the time to revisit the fictional characters I'd left on the Darwin beach. In the warm evenings at Nusa Tiga, I found a willing audience for the opening scenes from my then unnamed first novel, *Cookbook from Hell*. A Danish woman became completely enthralled by the tale and offered several suggestions on how to make a Hell that was unique and interesting enough to be worthy of my female Devil. I'm glad to say that her ideas survived intact through several drafts and are an essential part of the book. Thank you whoever and wherever you are.

You Can Never Go Back

After two weeks together on Gili Air, we had bonded into a tight-knit crowd. None of us could stand to leave or be left, so we all left together. I ran into Nusa Tigans all down the line in Bali, Java, Singapore, and even Germany.

In the crazed tourist town of Ubud in Bali, where buses overloaded with backpackers struggled along streets designed for oxcarts, I ran into Toby. He was as hyper as ever and still quoting Nietzsche. I had dinner in the night market with Jonathon, my savior in the marketplace on my first day in Indonesia.

The next day I walked the streets of that congested little town attempting to sort out the past from the present; the woman in the beautiful sarong marking her doorway in an age-old daily ritual of protection and the hawking vendor trying to sell me a batik. I stumbled to a halt.

In a shop window was a little book, *The Butterflies of Ubud*. Christopher, of the years-earlier "Sell everything and go now" advice, had spent four years on the road. Before I left, I asked he and his wife where was their favorite place.

"You have to find your own trip. You can never go back." Christopher was emphatic.

His wife leaned forward but she wasn't looking at me. Her eyes were focused somewhere far away. "Our favorite place was a little town halfway up a mountain. No electricity. No cars. No television or radio. Bullock carts in the streets."

"Just rice paddies and jungle all around." He looked as dreamy as she did. "We went walking one afternoon up into the surrounding hills and we came upon this beautiful field, every color in the world."

"Wildflowers. A carpet of wildflowers covering the whole meadow. There was this huge, old volcano in the background."

"We just had to walk there hand in hand. It was as if we were in *The Wizard of Oz*. When we entered, it seemed to explode. It wasn't flowers. It was butterflies."

"A cloud of butterflies. They almost blocked the sun."

Christopher's eyes came back into focus. "You can never go back. It will never be the same."

They hadn't told me the town's name, but there I was. Of all the different paths around the world, my path had crossed theirs. I looked around at the noisy trucks and the throbbing dance halls. I peered north between a bar and a souvenir shop. The great, volcanic peak of Gunung Batur was mostly hidden. Far from the center of town I did find some rice fields, but was told that it had been a long time since the butterflies had filled the sky. I wondered if I were to return to Maumere in a decade, would I find a dirty fishing village or would I find the charming town only too aware of the importance of the moment and of each other?

I sent a postcard of a butterfly to Christopher postmarked Ubud: "You can never go back. I understand."

Again, wallow in past memories, or use them to inspire and then face forward?

Life gives us the lessons if we listen hard enough. And if we don't listen? Sometimes life will repeat them—loudly—until we finally do.

A Happy Man

I left Ubud in the morning and rode up to the volcano's rim. Lines of tour buses were parked on the road between the view and dozens of souvenir shops. I wandered past all this until I found where the bus drivers were eating. I purchased a bowl of *bakso,* sort of Indonesian chicken noodle soup with dumplings, from a merchant who was miffed that I wouldn't pay the foreigner price. He calmed when I squatted Indonesian style and began haggling with him in Bahasa.

I wandered into a grocery store well away from the crowds and began chatting with the store owner. He had a television tuned to CNN. He didn't understand much English, but he could follow enough to know what was going on in the world. He was thirty-seven, illiterate, and the father of four children.

This sentence conjures very specific images for me even now, none of which fit this man.

He'd managed to send his first two children to university

and hoped to do the same for the other two. He'd dedicated his life to making opportunities for them that he couldn't dream of in his own youth.

"Why do you have your store so far from the tourists?"

"Here I serve the local people. It is easier."

"Do you barter among yourselves?"

"Not much, unless it is very expensive. When I was young, we bartered for everything, because we all had nothing. Now we are too busy. Too fast. Set a price and buy it or not. Up on the hill selling souvenirs, it is too fast. I work hard but like the quiet time as well."

He pointed down the western slope of the mountain toward the nearest village. "It took a year for my wife and me to buy our first cow. Four more years to make a herd of ten. We built a house and added more cows. We sold it all to buy this shop. It is lonely because my wife must work another job even though I could use her help.

"You see, we only wanted two children, couldn't afford more. But doctor didn't help, and we had third and then fourth. Fourth has polio. We paid for hysterectomy, which cost about a million Rupiah (about $500 US), my earnings for a year."

I asked about vasectomies. They are cheaper. Actually I said something like, "Why no male cut medicine?" then I nodded toward his lap. We were relying heavily on my six weeks of Bahasa.

"Not available in Indonesia. Most men would never let such a thing be done. Now I must work a double shift to pay the debt. I must pay for children to go to school. My father had no school but sent me for four years. I give mine university. I have grown a good family. I have had a successful life."

He was only two years older than me. If I had a fourth-grade education and had been too poor to own a cow in America, could I have put four children through college as he was doing? Could I grow a family and declare my life a success?

He wasn't content yet, but he was definitely pleased with his achievements. By contrast, I was traveling around the world, taking two years to find myself on a bicycle that would have paid for his wife's operation three times over.

"I try to live each day better than the day before. That is my goal; and look how far I have come."

I looked long and hard at the small store and its proud owner.

My life had so many more "advantages," yet he was the one who was happy. Was that because of the things he'd done, or perhaps for the family he'd given so much for and loved so dearly? I had finally learned enough, after losing home, leaving friends, and traveling for three-quarters of a year, to consider that it might be the latter.

Maybe I was learning. I just wasn't there yet.

Playing the Game

I arrived in Solo (Surakarta) at 3:00 a.m. My first big city, it lay near the center of the main island of Java.

The night bus operator shook me awake, and thirty seconds later, Junior and I were on the sidewalk and the bus was gone. I mounted up and slowly rode the night-filled streets of an Indonesian city of over a quarter million people waiting for the dawn. I'd been riding for a good while before I was nearly startled off my bike by a revelation. I wasn't in the least bit worried. If there was danger, I was blissfully unaware of it. Solo was certainly not an American city.

Around 4:00 a.m. the *warungs*, food stalls, began firing up. I rode out past a batik factory and eventually stumbled once more on the bus station. I could make out a few vehicles in the darkened yard, their drivers asleep on the roofs, awaiting the *jam karet* of "rubber time" when their bus would once more be jammed with people, upside-down chickens, hogs, and perhaps a bicycle.

Around 5:00 a.m. I passed the field of *warungs* again. Now they were busy with the people who'd been sleeping in the *becaks,* cycle rickshaws. They clambered slowly from their "bed" on the bench barely wide enough to seat two tourists, bought some food, and gathered in each other's vehicles to chat over breakfast.

I made a long loop in another direction. I passed hundreds of narrow houses, with women just starting their cookfires. I toured the well-to-do district, large Dutch Colonial homes behind freshly painted gates. It was here that I encountered the first *becak* drivers, seeking shop owners who needed a ride to work.

The *becak* drivers live in their tiny, three-wheeled vehicles, which they rent for some outrageous sum, about 2,000 Rp ($1 US) per day. A typical fare nets 2–300 Rp. Once they make the first ten trips to pay the rent, they can then worry about food. Very few have a home beyond their three-wheeler.

And when they aren't out hunting for paying passengers?

They play chess.

I occasionally stopped to watch a game between two drivers. I soon learned that the more drivers who stopped to spectate, the better the competitors were. I once saw a game surrounded by a hundred *becaks;* there was no hailing one anywhere in the area for over an hour—not that I wanted to. I liked walking everywhere in the places I visited, but there were a lot of irritated people that day. The chess moves were passed outward in whispers and those at the back of the crowd set up their own boards so they could follow the moves and debate them in whispers.

"Once there was a Russian chess master in town," one of the drivers told me on the fringe of a particularly heated match.

"It was Karpov."

"No, it wasn't," a nearby driver interrupted him. "It was Spassky himself."

"You don't know anything. It was Karpov. Habbie, a *becak* driver and a good friend of mine," the storyteller scowled at the other driver haughtily, "took him from the train station to his hotel. He even carried his bags up to his room for free. When Karpov dismissed him, he wouldn't leave, or take any money."

The other driver leaned in, and I noticed more and more of the nearby drivers were listening to the tale. "He said he would not go until Spassky played a game of chess with him."

"Finally at a loss, *Karpov,* because that's who he was, agreed to play."

"Habbie won."

The tale was told in a hash of Bahasa and English with a lot of translating going on in both directions.

They all waited for me to finally ask, "What happened after that?"

"Karpov was suddenly too sick to play an exhibition game the next day and he left Solo with no one seeing him. Some say he left Indonesia without playing a single game."

"Swore never to return."

"Habbie went back to his *becak.*"

"Is that him playing now?" I pointed toward the center of the massive jam of *becaks* now blocking most of the main street.

"Oh no. He is working over by the hotels today. These are not good enough to play against Habbie even for practice. The greatest chess player in the world is a *becak* driver." Everyone seemed very pleased that the story had been well told despite the translation challenges.

I watched the game to its conclusion and probably understood a hundredth of the nuances in the strategy. My storyteller and his friends debated each move that was whispered back to them. True or not, it was dazzling to watch them play. They move with a speed and certainty that I don't feel when faced with a set of checkers.

For three years I had commuted through the silence of the early morning streets of Seattle. As I rode through the equally silent streets of Solo that first morning, I couldn't help but make the comparison. Urban skyscrapers were replaced by two-story buildings. The large motorized street sweepers by ambling goats who will even strip movie posters off the walls to eat the paste. The Seattle city police cruisers who eventually recognized me well enough to wave were now sleeping *becak* drivers. The banks frantically exchanging carloads of canceled checks so that they could be returned to the proper customers were replaced by...no one. The bright streetlights placed every hundred feet were replaced by the moon, and half a hundred stoplights weren't replaced at all.

The pavement was about equally rough.

Once again, I looked at the man traveling these roads—at myself riding the bicycle. And another as if he rode beside me, a mirage in the moonlight.

One of us had been up all night because of the rough ride on the bus and no *losmens* being open at such an hour, pedaled lazily along the streets as the city slept.

The other—my parallel self of three years before—riding back to work at a hard sprint due to a failed backup of his newest server. The latter would be sleeping under his desk the next night, in between troubleshooting the problem.

Now my day's prospects included writing in my journal, working on my book, eating some *bakso* from a street vendor, and perhaps touring a batik factory. And meeting new people.

The world is an amazing place. And the lessons that we need to learn are constantly thrown right in our faces. Thank god, or how would we ever learn. Of course, that wasn't quite my perspective when I rode the Seattle streets. Then it was, "How am I going to survive this?"

Defining That Word

Once the sun was well up, I found Mama's Solo Homestay. *Losmens* had given way to homestays. Past and future tense entered the language, much to my confusion. And I began meeting folks other than locals and travelers. A young Swiss woman was volunteering at a limb replacement clinic to teach them paperwork management—a hopeless task, she assured me. A pair of Canadian missionaries were also in residence. I met, finally, travelers who were older than me; past twenty-five is a rarity on the long road.

Somewhere in Australia I began asking people where they called "home."

"Well, me stuff's at Mum's so I guess that's 'ome."

Others named a town. Travelers who'd been out three to four years would open their mouths and then close them again uncertainly. A worried expression crossed many of their faces as they realized they no longer had an answer.

I learned that there is some magic threshold at four years. Beyond that limit they are simply travelers with no other home. When I'd been in New Zealand, I camped with a man who'd been on the road for thirty-five years; he'd started in his fifties after his wife died shortly after he'd retired from the merchant marine. Now in his eighties, he informed me it was time to get moving.

"There are these two women who are chasing after me, and the seventy-four-year-old is pretty cute. If I want to keep moving, I'd better be going." We left camp together, but the wiry little man rode easily away from me on his clunky old ten-speed.

I met a couple in the Outback who'd been moving along for seven years and didn't see any point in stopping. They worked when they had to, wherever they were, and then moved on.

At Mama's I met Claud and Caroline, both in their fifties

and twelve years on the road. To my inquiry of where he called home, Claud, whose thick French accent was usually lost in the depths of his flowing gray beard, simply pointed over his shoulder at Caroline, who was reading a German novel.

He returned to cleaning his camera, which paid their way with thousands of photos sold to postcard companies. He didn't even turn to see her expression, perhaps he didn't need to. I felt voyeuristic watching her smile.

I stared out into the central courtyard of Mama's. A deluge that had no word in the Pacific Northwest (but was called monsoon here in the tropics), pounded from the sky until the lower area of the yard was six inches deep in water. A matter of minutes.

I was so far from home.

But in all my asking others, I'd never thought to define home for myself. I floundered on the dry land, watching the small inland sea swell and then subside as the drains caught up with the tapering downpour. Long after Claud had finished his cleaning and departed, I stared at that drying courtyard.

I wanted what he had. I wanted to be able to point to someone and say I was home. Where was it? What did it look like? I knew it wasn't Seattle, or Maumere could never have been so tempting. And I knew it wasn't in my head, because home was definitely not with *me;* it was behind me in Seattle even if that wasn't the place.

At the end of a long letter to my friends, I finally concluded: "Home is neither a place, nor a state of mind. It is a family of friends, and a bed without bedbugs."

But then there was Caroline's smile. Someday, I promised myself, I would see that expression in someone's eyes when they looked at me. Perhaps, if I was truly lucky, I wouldn't even have to turn around to know it was there. Maybe when I found that person, I'd know what home really was.

Who's Crazy?

More people drifted into Mama's Solo Homestay. A couple of Dutch cyclists, headed the other direction of course; a Swedish college student taking a semester off; and a wiry, hyper Austrian recovering from heroin addiction.

In my typical day, I toured the city before the afternoon rains and spent the rest of the time writing for hour upon hour on my story. It had begun as a vignette, turned into a few scenes, then a short story, and it was now totally out of control. Or perhaps in control—I simply had to write six to ten hours a day. I couldn't stop myself.

"Why did you come all the way to Indonesia only to sit here and write? You could do that at home." Dominic looked terrible. His eyes, horribly bloodshot, were set in a face gone gray with withdrawal symptoms. The others had avoided him, but I'd watched him go through three days of cold-turkey hell on his own. That had to be tough and I'd offered what encouragement I could.

He wasn't satisfied as I told him of my travels and the people I'd met.

"You're missing Indonesia."

"I tour around in the mornings." I told him about a batik factory and the chess game.

He scoffed.

"If I were at home, I wouldn't be getting the writing done at all."

He nodded. "Okay, I'll buy that. C'mon." He respected my afternoons, but the mornings became his. He loved Solo and had been sent here by his upper-crust Jakartan fiancé to dry out or go away. He'd chosen the rough road, for their future together.

He led me to "the best Padang food south of Sumatra." We went into this grotty little place with four tiny, peeling Formica tables. He walked to a display window where dozens of small trays of food were neatly stacked. Dominic flapped away some flies and pointed at half a dozen dishes, holding up one or two fingers as he pointed at each. The owner plopped a big scoop of iridescently white rice into a bowl and began selecting the items Dominic had indicated. He didn't reheat them or anything, just dropped them on the table. I did my best to emulate my mentor's decisiveness and ate a wonderful meal I would never have dared try on my own. And I wasn't sick at all: not even the runs, which was a pleasant change.

He took me to palaces and old forts. He took me to a Gambyong dance performance at the old Maharaja's palace. We were the only foreigners. The Wednesday morning concert tradition is of such a caliber that it is radio broadcast throughout Java every week. We sat in the gardens, listened to the sharp pings of the percussive orchestra, and watched what the vast radio audience could not: the powerful yet floating women, the best dancers of Solo, as they turned music into motion.

"Why me?" I asked as we toured the old harem room of a palace now lost in the middle of an outlying suburb. "Why pick me out of the crowd?"

"I need to think about something other than how much I'm hurting and because you're the craziest motherfucker in the homestay. Who else would leave their comfortable little existence and bike around the world? That's balls."

Having an ex-heroin dealer call me crazy left me a little unsure of the weight of the compliment.

And I still don't see myself as brave.

The night before I left, Dominic took me to the wedding of a local royal princess (not sure exactly what her title implied) and a British software engineer. Because I was a Westerner, I was automatically defined as rich (and I had put on my best clothes, though for a traveler that isn't saying much).

After some questions to Dominic that I couldn't follow, the mamas across the aisle began making a big fuss. Dominic explained, "I told them that you weren't just Western, but you were from the US. They want you to marry one of their unwed daughters and make them rich." The wedding went on for hours and they never quite gave up. (Thanks so much, Dominic.)

Indonesia: 59 days / 522 km (324 mi)
Elevation Climbed: 3.8 km (2.4 mi)
Total Distance to Date: 8,947 km (5,235 mi)
Elevation Climbed to Date: 44.3 km (27.5 mi)

6
SINGAPORE
7 DECEMBER 1993 – 23 DECEMBER 1993

English: *I'm traveling around the world by bicycle.*
Translation: *Fine. Just don't break any laws.*

B.L.T. Heaven

I went to Singapore for a few days to pick up my mail, get a new bike rack to replace the one that had shattered, and obtain an entry visa for India just as I had for Australia five months earlier. Twenty-four hours had been plenty, and I didn't want to stay longer than I had to...

It ended up taking three weeks.

Thankfully, as I was getting my last physical exam back in Seattle, my doctor offered me the name of a friend in Singapore.

"Lyndon?!" I was shocked. Lyndon and I had been in a songwriter's group together for several years in the 1980s. I had lost touch when he set off around the world with his family but, my doctor informed me, Lyndon had wound up in Singapore. The world really is a very small place.

Lyndon and I met for lunch on my first day in the country. I rode an elevator, my first in nearly a year, to the twelfth floor, the highest I'd been off the ground outside of a jet in even longer.

The receptionist guided me to his office and then plunged back to the jangling phones.

People trotted along the hall in hurried conversations.

He waved hello but was busy on two lines at once.

I struggled in vain to keep up with the three or four separate conversations rattling around me as people ducked in and out of the office.

Lyndon was a doctor for a med-evac firm, and they were working on extracting a seventy-year-old Japanese man with a broken leg and possible internal injuries from where he'd fallen off a trail in Laos. A French surgeon across the hall shouted out a question about present relations with the Burmese hill tribes as two packages were delivered, one by DHL and another by private courier.

Once the calls cleared, he turned to me. "Hi, Matt. How've you been doing? How long are you in town? Been having a good time?"

"Squeak."

He narrowed his eyes for a moment, left briefly to fetch some tea, and closed his office door behind him when he returned. I'd pushed my chair completely behind a large plant and had both feet under me on the chair. It required a force of will to scoot back to his desk and sip the scalding liquid.

"I haven't been in a hyper-office scene in over a year. And it feels way too familiar." I shuddered. It really was a deep visceral shock—far deeper than the early morning riding beside my Seattle-self through the sleeping streets of Solo. I had lived in this kind of pressure cooker for over a decade as if it was the most natural thing there was.

Once my hysteria had been washed down with the tea, he

toured me around his office. It was a crisis center that had been beautifully designed.

My specialty in my corporate days was information engineering, how information is created, flows, and is updated within a corporate structure. I was able to tell him why his office worked as well as it did at a level he'd never noticed. I even offered a few minor suggestions that he liked. He offered me a job on the spot; I chose to assume he was joking.

The real hit was lunch. I'd been happily eating Indonesian cuisine for two months.

He took me to Raffles Hotel, which had just undergone a massive restoration to its early 20th-century glory. I'm not sure I'd ever been in a building so glitzy and glamorous that wasn't a museum along the French Riviera. Writers, war correspondents, and the glitterati of the last century and a half had been through this hotel. It's said that when the Japanese occupied Singapore, they found the patrons there doing one last waltz. It was just the sort of place where that wasn't hard to imagine.

To me, the traveler? A bacon, lettuce, and tomato sandwich, real onion rings, and fresh lemonade was...ecstasy.

What's Missing

Over the next few weeks I worked to get my visa and toured Singapore. Great zoo, the best I've ever seen. Many of the animals have simply been coaxed to live there.

The National Library, a terribly noisy hangout for teenagers, claimed eight copies of Dante's *Inferno*, which I wanted to read for the book I was writing. None were checked out, yet none were on the shelves.

The city's core is dedicated to shopping in those massive vertical shopping malls that I'd discovered during my first pass through.

Singapore has incredibly restrictive laws. It was illegal to:

- Spit.
- Litter.
- Jaywalk.
- Graffiti. A terribly controversial caning of an American vandal had happened not long before I arrived. Controversial to us, not to Singapore.
- Import *Cosmopolitan* magazine.
- Chew gum on the subway.
- Eat or drink anything in a movie theater. Eat your popcorn before you go in.
- Not flush a public toilet, and yes there are people who check.
- Ride a bus without a ticket. No one ever checks, but there is no need, everyone has one.
- Smoke almost anywhere.
- Import *Sgt. Pepper's Lonely Hearts Club Band*. At least until 1990 because of the drug-promoting song *Lucy in the Sky with Diamonds*.

Lyndon countered my observation that the government was a tad bit fascist.

- His 14-year-old daughter had been riding the bus alone at night since she was 12. It is the safest major city in the world other than Tokyo.
- The low-income, government-assisted housing isn't for rent. At the end of the payments, the family owns it and it becomes a family asset.
- Free medical care of top caliber for everyone.
- No starving poor.
- One of the highest literacy rates in the world.
- The government decided that computers were the

way of the future, so they wired the entire country with fiber-optic cable in the late 1980s. This at a time when I'd been "incredibly cutting edge" for installing it to connect the three floors of a firm I was automating.
- Singapore has an 80-billion-dollar trade surplus. In 1992 the government stated they would give everyone a renovated bathroom with the surplus. "There's one problem. If we aren't in power after the upcoming election, we can't do it." There's really only one party, but apparently, they got nervous at every election. They were elected and they renovated every bathroom in the country. To us this is the worst form of vote buying, but Lyndon asked, "Is it wrong? They're investing in Singapore. And they kept their word."

Perhaps there is such a thing as a benign fascism or a democratically elected, benevolent dictatorship.

In the end, I only had one major problem with Singapore: I missed my mail. The American Express office had held it for precisely seven days and then returned it, with depressing efficiency.

That was the same day I'd arrived.

My last mail was in Darwin, and my next mail would be in Greece. Six months without hearing from my friends. Singapore's efficiencies do have their drawbacks.

Thankfully, Derek was a couple days late mailing the bicycle parts I needed, so I got those just fine.

Singapore: 16 days / 4 km (2.5 mi)
Elevation Climbed: 0.1 km (0.06 mi)
Total Distance to Date: 8,951 km (5,562 mi)
Elevation Climbed to Date: 44.4 km (27.6 mi)

7
INDIA
23 DECEMBER 1993 – 5 FEBRUARY 1994

English (the lingua franca): *My bicycle and I are riding around the world together.*
Translation: *Yes, but through India? Really?*

Turn the Dial to Eleven

India had me worried.
    Okay, scared.
Okay, as scared as before Japan.
This country generates traveler's tales like nowhere else in the world. Each one scared me even more, but they always ended with, "I can't wait to go back."

- "It's really hard to ignore all the beggars, especially the lepers. And if you see someone beating a child, don't interfere. They just want them to look more pitiful so they can beg better."
- "I always tried to be busy somewhere else when the cart for the dead rolled through the streets of

Bombay. I can still hear the thud of bodies that had died during the night being piled up."
- "Don't ride a Red Lion bus near Delhi. In their first year, they got ten thousand traffic violations. This is India. It's hard to get just one."
- "I read a story about a bus that drove through not one, but two crowds of people killing over twenty. It said, 'Driver and bus remain unidentified'."
- "Be especially careful in the north. Robbers will gas a whole bus or train car and rob everyone while they're knocked out."
- "I met someone who felt so guilty watching the people starve he basically stopped eating. They finally had to med-evac him out because he was too weak to even stand."

And there were hundreds more like them.
I was told three rules for surviving in India:

1. No mattered how prepared you think you are... You aren't.
2. You will be desperately sick for at least two weeks, just accept that now.
3. You have to commit to at least six weeks. For the first three, all you will want is out. After that, you'll have time to decide. But under six weeks, you'll never know.

All true.
I landed in Madras (Chennai) after an uneventful flight.
(Note: between my trip and this writing, India renamed most of its major cities—yet another stage of throwing off their English colonial past. The names in parentheses are the new names, but for me, Madras will always be Madras.)

Mid-Life Crisis on Wheels

Within moments of the plane's door opening, the smell of India slammed into my lungs. I sneezed painfully a number of times. It was spicier. It was richer. It was thicker. It was dusty and hot.

I had the normal audience as I assembled Junior on the dirty airport floor. As I prepared to roll away, a man shook my hand solemnly.

"Welcome to India."

I smiled back. I'd learned to deal with crowds and to be on display. I had grown. I could deal with this country. I kicked a pedal high, clipped in, and rolled out into the searing heat. "No worse than Indonesia," I kept repeating.

At the airport gate, there were no road signs. I asked the gate guard which way to Madras.

"Do you have American money?"

"No. I am in India, so I only carry rupee." Not true, but I wasn't going to tell him otherwise.

"May I see a 20 rupee note?" About $3 US.

"No, I just want to find Madras." I had been warned that India lived on *baksheesh*, bribes to do any service. I was willing to pay some, but this was silly. After a few more fruitless negotiations, I followed the bulk of the traffic to the left and rode toward the heart of Madras.

The cheap hostels in India had a distinctly unique flavor that I hadn't met before; a large percentage of the occupants were primarily interested in one topic.

"Man, the opium in Rajasthan is awesome, dude. They just pack a sock full of that shit and soak it in hot water. When the tea is strong enough, they toss all that great opium away over their shoulders. It's wicked. And Kerala, man, the coke there is the best. Out of this world."

"No way. The good coke is in Calcutta (Kolkata), but the hash in Delhi, oh my god, you won't even know what planet you're from, never mind which one you're on."

I'm one of those oddballs who never tried any drugs other than alcohol, and except for my senior year of college, had avoided most of its pitfalls. So, why did so many of these people decide I was their bosom buddy?

I could practically hear Dominic, "Because you're the craziest motherfucker here."

They preached peace and brotherly love until the power failed and blew out their ghetto blaster. The bliss-freaks then burst out with a stream of invective that was awe-inspiring to hear as they searched for someone to blame. I went out and walked the streets a great deal in my few days there.

Madras is a city of nearly seven million, about the size of Philadelphia or San Francisco, and the tallest buildings are the four-story train station and the enormous steeple of the Catholic church. All of the rest is sprawled across the broad, coastal plains. Much to my surprise, I encountered a truly fantastic English-language bookstore along the main road. One of the clerks explained it to me.

"In India we have 12 official languages, and soon the government will be adding another. We have 30 written languages and three hundred spoken and oh so many of dialects. If one Indian wishes to speak with another from different province, they must use English.

"This makes us very crazy, very schizophrenic, yes. We hate the British Raj and threw them out decades ago, but we must use their language to run our country. So, in India, we have the largest English-language publishing houses outside Britain and America. If publisher is smart, we get titles same time as America, before other countries. If not, we pirate book and get it anyway, but they do not get their royalties."

And best of all, the books were wonderfully cheap. Where $0.30 US will buy a meal, $2–4 US will buy a paperback novel. I departed Madras with a large and weighty stack.

The poorer sections of the city made even sad, little

Maumere look well off. Large signs surrounded water fountains where people fetched their drinking water. "Boil it before drinking it." I saw a little girl lift her dress, poop out a whitish mass in the middle of a street, and then turn around to inspect it, clearly wondering what was wrong this time.

An empty bridge arched over a slow, brown river.

As I watched, I saw some patterns I'd read about but not really given credence. At the head of the stretch of river, water was drawn. Next downstream, men wash themselves, then women. Below that, men defecate, then women. All very efficient and well-organized, if you aren't female. The problem is that the next house downstream follows the same pattern, taking their drinking water immediately below the toilet of the upstream neighbors. And nobody argues with the giant water buffalo who wallow there through the heat of the day.

And these were the ones lucky enough to have homes. I heard stories that in Bombay (Mumbai) and Calcutta (Kolkata), you can't walk at night for all the people sleeping on the sidewalk patches that are passed down from father to son. I saw no such masses of humanity in Madras, except on the buses. The rusty old crafts swayed and weaved beneath the weight of humanity that was forever perched atop them.

Then I noticed the high-water marks along the river. Come the monsoon, these houses would be gone in the resulting torrent and the residents would migrate up to the roadbeds until the waters receded and they could build again.

I splurged 300 INR ($10 US), a month's wages for the average Indian worker, on a Christmas dinner along with a Belgian, two Canadians, and a few other of the less-stoned folks at the rooming house. I tried not to feel guilty as I looked at the banquet of food spread before us.

"Has anyone seen a kid that wasn't in bare feet?"

"I can't believe there are lepers begging on the street with no one to care for them."

"Their population is growing so fast they don't know what to do. For a while there were press gangs who would grab women off the street and force them to have hysterectomies. They were finally stopped, but not until several hundred thousand women had been forcibly neutered, some multiple times."

Dinner conversation when traveling in the Third World requires a little explaining. There are no rules regarding "acceptable" topics. The worst offender is health.

"Which malaria regimen are you on? Oh, that one makes your hair fall out. I just carry a cure. It will kill off almost anything except for cerebral malaria. If you get that, you're dead in forty-eight hours anyway."

"My pee is white. Anyone know what that means?"

"So what's the sure indicator of dysentery and which antibiotics should I take for that?"

"Anyone have a spare clean needle? I need to go and get a cholera vaccination, but I ran out of needles and I'm not about to trust theirs."

I often joke that India is the only country where a pickup line among travelers might be: "So, what was the color of your stool today?"

It's not far from truth and it was certain to come up at any meal eaten with down-and-dirty travelers. Most of us carried large medical kits with malaria pills, syringes, several types of prescription antibiotics, as well as various other supplies. I also had eleven different vaccinations winging around my bloodstream already, some of which needed booster shots in Australia, Singapore, and Germany. I'd even gotten a cholera injection in Singapore. The doctor admitted they were only thirty percent effective, but the Singapore National Health Plan paid for it even though I was a foreigner. I was in their country and preventative medical was covered. Period.

Mid-Life Crisis on Wheels

My med kit. The big bunch of pills front and center? Antidiarrheal. (more details in Appendix I)

Upon ordering a meal, the first thing I'd do was touch it. If it wasn't hot, I sent it back. If it was hot, I'd look at the large steel plate it was served on, still dripping with wash water. Would I catch some disease from that? Was I hungry enough to risk it? Was it safe to just leave a thin layer of rice so what I ate never actually touched the plate? Eating as an extreme sport was a new perspective for me.

It wasn't until I reached Thanjavur that I learned to follow the general flow of locals in the early evening. We trooped into a tent and for 8 INR ($0.25 US) I purchased three tickets. I sat at one of the long tables and a young boy dropped a banana leaf on the table. A man placed a large pile of rice in the middle of it and took one ticket. Another left a goodly scoop of dal, a lentil and spice blend, and some yogurt. The last ticket went to a man wielding half a dozen different sauces. I pointed to a red curry, a yellow one with green flecks, and a green cilantro something. He indicated the second and made a face like a dragon breathing fire. I aimed my finger at a pinkish mixture, and he ladled a scoop of each around the perimeter of the rice, and a little of the hot one just for the fun of it.

I watched those around me as they used their fingers to mix the dal, yogurt, and sauces in varying proportions with the rice, stir it up well, and with a deft scoop, deliver it to their mouths on three fingers as the spoon and using the thumb as a scraper. When I finished, I fed the banana leaf to a goat who was wandering the tables for just that purpose. Twice in India I splurged on nice restaurants and found the food bland and Western. I hunted down the dal and rice stalls whenever I could.

Meals were always topped off with a visit to a *chai* stall. My favorite was in Kerala. It was full when I arrived, so I squatted outside the six-by-ten-foot space with a few others and waited. Over a dozen people crowded on the three benches under the stall's soiled canopy. The burner stood in the middle and the fourth wall was the open street. A long, thin man in his late twenties poured great streams of glittering liquid from one pitcher to another and back as he mixed the milk and copious sugar the Indians put in everything. Only those on the benches were served. Perhaps he could have served those waiting, but it didn't matter. It was evening time in India.

But it wasn't the *jam karet* of Indonesia, the indolent movement performed only when necessary.

Indian cities are filled with a bustle and hum of humanity and activity that would challenge downtown Manhattan. Everything is done quickly during the day, though perhaps to no clearer schedule than Indonesia, but certainly with a First World intensity. Only in the evening does it slow down, and we squat and tell jokes while waiting our turns.

The merchant's seven-year-old son indicates who gets to replace those who've left. He keeps perfect track of who arrived when.

"I cannot pay to send him to school, but I teach him to make *chai*. My father made *chai* and my son will too."

The boy served the blazing-hot *chai* in little stainless steel cups set in stainless steel bowls. I watch the locals pour it back and forth between cup and tiny bowl to cool it. My "Ooh! Aaah! Ow!" attracts his attention and the boy showed me the art of catching the edges of the red-hot cup—at least it felt that way—on the hard skin of my finger joints. With a little practice, and much good-humored advice from the locals, the clumsy, burnt-fingered thirty-five-year-old traveler finally mastered this skill, thanks to the patience of a seven-year-old magician.

He leaned back against his father's legs while we drank and chatted, right where he belonged. He was home. There was a piece of my definition of home, the way that child stood with his father.

He was also perhaps the quietest kid I saw in all India. Healthy, fit, well-clothed kids always ran toward me, just like their Indonesian counterparts. But instead of waving and yelling, "Hallo, Mistah!" they held out their hands and yelled, "Pen. Pen." or "Rupee. Rupee." Some even carry schoolbooks, meaning their families are very well off indeed, and still they pulled at me. They especially wanted pens, pencils, and paper for their schoolwork.

One traveler told the story of offering a child a candy bar from his pack. "They swarmed me. Within seconds, they'd gone through everything I had. They didn't steal anything except the candy…oh and the pens, pencils, and paper. Every scrap."

And it wasn't only the children. I'd stop to rest along the road and four workers would come up out of the fields. I'd watch them drop their lunch pails and head toward me. I knew what was coming and by the time they arrived, I'd be leisurely back aboard Junior. "Hallo? Where from? Food? Smoking? Pen? Candy? Rupee? American money?"

I learned to stop only long enough to pull out an orange,

though it took some time to figure out how to peel one as I rode.

A New Year

New Year's Eve in Pondicherry (Puducherry), Tamil Nadu, India. At home, Mac and Ruth would be spending the night babying their dogs through the loud booms and bangs. Others, well bundled up, would be down at the park atop Queen Anne Hill watching the fireworks run the length of the Space Needle before heading through the chill morning to warm homes.

I was squatting on a breakwater drenched in my own sweat from the thick heat. I stared out at the setting sun and tried to imagine how in the world I had ended up here—alone. I hunched instinctively away from the four Indians who descended upon me.

They had very little English between them. It took me a while to unravel that the two jewelers didn't want to sell me anything; the bus conductor wasn't offering me a ride to anywhere; and the mechanic, who spoke no English at all, simply wanted to smile.

A lot more word-sounds went back and forth to create a little more understanding.

They simply wanted to welcome me to their country.

We took photos and attempted to tell jokes as darkness descended. They invited me to their party, but I'd arranged a late dinner with a French cyclist, once again headed in the other direction.

With their great hugs and friendship and good wishes, and my faith in humanity being bolstered by still being in possession of my camera and money belt, I happily met with the cyclist. As we shared tales about the road ahead and the road behind over Tandoori prawns and a large beer, I still couldn't believe how easily my mood could swing. It was going to be a very good year.

| New Year's Eve, Pondicherry.

Step Right Up

After two weeks, I could still smell India. Any new place has a smell that I notice when I step off a plane, but usually in a matter of minutes the difference fades into familiarity. India was different.

It wasn't the rotting garbage; the goats and cows ate all that before it could get too nasty.

It wasn't the cows walking down even the busiest streets; I grew up in dairy country and was used to their smell.

It wasn't the cooking spices or the clouds of diesel exhaust from every truck and bus.

It was all this mixed together and yet something more. I asked another traveler and he could only shrug, "India smells funny to us foreigners."

The roads were different too, jarringly different. Some of the problems had been eased by the last-minute addition of a shock absorber to my handlebars (the reason for the loose handlebar bolt that laid me out on the ground my first day). But my kidneys took a pounding. There were some sections of road where I could barely outstrip a walk, and the ruts were so deep that buses barely achieved a slow trot. This could continue for twenty or thirty kilometers.

And the traffic. It was a constant shock to someone like me who learned to drive in timid localities like Boston and New York. A local was nice enough to explain it to me.

He'd read about me in the Rajapalayam morning paper. I was probably the only white person in this city of a hundred and ten thousand. He introduced himself over breakfast in the restaurant nearest my hotel. I sorely wish I had purchased a copy of the paper or could have read the curlicued Tamil he showed me. Some reporter had turned my hotel check-in information into a dozen column-inches of newsprint with a half-inch headline. I'd love to know what it said.

"An Indian who owns a vehicle is a very proud person," my unexpected breakfast guest explained. "He will blow his horn saying, 'Look at me. Look at me.' An Indian person who hears this horn for the third or fourth time will think, 'Why should I care?' But still we blow them proudly."

All I know is that when I heard a loud horn, I dove for the shoulder, even when there wasn't one. Buses shimmered past at immense speeds, when the roads allowed, leaving a maelstrom of dust and diesel fumes in their wake. In Tamil Nadu I saw two wrecked buses and three destroyed trucks in the same day. There appears to be no one to tow them away. Each had a line of fist-sized stones placed around them as some sort of a warning. On four of the five, the front windshield was blown out from the bodies hitting it from within. The bus that was rolled over in the ditch left me to wonder about those who were perched on top. India has one percent of the world's vehicles and six percent of its traffic accidents. (Since then, I've heard that a powerful middle class has emerged and with them there's been a flood of cars. However, in the first days of 1994, traffic was ox carts, scooters, trucks, and buses.)

Another helpful road sign. The oxcart hauling squash was slow, the truck hauling hay was fast, and the buses were lethal (this one almost clipped me, though I was stopped well off the road's edge, because he was avoiding the fast approaching hay truck that was out in the wrong lane to get around the slow ox).

I learned to recognize the vehicle by the sound of the horn and was only taken by surprise once.

A truck horn blasted close behind and sent me diving into rough dirt and gravel. A scooter zipped by and waved merrily before releasing another blast, this time spooking a harnessed team of oxen. I waited in the gravel until the oxcart driver got them calmed down. Their horns looked even fiercer than the scooters.

Being alone was nearly impossible. At times I would retreat to my room for some peace and quiet. In Quilon (Kollam) I was such an oddity that every single person who worked in the hotel must have knocked on my door in that very long night, offering me services I often didn't even understand. They were all clearly there to see the American and his weird bicycle.

The guidebooks estimate that fewer than a thousand foreign cyclists arrive in India each year (that's in a country of a billion people). I would guess there are at least that many on the roads of New Zealand (four million people) every day of their summer. I was beyond a rarity in a cheap hotel in the great vastness of India, the seventh largest country in the world.

Crow Travel Agents

I took a ferry boat through the Alleppey Backwater—often called the "Venice of the East" and locally called the Swamps of Alleppey. After a long debate with the skipper, he agreed to take my bike without *baksheesh,* but he was not happy.

Several times during the trip, he would offer to throw my bike overboard. I'd counter with an offer to remove his steering wheel and do the same. He'd lift a floorboard and point at the emergency tiller. I'd shrug and he'd laugh wildly. He'd won that round, until the next time one of us thought up a new strategy.

Some American passengers had joined us at an ashram, a meditation retreat, without my noticing. At a tea stop, one introduced herself.

"Are you the one traveling with the bike? Well, the crows were eating your cookies, so I slipped them inside your saddlebag."

That was how I met Rollie and Meegan, a couple of chefs from Seattle. They weren't cyclists themselves, but they'd met *another* Seattle cyclist and he was on the boat. That made four non-Indians on the entire ferry, and we were all from Seattle! Three-quarters of the American travelers I met were from the Pacific Northwest, none from the South except for one lone Texan in Greece who had sassy blonde cowgirl honed to a fine art. (Hands down she won the most-exotic-headgear award for any traveler I met, a pristine white felt cowboy hat.)

Douglas was a spare, narrow man with bright, brown eyes and a matching ponytail that just reached his shoulders. His voice was quick, and he leaned forward eagerly to speak, punctuating each thought with sharp, precise hand motions. He reminded me a lot of Toby from Indonesia, just with "frenetic" turned down from eleven to maybe eight.

He'd given up on the Indian roads and had stored his bike in Goa for a month to travel by boat and rail.

The story got weirder the more we talked. Just six months younger than me, he'd burned out of corporate America as well. He'd flown to Japan within a week of my landing there. He'd ridden south into summer while I rode north into Hokkaido's winter. Our future journeys promised better, we were both headed for Greece and from there to Vienna. I'd planned to ride through Italy and Switzerland to get there. He planned to travel Eastern Europe because it was cheaper.

No-brainer.

"I'll join you."

"Great!" Douglas always had a positive word.

In that moment, I joined with my third fellow traveler: four days with a British couple in Oregon and ten days with a German in Flores and Lombok, Indonesia, three months earlier.

When we finally reached the end of the ferry ride, I gave the captain a nice tip for not tossing my bike into the murky waters. I guess *baksheesh* is just a tip for services yet to be rendered, but it still irritates me. He was suddenly my best friend, even parading around in my bicycle helmet much to the amusement of his crew and passersby. I offered to drive his boat next time out and he could ride my bike for a day. He quickly surrendered the helmet with a broad grin.

Writer's Motto

I left my new-found companions reluctantly, but made arrangements to meet up a week later. I was headed to places they'd been and vice versa. I slid into Kochi (Cochin) after exactly three weeks in India.

Honoring the advice I'd been given, I would spend six weeks in-country. But I now knew that was enough. My plans to ride to Nepal and trek were abandoned. My intent to take a week-long yoga seminar in Kathmandu from one of my fellow

Nusa Tigans (that same thatched-hut *losmen* on Gili Air, Indonesia) went by the boards.

Yes, I could travel in India. Yes, it was interesting. It wasn't that I disliked India as I had Japan. But did I really want to work that hard?

A resounding: No!

India should be traveled with a change of clothes, a mosquito net, and a med kit—all together weighing under five kilos—not on a touring bike weighing well over fifty. I bought a plane ticket and tucked it safely into my money belt.

I'd revel in my final weeks in India. I toured the Mattancherry Palace, a gift from the Portuguese to the local raja in the 1550s. Fantastic murals decorated the walls depicting scenes from the Mahabharata, the ancient Hindu text. I wonder how the Catholic Portuguese felt as they inspected the luscious, sensual depictions of the God Shiva and his voluptuous mortal wife Parvati. Oddly, I wasn't moved beyond a simple appreciation of the beautiful work. I finally recalled another warning I received before my arrival.

"Indian energy suppresses Western libido at first. It is only on your second or third trip to India that it will come to life. And then everywhere else will pale."

I don't know about the latter, but I realized that while I had certainly looked at women both native and foreign since my arrival, I hadn't felt attracted to any. Hadn't even a thought much beyond, "Oh, that one's pretty." I tried picturing the lovely Suri back in Maumere, Indonesia. Nope, nothing. India is the most different place I've ever been.

There was a synagogue next door to the palace.

Jews in India?

Not something I'd expected to find. To my astonishment (India had not suppressed that ability), this community traced its origins directly to the Diaspora, which followed the destruction of the second temple in Jerusalem by the Muslims in 58 A.D. It was the first synagogue I had entered since the age of six.

I am that oddity in modern America, a pureblood. I'm Jewish on all sides of my family tree from a region near the Black Sea of what is now Romania (one of those genetic tests lists me simply as 100% Ashkenazi Jew). And here I sat, half a world from home in a temple of my direct ancestors. Not even knowing my great-grandparents' names (my family wasn't big on history), I had nonetheless stepped into their world. After sitting in silence for a few hours, I was unaccountably at peace when I stepped back into the bright sunlight of southern India.

Something had been brewing in my writing from my time in Singapore and India, but I wasn't sure what. I finally put my finger on it in Kochi.

I went to see Director Devan's Kathakali Dance Performance. This is the tourist's introduction to a five-hundred-year-old art form that takes fifteen years of study to learn. He reduced one eight-hour story from the massive repertoire to a two and a half hour performance, enlivened with his running commentary in one of the most overwrought accents I heard in my journeys there.

"Hindu religion (ree-lig-ee-on) can be seen as two levels (lee-vuls). The first level is the religion. The religion is the stories of the myths and Gods (Gawds). This level is solely symbols created by the artists and it is enough for most people. It is all they need to survive, so it is all they see and understand.

"Ah! But the other level. Ah! This is the philosophy (phee-law-so-phee). This is what the stories make available to the people. It is the philosophy, not the religion, that is important."

It was exactly what I was ready to hear. As I'd studied different religions in different countries, I'd found that the core teachings were much the same:

- "Treat others as you would be treated." –Occidental

- "Treat a guest in your house as if it were his house."
  –Islam
- "Walk seven steps with someone and they are your friend." –Hindu

It's all the same sentiment. And whether it is Jesus upon the cross or the Buddha under a Bodhi tree who is worshipped, the lessons about how to treat one another are the same. I'm not going to start teaching religion, but in that unlikely place, a rooftop under the winter stars in Kochi, Kerala, India, I found the key to my first book. It was the "philosophy" I wanted to make shine forth.

Director Devan's simplified talk describing this ancient dance would go on to be at the very core of every story I've ever written—every single one.

My first writer's motto, which I didn't fully articulate for years but was nonetheless true was:

> To Champion the Human Spirit

I've been striving to honor that ever since, Director Devan. Honestly, I have.

Dials Turned at Twelve?

I struggled northward out of Kochi up the Western Ghats. What I had tackled with heart and enthusiasm on my way westward across India now towered before me like some insurmountable massif as I tempted to re-cross them. I had planned to cover eighty or so kilometers toward my rendezvous with Douglas and friends; I barely made thirty before I pulled into an expensive hotel and slept fourteen hours on clean-washed sheets.

The next day I crawled into a bus station after only ten

more kilometers and was instantly surrounded by a large crowd as usual. But for the first time, I didn't trust it. Sure enough, I literally had to strike out at them to keep them from picking the bike clean. I rode away and found a vacant lot to regroup. There was no way I could get through that crowd and onto a bus with everything intact.

I waited a few hours for the crowd to change, then rode back. Perhaps there were different people there now. It was worse, and I actually had to swing about with my bike pump to clear an escape route.

I ground out of town and managed to flag down a passing jeep. For an outrageous *baksheesh* of $10 US they gave me a lift to the top of the pass. It was a fortune I could have lived on for four or five days (including hotels), but I didn't care. Sharp stomach cramps set in and my legs were screaming.

I was a day late for our planned meeting and that added to my anxiety. I rushed as well as I could along the final kilometers toward our agreed meeting place.

A large sign announced my entrance into the Mudumalai Wildlife Sanctuary. A few hundred meters farther along was another sign so small and high up a tree, I'm surprised I noticed it:

Warning! Animals may scratch and bite.

That was it. No public-safety American fence surrounding the park, no gate, no rangers. I was simply in the park.

I didn't think much of this one way or the other. The tigers this park was known for were so rarely seen that some said they were extinct in this region.

A few kilometers on, I rounded a clump of trees and the cutest little elephant, no taller than me, popped up its head and made a little trumpet sound as if asking what I was. The baby began to lumber toward me as I drew even with it along the roadway. We were perhaps ten paces apart and I was wondering if I should stop to take a photo or not. But with the way my gut was hurting would I be able to restart?

Then I heard, or rather felt, a large bellow. The mother elephant was only a few steps beyond her baby, hidden at first by tree and brush, but now she was trotting forward.

She bellowed again, threatening to split my eardrums—it even echoed in my burning guts.

I bolted. Every ounce of power and bit of technique that I'd built up over ten thousand kilometers of riding went pouring into my pedals.

I zoomed into higher gears. "Trampled by an elephant" was suddenly a real possibility for an epitaph.

In my rearview mirror I could see her slow to a halt, not wanting to be too far from her tiny child. For a foolish moment I slowed and wonder if it would be safe to get out the camera. Another bellow and I was instantly back up to speed and gone. I've never seen anything look so big in my life.

My new friends loved the story when I met up with them an hour later. The next day we walked about the park. I couldn't have ridden if my life depended on it; even walking was dicey.

There was a wonderful sign along a narrow river near the hostel: "Fishing, bathing, and washing clothes in crocodile-infested river is prohibited. Survivor will be prosecuted." There were, of course, numerous locals doing all three. (The sign was in the singular, leaving us to wonder if that was intentional or not.)

The Indians have a casual relationship with the English language. We started naming our favorite misnomers:

- "Fried Children" on a restaurant menu.
- "Future site of proposed historic city" on a billboard.
- "My husband's hands can see in the dark. Can yours?" on a billboard of a beautiful woman

recruiting for the Air Force. (Night-vision goggles implied, making it a puzzle.)
- "Duck Insurance – another first from United India." It seemed funny until we realized that a duck herd might be all a person owned in the world. Well worth insuring.
- "For the man who isn't afraid to show he cares. Nivea aftershave." It took us a while to work this one out. It was a billboard of a pregnant woman sitting on a bench while a man tied his shoe. Oh! He was a man who cared. He was tying his *own* shoe instead of making his very pregnant wife kneel to do so.
- "We don't build apartments, we build complexes." A construction company ad and I bet they do.

Everything seems bigger in India. The Guinness Book of World Records loves India.

- Largest gathering of people: fifteen million at a Hindu festival.
- Most dead by natural disaster: one million in a hurricane.
- Most people eaten by a single animal: four hundred and thirty-six by a Bengal tiger.
- Most dead in a chemical disaster: sixty-three hundred at Bhopal.
- Largest bicycle manufacturer: three million one-speed clunkers in 1992.
- World's largest public utility: the Indian railroad.

Everywhere I turned in India there was life. Not just crowds, but crowds doing things. I spent an afternoon recording what passed me on a street in the little town of barely barely a half million people—little only by the standards of this immensely populated country. A city below fifty thousand is called, and feels like, a village.

- A group of dancers and musicians in brilliant blues and glittering golds parade through the streets burning incense until the air is thick with clouds of it. It is a funeral. A happy time. It is not that life is cheap here, it is that in most of the religions this is not the only life. The dead have survived this mortal dance and are on to the next.
- A leper scoots by on his bottom with only his loins wrapped in brown burlap. He uses the stumps of his wrists to lift his body high enough to move his butt forward, then reaches forward with his ankle stumps and repeats the process. Middle-class businessmen with briefcases step around him. He isn't begging. He pries a few coins from the folds in his waistcloth, drops them in a vendor's bowl, and turns back with three fresh bananas in his lap.
- A dye vendor hawks his bowls brimmed high with brilliantly colored powders. Each bowl glows like he caught of bolt of light, his magentas and yellows so pure they beckon me to play with them like a child.
- Across the street, a group of women squat in elegant saris and wield sledgehammers. The sharp odor of cracked granite temporarily overwhelms the roasted nut vendor. Boulders are dumped along the road and these women crack them into gravel for refinishing the road. Rock crushers are illegal in this state because they would put too many out of work.
- An elephant, wrapped in gold cloth and led by six drummers, carries a sign announcing a book fair.
- On the sidewalk there are fruit vendors, beggars,

shop clerks, shoppers, tailors sipping *chai*, and hordes of children playing with a passing monkey.
- An actress rests during a break in a new Bollywood film.

The parade never ends and this is no special city. I've heard that the big cities of the north—New Delhi, Agra, Varanasi, and Calcutta (Kolkata)—are much more dramatic.

The Eye of the Beholder

There was no way I could ride through my gut cramps the next day, but with my friends' help I managed to get Junior atop a bus for the short, steep climb to Udhagamandalam (Ooty) hill station over a thousand meters above sea level. This was one of the towns that the British used to retreat to during the sweltering summers.

I collapsed at the motel, feeling worse if possible; 102°F fever (39°C), and someone whipping my innards with an elephant prod. I finally thought to drag out my medical book. (Why so slow? Japan had been eight months ago, and I was sick, so give me a break.)

I read a number of pages through tear-streaked eyes as I squatted over the toilet, then lay shaking and sweating in my sleeping bag. My friends tried to help, but they knew as little as I did. I finally narrowed it down to two possibilities. One required immediate hospital care, not something I wished to experiment with in the heart of India. The other was dysentery.

I remembered the simple test I'd once heard in "polite" travelers' dinner conversation. I rose shakily to my feet. I steeled myself. I hopped on one foot, perhaps a finger-width high, just a little hop.

I was slammed to the floor doubled-up with pain. Dysentery, positive diagnosis. When I could focus my eyes again, I checked the book against the Travel Clinic's doctor's notes when he'd given me the antibiotics a year before in Seattle. Cipro. The big gun. A three-day regimen.

By Day Two I was able to leave the room and sit in the sun during the warmest part of the day, but couldn't keep down even a banana. By Day Three I could actually walk into town and eat dinner. I felt light-headed and ethereal, but okay. My friends were now bored of a town I hadn't even seen, but there was no way I could ride. So, we all took a bus up to Mysore (Mysuru).

As we traveled, we learned more and more about each other. Douglas hadn't noticed any of the gender bias I had found so irritating in Japan. And the constant gifts hadn't bothered him in the slightest. It was their culture. If he didn't want it, there was always an unused garbage can somewhere out of sight.

And he was *always* in more trouble than I was. Instead of being a babe magnet (which he would have liked), he was a total trouble magnet. In northern India he'd pulled out a can of mace during an attempted robbery at knife point. He'd also had to bribe himself out of trouble any number of times. I hadn't even thought to bring pepper spray because I was never going into the types of situations that seemed to materialize around Douglas.

Rollie, it turned out, had been the chef at the restaurant for one of my going-away dinners. After all, how many 6'3" men have blond hair down to their waist and cook in the same small Seattle restaurant? I'd eaten one of the last meals he cooked before his own departure. Rollie was a photographer by desire, a chef to pay for it.

I'd always been convinced that I had no eye for art. He scoffed at that.

"You are trying to follow what other people say is good art. Go and listen to yourself, not others. If Monet looks liked he spilled his paint set to you, walk away. If a child's drawing with watercolor arrests you, then look and appreciate. Don't trust others. Art is personal."

He found a couple of art museums in Mysore and I followed reluctantly in his wake. In a huge photo exhibition, I only found three images I liked. Rollie named two of the three, although neither Douglas nor Meegan agreed.

"Art is in the eye of the beholder; we just have a common eye."

He always had a camera in his hand, and I began paying attention to the images he shot. They seemed nothing special, until I raised my camera to match his. Between two ramshackle wooden huts, a woman in a blue-and-gold sari shook out a child's sari of exactly the same color to hang on a clothesline. With the huts framed out, she was a busy mother against the backdrop of the green hills beyond.

I learned more about photography in that one day with Rollie than I had in hundreds of rolls of film over the last few decades. We saw the same world; he just knew how to capture it. I still achieve mediocre at best.

Douglas looking for a role in Bollywood central casting. Children were endlessly fascinated by the towering Rollie and his camera. Never happy until each had looked through its viewfinder multiple times.

Challenges of the Dial Turned Full Up

That afternoon Rollie and I sat in a small park near our lodgings telling jokes and stories. Sometimes reading some poetry aloud and sometimes just watching the world go by. I think Meegan and Douglas were taking a walk.

"Are you brothers?" A man and his wife were holding hands on a nearby bench. They were our age and nicely dressed. He in the ubiquitous black slacks and white button-down shirt open at the neck. She wore a green-and-blue sari of obvious quality.

Rollie and I glanced at each other, the towering WASP and the short Jew. "No, just friends. New friends."

There was a long pause as he mulled this over. "You seem to have such a good time together. I don't have any friends like that. I used to. Then I started a house construction company. I lost friends because I founded it far away from my childhood home. Then I made new friends who disappeared when we competed for the same job and I won. I know people who work in construction, but not to laugh with as you two have been."

His wife leaned forward. "Even wives do not talk as they did when we were poor. We cook. We entertain. But there is no laughter in the kitchen. I must be very careful what I say or that, too, is used against my husband in his next business deal. Do you have many close friends?"

Rollie and I nodded together.

"Here in India we have a middle-class that is a hundred times as big as a generation ago. Now poor friends look for handouts and those in the middle class with us are terribly cutthroat. We don't want friends like either of those."

"You could join a group?"

"The business groups are often vicious."

"How about chess, golf, or a reading group? Nothing to do with work."

"I don't know of any."

"We could form one." His wife clearly liked the idea and held his hand tighter. "We could try."

He thanked us for the idea and they began to talk it over among themselves.

That night I explained the problem to Douglas and Meegan. "They've imported the American corporate ladder all at once without any time to get used to the problems."

Douglas laughed. "Yep. The good and the bad. WAY UP!"

A Different Kind of High

One evening, Douglas and I headed north by train. Rollie and Meegan turned east. Again, new friends, who I would stay in touch with for years.

At sunrise Douglas and I slid open the train's door and stuck our heads out into the wind to wash away the last haze of sleep. Perched on the steps, the broad plains slid by beneath a pastel pink and gold glow. The rolling green grass could have been in America as easily as India. For an hour or so we sat in the wind and watched the world in silence.

At Hospet (Hosapete) I went trotting back to the baggage car for Junior, only there wasn't one. I found the station master.

"Where's the baggage car?" I was perhaps a bit abrupt.

"You turn west in night. Baggage car go north to Guntakal."

I had woken in the middle of the night at the switchover. I'd even thought to go and check on Junior, but I'd let sleep win. Stupid. Stupid. Stupid.

I switched to a pleading tone, which failed to impress the station master. Finally, I looked him square in the eye.

"My bicycle is worth 60,000 rupees (about $2,000 US). I couldn't replace it in your country even if you gave me the money. I want my bike."

I finally had his attention; it might be more money than he

made in a year. I didn't know. I didn't care. He promised to look into it, but it would take at least a day.

The next morning, I went down to the luggage warehouse—and there was Junior, leaning casually against a wall, no worse for his adventure. I had long since covered his bright-blue frame with black duct tape and scuffed that up with dirt and the edge of my knife. He didn't look like much, but I was glad to have him back. Unable to find the station master, I left him a note with several hundred rupees (about $10 US) wrapped inside.

I locked Junior in the hotel room, and we went into Hospet. Drugs flowed around us as we went. I was offered coke twice before I realized that, "I'm not thirsty," wasn't the expected response. Though it did gain me many surprised and bewildered looks. I decided to keep using it as an easy out. They must have decided that my brain was cooked from too many drugs rather than addled by simple naiveté and lack of interest.

Ads were posted for rave parties in the hills beyond the temple, hash and music provided for one low fee, coke and opium were extra. Sex was probably a given, but I didn't go to find out.

We opted for the quieter life of exploring the expansive ruins of Hampi. The ancient temple spread over a large area. The chariot of Ganesh, pulled by three-foot-high elephants all carved in stone, stood much as it had 1,500 years before. Shapely goddesses, bedecked with sandstone jewels, welcomed us through arches to temples that no longer existed. Water buffalo bathed in the same lake that had once been the center of a city of half a million and had ruled southern India.

We climbed high into the rocks. I found a shady spot to work on my book while Douglas napped and explored. We climbed a nearby peak for sunset and were both content when we descended back into the madness below. The full moon in

Hampi is a time of immense parties. Hundreds upon hundreds of foreigners, pretty much all under twenty-five, and, as far as we could tell, all stoned or wishing they were.

I preferred my "crowd."

Goodbye, India

My last stop in India was the beach resort of Goa, an old Portuguese port. The parties here were active as well, if less drug oriented. Fighting a second round of dysentery, I spent most of my time in a beach chair beneath the palm trees.

Douglas would tell me tales of where he'd been over breakfast each morning.

I spread the antibiotics out by a day so that the last pill would enter my system just as I was leaving India.

He planned to stay in India for another three weeks, I was continuing on to Israel. We agreed to meet up in Athens at a particular hostel for our two-week ride up to Vienna.

It was only on my last night that I felt well enough to even stay awake after dark.

Over dinner I fell in with Helmi, a Danish journalist on holiday after spending half a year straightening out her ex-husband's estate. Apparently his second wife had stabbed him to death when she caught him cheating. We talked about writing, the books I was thinking of, and the story of her husband's life; he'd apparently been quite prominent in addition to being a shmuck.

We spoke of the need to hope for the future rather than dwelling on the past.

I told her tales of Maumere and Antonio, "Good heart, good thoughts, automatic good actions."

"*Gøt Heuge!*" she offered. "It roughly translates as 'being yourself with friends'."

We floated for hours beneath the waning moon in the warm

waters of the Indian Ocean as we continued to talk. Around 3:00 a.m. we kissed goodnight, just four hours before I had to ride to the airport. We had to cling to each other until the shakes stopped; it was the first time in three years either of us had been kissed.

I thought about that moment a great deal over the next few days. I didn't have to be alone. I just had to "be myself with friends." That is what had drawn us together. Of course, why I didn't just delay my plane ticket by a few weeks is a question I've never been able to answer.

After six weeks in India, everything else had been stripped away. My arrogance about how well I understood the world. My expectation of always receiving decent treatment. My belief that my own health was secure for decades to come. In those few moments of that long spring night as I held an attractive, intelligent, worldly woman in my arms, I was more myself than I had been in a long time. Perhaps ever. I hope that I opened a path for her back to her heart, as Helmi did for me.

I think India is a land of truths. Life is very exposed there. The comfortable Western facades are few and far between.

- The children would leave the sides of dying relations to come and play with my bicycle.
- When a salesman finally accepted that I wouldn't be buying anything, he'd sit and talk about the seasons, his family, my country.
- Two guys rode beside me for hours on a scooter once, friendly as could be, chatting up a storm—until they tried to tear a pannier off my bike as they roared away, which failed because the bags were locked onto the racks. They did dump me hard onto the rough road as they raced off.

Cutthroat and kindness live side by side there. Sorrow and

joy are not separated by the great chasm that it is in the West. I have seen a country that believes in celebrating a funeral.

Without question, India is filled with life.

The contrasts are overwhelming...and I could do with a slightly lower volume setting.

India: 36 days / 1,419 km (882 mi)
Elevation Climbed: 3.8 km (2.4 mi)
Total Distance to Date: 10,370 km (6,443 mi)
Elevation Climbed to Date: 48.2 km (30 mi)

8

ISRAEL

6 FEBRUARY 1994 – 17 FEBRUARY 1994

English: *I am traveling around the world by bicycle.*
Translation: *Are you seeking to reconnect to the community of your religious heritage or are you seeking a path to God through...*

The First of Three Cities

There is a saying in Haifa: "You go to Tel Aviv to play, Jerusalem to pray, and Haifa to work."

After a kiss, three hours of sleep, and a fifty-kilometer ride to the airport, I thought nothing of riding through the interior of the Indian airport terminal—dodging travelers, suitcases, squalling kids who suddenly stopped and watched me pedal by in wonder—until I found the check-in counter (it's India, after all).

Three planes, twenty-five hours in transit, and another fifteen kilometers on my bike later, I arrived in Tel Aviv at 10:30 on a bright, chilly winter morning. I hadn't slept but those three hours in two and a half days, and the youth hostel was closed for another six hours.

I also hadn't been anywhere this cold since Hokkaido. I

pulled on every piece of clothing I had and sallied forth to see the town.

And get some food.

I'd spent my last 6 INR ($0.18 US) to buy a candy bar for dinner over twenty-four hours earlier. That and airplane food was not enough to assuage my post-dysentery, cyclist's hunger.

I discovered a small grocery store and ducked out of the rain.

And jolted to a halt worse than any deer in the headlights.

It was a little place, but everything was neatly packaged and labeled in English and Hebrew. There wasn't just one type of bread, there were a dozen. Cookies, cereals, everything had a choice. I wandered the aisles in a daze, sometimes picking up a box to inspect it. I could actually read what was in these packages, rather than just trying to interpret the pictures. And the ingredients as well!

I must have been a sorry sight: long hair and beard, clothes that had seen far too much of the Third World, and a wild look of panic in my eyes. I finally purchased some dried apricots; it was the only thing they were selling bulk—the only thing my world-shocked mind could understand how to purchase.

I went back onto the street.

I had left an Indian beach town of barely ten thousand souls and had arrived in a throbbing metropolis of four hundred thousand Jews. The wealth around me was mind-boggling.

Cars were everywhere.

Teenage girls, in the latest styles with their hair done just so, pranced down the sidewalk in clusters of giggles and flashing fingernail polish.

A beggar sat on the sidewalk dressed in blue jeans, a flannel shirt, and decent hiking boots: all signs of middle class or better in India.

There, I had traveled for six weeks on $200 US for food,

clothing, hotels (cheap ones), and transport. Here, most people's coats probably cost that much.

I dodged my way past bars and discos, auto repair shops and sporting goods stores, booksellers and fast-food places like some puck that was being batted about an air hockey table—but with no net to land in. I finally found safety on the windswept beach, barren in this midwinter month of February. There I finally found a haven in which I could eat my apricots.

The next day I was better able to brave the grocery store. I also left town as fast as I could for the ride to Jerusalem.

Finding Faith in the Second City

Two rounds of dysentery had knocked off five kilos (over ten pounds) and much of my conditioning. The easy one-day ride up into the hills to Jerusalem turned into a grueling two-day grind. I was healing, but slowly. And it was even deeper winter at eight hundred meters than it had been at the coast. I was never warm in the week I was there.

It didn't take long to learn that there are only two topics of conversation in this city.

- If two people are standing toe-to-toe and screaming at the top of their lungs, it is just a friendly chat about politics.
- If they are sitting quietly in small groups for hour upon hour, it is a religious discussion.

All other topics have apparently been outlawed within the old city wall.

There in Old Jerusalem, a space barely a kilometer across, is the holiest city of the Jews and Christians and the third holiest of the Muslims. The Armenians also have a well-tended, quiet corner, a silent haven from the storm of emotions elsewhere.

The ever-present, twenty-year-old, Uzi-toting members of the Israeli army failed to instill further confidence.

I started peeking around the edges of buildings before I crossed into a square.

One afternoon I traveled out to Yad Vashem, the Holocaust museum. I wandered through pictures of death camps, charts of how many Jews were in each European country before the war and how few afterward, and endless photographs of survivors, gas chambers, and burial pits. Prison art overflowed the room allotted and left nightmares in its wake.

It was impossible to not draw parallels with the Hiroshima Peace Memorial Park. The Japanese museum left me with two messages. One written: *Never let this happen again.* One unwritten: horror that mankind had ever ranged so far out of balance that such force had been deemed necessary.

The Yad Vashem Memorial has but one single, very clear message: *Be vigilant. Stay armed so that it can never be done to us again.*

The same war, World War II, and two equally horrifying devastations perpetrated upon humanity by humans. Israel is an armed state. Do they train their soldiers for peace? It didn't feel that way.

Yet, I belonged in Jerusalem. Belonged in a sense I'd never felt before or since. I've mentioned it to other travelers and many of them had found such a place.

"I went to Croatia and everyone looked like me."

"Scotland is amazing. I want to live there someday."

"I was in this remote corner of the French-Italian border, at the very center of my family's history. And though they'd been gone for two hundred years, somehow I was home."

I'm not particularly aware of being Jewish. I often say I'm of the Hebrew race but not the Jewish religion. Yet with my pureblood Ashkenazi heritage, I absolutely *looked* as if I belonged.

Many natives refused to believe that I didn't speak a word of Hebrew or Yiddish. But that wasn't of real importance.

I *understood* these people. Somehow, despite three generations in America and living most of my life among *goyim* (non-Jews), I shared beliefs and values and ways of seeing the world that couldn't be articulated.

And didn't need to be.

They simply were the same.

I stood one evening near the West Wall, the remains of a temple destroyed over fifty of my lifetimes ago. I was contemplating the barrenness I'd felt in the Japanese religion and wondered about finding the same thing here. Religion was an intellectual topic but seemed little more.

Then I heard the singing. I asked a fellow traveler what that might be.

She pointed up the road. "It is the men coming from the synagogues. They have just completed the Sabbath prayers."

I hadn't even known what day of the week it was.

The men came down in rows ten or more across with their arms over each other's shoulders. Voices raised in unison, they sang and danced as they came, laughter and joy filling the air about them. They danced to the open space before the towering West Wall.

At that moment, high above, Muslims gathered in the Temple of the Dome of the Rock for the first night of Ramadan began jeering the Jews far below. They were ignored by the dancers as they cast nothing heavier than insults, perhaps deterred by the ring of soldiers who stood in the shadows with their weapons unslung and aimed at the sky.

The West Wall and the Dome of the Rock. I got in a lot of trouble for visiting the Dome of the Rock—not from the Muslims, but from the Orthodox Jews. They weren't happy that I had gone among Muslims, but they feared that I might have unknowingly tread upon the Holy of Holies where the Ark of the Covenant had once been stored—even though its exact location was lost millennia ago.

When at last the dance broke, people turned for home. A man in yarmulke and black frock coat approached me. "Have you a place for Shabbat?" first in Hebrew, then English.

Rabbi Mordechai led me and the young English traveler next to me, along with a dozen other strays of various countries and religions, out the city gates and up the streets of New Jerusalem to his wife Henni and his seven children.

We ate.

We danced (men and women separately, of course).

We sang.

We thanked God, an act that had always made the agnostic part of me cringe, but not on this Sabbath night of all nights.

We talked of hope, of a good week gone by, and prayed for a better one to come.

I talked of my journey with another of Rabbi Mordechai's guests, a Rabbi Stone visiting from New York, a prominent scholar and leader there.

"You have come back to find your roots; that is good."

"Actually, I had not planned on coming to Israel until a month or so ago. I'm a little surprised to be here." I'd always despised the wars and intolerance in the Middle East, but I'd done it from afar. Now I was in the middle of the country, surrounded by people who were filled with a faith I knew little about and understood even less.

"Yes," he nodded happily, his great gray beard billowing down the front of his dark woolen vest. "That is the way it works. Your heart knows what your mind does not."

"Do you study other religions?"

"I have no interest. There is no reason. All I need to know is in the Torah and the Talmud."

"But are there not many paths to God?" I might not believe in God, but I had studied. "An Indian saint once said, 'There are many paths to enlightenment. You may eat a cake upside down or sideways, but is it not still sweet?'"

"There are many roads to Jerusalem, but there is only one path to God and that path is in the Torah."

I do not believe in that one path, yet something had brought me to this city, and though I don't believe in fate, something more than chance had brought me to this very table to spend an hour or so debating learning with one of the more notable Jewish thinkers of our time.

"Traditions become a part of your life without your knowledge. That is what makes you Jewish. And here, you are no longer one Jew out among the masses, able to forget yourself. Here you are one in the midst of thousands like you. That is why people come to Israel from the four corners of the globe. Here you are with your own."

I did choose to ride away from Jerusalem. Their battles are not mine, a life bounded by a religion is not for me. Yet I won't forget the passion for life and knowledge, and the feeling of perfect community I reveled in during that long, fascinating week.

I didn't find religion.

But I may have found faith.

Faith that the Universe does indeed work in strange and interesting ways. That by putting myself out there, I would meet interesting and wonderful people.

A Third City

I rode to Haifa to catch the ferry to Greece. It is a small, busy, modern port town. None of Tel Aviv's discos, pubs, and beauty salons line the streets. The shouting matches of politics and the probing investigation of religious discovery were also far from Haifa's bustling streets. Yet it is still Israel, religion is never far away.

Atop the cliffs overlooking the Mediterranean Sea sits the Shrine of the Báb. It is here that the ashes of Bahai's founder rest, one of the most recent of major religions. Amidst the beautiful gardens and the elegant shrine, I found a small brochure explaining Bahai.

"There have been many wise people upon the Earth. Buddha, Christ, Mohammed, Confucius, Einstein... So, let us learn from them all."

It sounded interesting but that was the scope of the brochure. There were no others. No gift shop. No book kiosk. At the base of the hill, I discovered a typical Israeli bookstore. Its shelves were lined with religious texts and discussions, even a complete copy of the massive, hundred-thousand-stanza Hindu Mahabharata much to my surprise.

Not a word on Bahai.

Haifa was far too busy with the business of the day to worry about such things.

But my stay in Israel was brief. It was time to meet Douglas in Athens. A chance to ride with another cyclist for a few weeks was a blessing not to be turned aside from lightly.

Israel: 11 days / 266 km (165 mi)
Elevation Climbed: 1.9 km (1.2 mi)
Total Distance to Date: 10,636 km (6,609 mi)
Elevation Climbed to Date: 50.1 km (31.1 mi)

9

GREECE

18 FEBRUARY 1994 – 18 MAY 1994

Greek: *I, uh, Ehgho keh podheelahto, er...bumi, no, that's Indonesian, sikai, sorry, Japanese, crap, oh sorry, um, world. I can't remember the Greek for "world."*
Modern Greek (i.e. Tourist English): *Oh, you're traveling around the world on your bicycle? Is that what you're trying to say?*
English: *My brain hurts!*

My Mother's Footsteps

Eliciting a smile from a Greek native is a major accomplishment. This country is inundated by over seven million tourists a year. Until this point of my journey, except perhaps along the western US, I was such an oddity that I always caused interest.

Not so in Greece.

Many travelers describe Greece as a Third World country in First World clothing. After having wrestled with its postal system, banking, and telephones more awkward than Indonesia, I was forced to agree. Yes, the streets were clean. The prices were fixed in the stores—though they were all jacked up so high for the tourists that I was often required to barter things back down to a reasonable range.

"Nothing happens when you're locked in a vacancy." Some friend used to always say that, and it summed up how I felt.

I was exhausted emotionally and physically. I was just doing time until I'd get home six or eight months from now. I was tired of the road, tired of learning new languages and customs, tired of being treated like a tourist mark to shake down for a quick drachma (Greek currency at that time).

Perhaps Greece and I just got off on the wrong foot. In Athens there was no word from Douglas; we'd left India two weeks apart. And, after six long months without, I finally received mail.

There was a letter from my dad.

I debated a long time about opening it first or last, his previous one had been so harsh and accusatory. I opened and answered all of the others until only his lone envelope faced me. It was perhaps the longest letter I ever received from him, a full page of single-spaced type.

> *Like many others, during my undergraduate years I tried to assess the world around me and how I should fit in. Frankly, the world stank....*
>
> *While none of the Buchmans are constitutionally happy (I would never claim to have been so), I don't feel completely discontent with what I have done. With the satisfactions of living being so meager, that's not too bad.*

I was stunned.

First, I wasn't being eviscerated.

Second, I'd found why we were having such trouble communicating.

Our worldviews were *polar opposites*.

I stepped out of college with the clear belief that I could do anything I wanted; my problem was that I didn't know what that was. I still (even as I write this in 2019) see the world as a place filled with opportunity and hope; a place where joy is to be striven for and good will spread about like fertilizer. I wrote pages and pages like this back to him, thrilled that I could now see his world and attempting to explain mine.

I pointed out that I hadn't run away. I lived in an age where, sick of the corporate grind, I had the opportunity to take a break and decide how I wanted my future to look. I was giving myself the gift of time before I plunged into the next thirty-five years of my life.

I was beside myself with joy. My father had spoken to me, for the first time in my life, of things that mattered. Of how he thought and how he saw the world. This trip was worthwhile in more ways than I had imagined.

The day was further brightened by running into Douglas. He'd forgotten which hostel we'd agreed to and had gone to the wrong one. Before I sent the letter, with a sense of caution creeping in, I asked Douglas to read my reply.

"Wow, this is great. I'm going to write some of this stuff to my dad. He's a minister and runs a Bible camp every summer. He sure as shit doesn't know what to do with his divorced, dropped-out, burned-out son. This is so cool."

I also thought of my mom. She'd died five years before—divorced from Dad and not on speaking terms with me. But she would have loved my trip. Not long after she was separated, she'd come to Greece and Turkey for a month, her first solo vacation in thirty years. She'd bubbled about the art and the architecture. Her eyes grew misty recalling strong coffee in small *tavernas*.

As I stood at the threshold of the Parthenon, I knew that here we had crossed paths. I looked at the soaring columns and their massive marble cornices. I shifted sideways a little until the columns lined up so neatly that I knew she'd done the same. We were now standing on the same spot. Through that tenuous connection of two travelers separated by over fifteen years of time, Athens became a little less wearisome and a little more filled with hope.

Over the years I've grown to regret that final fight that drove us apart. Its reasons are inconsequential and its resolution sad. Four years before my trip, I had drafted a letter reaching out to her across that gap of the prior five years of silence. The final draft had been sitting on my desk. I wanted to take another day, then read it one last time before sending it.

My sister called that night and I was too late.

At the memorial service, I was the unknown to her new friends and a pariah to her old ones. The son who didn't speak with his mother. Only my sister and uncle spoke to me at all.

Her best friend, who I'd never met, did call me that weekend—too exhausted to come to the service. "Your mother said to say that she understood. And to acknowledge that you were definitely her son—because who else could possibly be so stubborn other than herself."

It took that, and years more, to understand my mother even a little.

Yes, she would have loved this trip. And the fact that I've become a full-time writer would make her so proud that she'd never have stopped talking about it.

I do take a little relief in a cassette tape I found at her apartment. She always loved me playing my guitar music (even off-key, as I got my tone deafness from her). Six months before she died, I recorded all the songs I'd written both before we stopped talking and since, including one about a mother and son reaching for each other.

I sent no note with it.

She sent no thank you.

But when I found the tape in her apartment, it had been badly worn from so much playing.

And in Athens, I also found where she must have sat at the base of the Acropolis.

| My mother and I crossed paths right about here.

The Play Was the Thing

I spent most of my time in Athens sitting in one of the true wonders of my entire trip.

Not the Agora where Socrates had expounded or the Acropolis where the gods resided. Nope, not for me.

For days I sat working on my novel in the seats of the Theatre of Dionysus. For hour upon hour I imagined the ancient choruses of two thousand five hundred years ago striding forth in their great masks to intone the opening of the tragedy awaiting Oedipus or the humor of Aristophanes' attack upon Socrates in *The Clouds*. Here Aeschylus philosophized and Sophocles revealed the "self" in crisis.

For one of the first times on my whole trip, I wasn't in crisis. I wasn't surviving Japan or India. My butt wasn't torn up in the Outback. I wasn't miserable in some Australian paradise.

I was sitting in the most important Greek theater ever built, perhaps the most important theater ever—in many ways, the

Western traditions of theater had all been born here. I was resting on the tiers of seats slowly giving way to the dusty green weeds, enthralled by the semicircular stage below, upon which so many farces and tragedies had been played out.

I had worked in theater for seven years, including four in high school and three professionally. I had taken several courses in Greek mythology and history in college. I stood on perhaps the most familiar ground since I'd left home. I understood, as much as any modern, non-Greek speaker could, the place where I sat in space and history.

It was magnificent.

I can still see it when I close my eyes.

A last bit of good news sent me right over the top. A good friend from Seattle wanted to come ride with me in the summer. Not able to wait for mail, I called Ken right away.

"I'll meet you anywhere in Europe, just say when. Though not France in August. The French are all on holiday then and I've heard it's nuts."

"Okay, check with me in May."

"Fantastic. I can't wait."

Even the youth hostel was fun. Douglas and I, now sharing a room, were playing a vicious round of the national sport of Greece, backgammon, when another traveler asked where I was from.

"Seattle."

"What part?" Jamie sat waiting her turn to tackle the winner.

"Ever hear of Greenwood?"

"Yeah. I just sold a frame shop there to my ex-boyfriend ex-business partner six weeks ago."

"Which one?"

"Greenwood and 74th."

I used to lean on her window while waiting for the bus to commute to downtown, before I started bike commuting. I'd lived at 76th. So, even if we hadn't met, we'd been within a dozen feet of each other hundreds of times. She filled me in about home. It was so good to hear that even news of the gray weather left me foolishly happy.

We all three made plans to meet up in southern Greece. Regrettably she circled the wrong city on my map—we were there, she wasn't. Jamie and I weren't to meet again until I returned home. But she became a good friend in an incredibly small world.

I called my sister. I racked up some nasty phone bills on the trip, but I don't regret that expense. It's part of what kept me sane.

"You sound so much better, maybe you finally found your traveling feet."

"If I haven't by now, I'm in deep poo. Besides, it's Europe. Europe is easy."

It's true. Europe, First World travel for that matter, is easy. But would it be enough to keep me interested and learning? I couldn't bring myself to learn Greek. Oh, Douglas and I flailed at it a bit, but even after a month I was never able to use it. My Greek was worse than my Japanese, which was a sad statement.

To mark our departure from Athens, Jamie, Douglas, and I teamed up with an Argentine woman, a British rugby player, and a Croatian refugee. We walked around until we found a nice little *taverna;* half a dozen tables filled the brightly lit interior. A small stereo played a radio station of traditional Greek music.

After a great deal of eating and drinking, there was a sudden clatter.

A young Greek at the next table stumbled to his feet and turned up the radio with a sharp twist.

The hostess and other restaurant patrons cleared the tables to the side and began smashing empty wine bottles against the floor. They covered the red tile floor with glittering green shards. A single wine glass was filled and set in the center of the floor. The man danced and whirled about the glass, sometimes bending low over it, sometimes dancing away, but never reaching for it. The hostess explained that this was a very traditional dance. After a great, wonderful display, he finally leaned low over the shard-covered floor and lifted it with his teeth. He tilted his head back and drank down his reward.

None would follow his exhortations to do the same. His friends all declined to challenge his success.

I jumped to my feet, bearded traveler in Birkenstocks.

"You must dance like there is nothing more important you can do," he had someone translate for him.

I mixed in the steps he'd used with Kathakali poses seen at Director Devan's in India, from the Gambyong concert Dominic had taken me to in Indonesia, good old Australian hoedown, and basic American rock 'n' roll I-don't-have-a-clue style. On my third attempt, I successfully raised the glass without touching the hazardous floor and the crowd went wild.

We all danced and drank until well past two in the morning. That is a proper way for a dinner party to go. Now all I need is a red tile floor...

The Three Ds

We crawled out of Athens the next day and down the Peloponnesian Peninsula that is southwestern Greece. We wanted to tour a bit before we pushed north to Vienna in a few weeks. It felt good, albeit a bit of a shock, to be back on the bike. Except for a ride to an Indian airport and four or five days in Israel, I hadn't been on Junior in the two months since I'd first contracted dysentery.

The best part was that for the first time in a year, I was riding with someone else. On my own, I'd buy food that was familiar and cook it up. With Douglas, we'd prowl the store shelves looking for different and entertaining local goods to try —egging each other on. I don't think I built a single campfire for myself, but together we scrounged wood and made many.

We studied the fortifications of Agamemnon at Mycenae, the king who had launched a thousand ships against Troy for the kidnapping of the fair Helen. We played backgammon with the old men sitting in the village square of Kosmas at the top of the Parnon Mountains. We slept above the snowline, in southern Greece. Douglas, who usually slept with his feet outside his bag, suffered a minor case of frostbite that bothered him for weeks until the temperature warmed.

The nights were chill and the days drenchingly wet. We decided that Vienna could wait another week or so and we hopped a ferry down to Crete. We reached the southern shore and camped on a broad sand beach—the only occupants other than a few fishing boats.

Douglas was getting worried because he was running out of money and even our lowly $3–5 / day was stretching his resources. He was headed to Vienna to find work as an architect, but the passes through the Carpathian Mountains were still snowbound and neither of us was eager to try such a crossing.

"I've got an idea."

Douglas looked up from the soup he was concocting on the stove.

"You're an architect. I own a nice little piece of island property in Washington that I want to build on when I get home. You help me with the design, I can do the technical drawings, and I'll pay your expenses as long as we keep them at this level."

He poured two steaming mugs and handed one over. He doused the stove and looked at me over the campfire.

"Describe the site and the view... Fine. What do you like in a house?... Uh huh. Why aren't you as homesick as you were in India?"

That pulled me up short. He was right. "Damned if I know."

"Just checking."

"No. Seriously. Maybe it's having someone to talk to without going through the nine standard questions."

He mocked a Japanese accent, "Ah, where are you going, *desu-ka?*"

"Where ya from, mate?" I riposted.

"And why are you traveling through our country on a bicycle?" He inquired with a classic Indian headshake.

We actually came up with fifteen or twenty of the questions that we'd answered hundreds of time over our year of travels.

"I always wanted to make a T-shirt that had the nine answers on the back so they could read it while I was walking away."

Douglas nodded, "Make two of 'em."

I'd become less and less talkative in camps because it saved me repeating the same weary answers. For the first time since Rainier in Bali, Indonesia, I was with someone long enough that we could discuss other topics, such as women.

Douglas had been married. "We just couldn't ever work it out. We really liked each other but hated who we became when we were together. Taken me a year on the road to figure that one out."

I'd never even lived with anyone. "I've always been scared to death of relationships. I try letting one go along naturally and it dies of boredom on both our parts. I attack another the way I attack my career, full-attention, all-out focus, and I scare the daylights out of her. I guess there's a middle ground; I may have found a bit of it that last night in India."

Secrets seemed pretty pointless when we were living just meters apart for every minute we weren't on a bike. So, we laid it bare and picked it up to see what we could learn about art, religion, politics, and relationships.

"The three Ds," Douglas would insist and then spit an olive pit into the ocean waves. "Diet, diary, and dialogue. Need all three to be healthy."

I read and wrote less while we were together, but I learned far more. My 36th birthday came and went unremarked. Didn't even notice it was gone until days later. So different from my 35th, launching myself in panic on a crazy bicycle trip around the world.

Time was not measured in dates, but in the melting of snow in the passes. Measured in how many days' ride to cross a place in four-days-on-one-day-off fashion.

Of course, it was to be months before we rode four days in a row again, but we didn't know that yet. Our two-week ride would ultimately be stalled for three months by an incredible late spring on the back side of a particularly harsh winter in Europe.

One Year Out

The day the beach turned warm, we abandoned the full-size house plans we'd been drawing and redrawing in the hard, wet sand and headed north. It was just as well; we were out of food and it had been over a week since our last store.

Full-scale house plan in the sand. We even drew plates on the breakfast bar by the window and sat cross-legged before them as we ate our last meal there before finally turning north. (Left to Right: half bath, big pantry cupboards (the Xs), kitchen, stairs foreground, deep bay window with dining table facing the view, living room, stairs down the front right to sweep onto the big deck.)

Clouds moved in as we rode. We pounded thirty kilometers along a gravel cliffside road and then up to a high pass through the mountains that isolate the southern corner of Crete. At the top we crested into a *brutal* windstorm. The blasts were so bad we'd often stand braced with both brakes on, just to keep from rolling backward. Once I was dragged, while lying on the road for traction, to within two steps of a hundred-meter drop. Hauling Junior inch by inch behind me, I crawled to the inside edge of the road and remained against the cliff the rest of the way regardless of which lane it was beside.

We cleared the top and bombed down the far side, finally dropping into a grove of orange trees as a camp. We had water and the fruit over our heads—nothing else. Douglas, despite being a stronger rider, was exhausted. I dumped my gear, emptied one pannier, and rode another ten kilometers to the nearest town. I purchased a couple of days' food and restocked all the staples and emergency supplies before pounding back to camp.

"What happened to you?"

"Don't know. I should be wiped, but I feel great. Well, tired as can be, but not sore or aching. That's the best ride I've ever done."

Douglas made a Greek salad of olives, feta cheese, cucumbers, tomatoes, and dressing. He also cooked a huge pot of pasta as I pulled out my journal to record the windy passage and the feeling of power that had come over me on the road. I really could do anything I wanted to.

"Hey, today's March 27th. I've been on the road a year today."

"And?"

"Well, a year ago I headed out on a four-year journey to conquer the world. Six months ago I cut that in half and shaved off another six months since then. Spring started last week, and I'll be home by this time next year. The weird thing is, I can mark all this time, but I can't tell you who that other guy was."

"Which one?"

"The driven, work-crazy guy. The one who thought it was a good thing to be working a hundred-plus hours a week in three cities a week, while his ex-girlfriend and her fiancé housesat for him and slept in his bed."

Douglas looked at me. "But you aren't changed by travel."

"What the hell? Wasn't I just saying how much I was?"

"Yeah, but you're wrong. Rollie and Meegan agree with me. We three are out here, totally screwed up. I lie there for half an hour each morning after I wake up trying to reinvent myself and figure out who in the hell I am today. I've watched. You're different.

"You roll out of your bag and you're the same person as the day before. You've got your shit together; you just don't know it yet. It's like you're tuning your values while the rest of us are still trying to make them up."

I couldn't even respond.

"Look, what's important to you?"

I pulled down an orange to buy some time before answering. It was still sour, but I sucked on its tangy juice while I thought about it.

"Friends. Home, whatever that means." I tossed a half to Douglas.

He pulled a slice free, "You like writing. A nice house."

"Family."

He spat out his chunk of orange and shied his half off into the woods.

"See, you already know all that shit. Just one thing, Matt."

"What?"

"Perhaps you shouldn't try to do it all at once this time."

The hill we climbed through a raging windstorm. No analogy to my bicycle or personal journeys, of course. None at all. Honest.

Former Southern No Longer Somewhere

We chased the cold north, island by island. We were following the leading edge of an incredibly late spring, so we were usually cold and damp, but at least not freezing.

The weather finally changed.

Overnight our chills turned into pouring sweat as we beat north up baking roads. Mykonos, Delos, and Delphi slid beneath our wheels. Three weeks had become three months, the house was long since designed, and my funds were feeling the strain. We rode a hundred miles a day at the top of our form. We pushed day after day without a break, glad to finally be laying down the miles. (Sorry, sometimes the distances just sound better in English units. Breaking a hundred-and-sixty kilometers a day just isn't as cool as riding an English-unit century.)

As we approached the border, the Greeks finally showed some interest in the destination of these two American cyclists.

"Where are you going?"

"Macedonia, then we'll—"

"There is no such country." The interruption had been rude even by Greek standards. "Why would you go to Former Southern Yugoslavia? It is Greek. Macedonia is a Greek name. Former Southern Yugoslavia is Greek land. It belongs to us."

"Are you from there? Or your people?"

"No, Athens. Now get out of my shop." He wouldn't let us even buy our food before we had to go.

We met similar, if less toxic reactions as we neared the border. I did a little checking and this Slavic country hadn't been a part of Greece since WWI, and not really since Alexander the Great a millennium before.

"There are terrible food shortages there and in Bulgaria and Romania. You must carry your own food."

This was a problem. We were both eating 8–10,000 calories a day and, with our recent burst of riding centuries, losing weight anyway. Near the border we purchased a massive grocery supply. Powdered milk for our granola. Peanut butter and jelly premixed and moved into a double Ziploc bag to save weight. Loaves of bread dangled off our saddlebags and dried pasta and potatoes rode in our clothes. We dragged to the border on our massively heavy rigs.

At the border we carefully filled out the transit cards with "Former Southern Yugoslavia" as several signs directed. Other than the guards, we were the only occupants on this main link between Greece and Eastern Europe. As we prepared to cross, a busload of Greek schoolchildren arrived and unloaded. They didn't move toward the barrier but lined up facing it. A field trip. We caught bits and pieces of the Greek.

"Evil people...stole from Greece... We kill thieves, yes?..."

When the teacher's vindictive finger aimed in our direction, we decided it was time to go. We rode into the hundred-meter no-man's-land with its tall steel watchtowers. We made a point of laughing as if at some wonderful joke and waved merrily to the glowering Greek guard. It was terribly depressing to watch the whole charade.

And this was a border with no war, only an embargo that our American passports allowed us to cross.

Greece: 89 days / 1,649 km (1,025 mi)
Elevation Climbed: 17.9 km (10.9 mi)
Total Distance to Date: 12,285 km (7,634 mi)
Elevation Climbed to Date: 68 km (42.2 mi)

10

MACEDONIA, BULGARIA, YUGOSLAVIA, HUNGARY

18 MAY 1994 – 4 JUNE 1994

Four languages in 17 days: *"Um..." Point to chest. Point to bicycle. Point westward. Move hand in great loop until it shows us riding up the road behind.*
English: *I and bicycle going thataway around a big circlish shape.*
Translation: *Shrug.*

"Ah. America."

We rolled across the no man's area and were greeted by the Macedonian border patrol. Our American passports elicited smiles and entry stamps. They wanted to know where all the stamps were from, but it took a bit to straighten out that Douglas and I had come to Greece separately.

Point to self: "America, Japan, Australia, Singapore, Indonesia, India, Israel, Greece."

Point to Douglas: "America, Japan, Thailand, India, Greece."

Finally, as much of their curiosity sated as our non-matching language skills could achieve, they waved us through.

It was only as we rode by the foot of the watchtower that we realized no guns were overseeing us. Blackberry vines were growing up the rusting ladder rungs.

We passed some workers out in the field and decided to test what reaction our bells would elicit. In Greece no one even looked; in India the merest ping evoked immediate and massive attention—"Pen! Pen! Pen!" In Macedonia the farmer and his wife leaned on their hoes for a moment and waved cheerfully in our direction before returning to removing the weeds.

We stopped in a little roadside hut and were thrilled to purchase a large bag of nuts at a very cheap price. We needed the protein. My very broken German opened a small glimpse of the country before us.

"Macedonia is the fruit bowl that has fed much of Eastern Europe until the Iron Curtain fell. Now that we are seceded from Yugoslavia, we have more food than we know what to do with."

We looked at our massively loaded bikes and tried not to cry.

In Titov Veles (Veles), we stopped by a yogurt store. This essential food is always safe in any country, and restores the intestinal flora that are killed by antibiotics. It is a staple for most travelers. As we reveled in the tangy, stiff, best yogurt I'd ever had, a cyclist rolled up. No saddlebags or racks; he must be a local.

Sasko took us to lunch after gathering up some friends along the way to "meet the Americans." Elana was twenty and had her sun-streaked, brown hair cut short and modern. Her T-shirt sported a Nike logo. Her best friend, Lissa, wore Lycra and a bright green scrunchie to hold back her long, dark hair. When I commented that they'd gotten the American look better than most Americans, they positively glowed.

"We are the MTV generation," Sasko sipped his iced tea. "We see it on TV. We are smart and know it isn't all real, but there must be some part of it we can achieve. We are well educated, school is free through university. But there is no work. A good job pays 150 DM a month." (Deutsch Mark, about $100 US—their thoughts were all of Western currency, not Macedonian denar). "What motivation is that, even if there were jobs?"

"You have a Greek embargo to the south and the Serbo-Croatian war to the north. Are you safe?"

"I'll tell you. World War I started in Sarajevo. WWII started there also, and now there is war there again. The Greeks are friends of the Serbs and are just waiting for a chance to overrun us. We have no army. We barely have police. There will be war here in less than five years."

A glum silence settled over the table, which Sasko finally broke.

"But, when everything is going right and we feel that all is luxury, then we fold our hands behind our heads, lean back, and say, 'Ah. America.'"

Elana and Lissa copied the phrase and motion with the ease of long practice.

War in this idyllic countryside was hard to imagine, but I kept my doubts to myself. A few months later I read one of the speeches given at the turnover of the EC presidency: "The Greeks are just looking for any excuse to overrun Macedonia. We must be watchful."

Four years later I wept as war surged over the mountains and crashed down upon this little country. I wish more than anything from my trip that I could take Sasko and his friends who looked at us with such longing and hope, and hopelessness, and give them a bit of the America they so richly imagine and deserve.

We stood to go and wandered over to our bikes. A shadow on the front rim caught my attention. A split. I knew from my experience north of LA some 10,000 miles ago that I had perhaps a hundred kilometers, perhaps less before it failed. Braking heavy loads in muddy, sandy, and other adverse conditions had ground through several sets of brake pads and finally another rim.

The only bike shop in town could do little more than pop it temporarily in place. Sasko rode to the edge of town and pointed us toward the big city of Skopje. In a single afternoon he had shaped our entire view of his country and his people. When we commented on his splendid 21-speed mountain bike, he explained that he needed it for work.

"It is the fastest in Titov Veles. I smuggle ceramic parts for weaving looms into Yugoslavia from my father's factory. They can't pay now, but they are friends and they need the parts so badly that I risk to go there. The bike lets me get away if I have to. Sometimes I can warn them through connections if the police are coming to kill their family and they escape. Once the ceramics saved my life when they stopped bullets, but the stupid soldiers broke parts that people needed. They nearly starved before I brought them new ones to make their cloth for trade."

He waved goodbye and we limped the sixty kilometers to Skopje, quickly but gently.

He was twenty-two and risked his life as a matter of routine to help others. The world is filled with amazing people.

Sasko dreaming he can ride all the way with us to America.

With a little friendly guidance in Skopje, we located the one high-tech bike shop in the country. After seating us at a nearby shop to enjoy tea and biscuits, the mechanic replaced my rim in thirty minutes and Junior still rolls on it today. One look at Douglas' bike was enough for him to recommend a replacement of his rear wheel as well, but Douglas declined. We were less than two weeks from Vienna, and after that he'd be off the bike for a long while.

...and again!

We'd been given a route through eastern Yugoslavia that was supposed to be gorgeous, and three hundred kilometers from the fighting. But the closer we approached the border, the more we began to worry.

The frequent, startling passage of the low-flying British Harrier jets on their way from Mediterranean-based aircraft carriers to enforce a no-fly zone unnerved us.

Then the BBC World Service News on my little shortwave

announced that the war had jumped half that distance eastward the prior night. Ten kilometers from the Yugoslavian border, we turned aside to climb the kilometer-high pass into Bulgaria.

Halfway up the final climb we were stopped by a group of road workers. They practically forced upon us a great bowl of lamb stew and a loaf of fresh-baked crunchy bread.

We ate as only cyclists can.

No common language to aid us here beyond: *zdravo, dogledanje,* and *blagodaram.* Hello, goodbye, and thank you can only get you so far. As usual, we retreated to sign language.

They were rushing to widen the road as it was now the only access to their land-locked country. This was the first winter they'd ever kept the pass open the entire season; there'd been no need until there was war across the lower Yugoslavian road.

As they were waving goodbye and trying to stuff another loaf of bread into our overloaded panniers, the camp cook pulled us aside. He proudly showed us the inside of his truck's door where a long, blonde Playboy centerfold graced the rough steel. All the men smiled and said the only words we were to understand the whole time: "Ah. America."

A New Deal

Ten minutes later I was laid up on the side of the road with stomach cramps brought on by the heavy meal and the hard climb. Douglas, with no patience for my slow riding, left me and shot up the hill. He was always a better climber.

The cramps worsened until I was considering if the possible easing of pain by curling into a little ball was worth the risk of moving at all. I had just decided that not moving was safer, when a large man strode out of the woods. His heavy, soiled jeans jacket showed his indifference to the heat of the day. Borders are always weird places that have filled me with caution and Bulgaria was barely half a kilometer away, up the very steep pass.

It took very little to determine that sign language was, again, our only common tongue.

"America," had some meaning.

"Do you have any money for me?" Such a common question that the signs are almost universal, though it was the first time I'd run into it in Macedonia.

"No, my friend up the hill has all the money. I have none."

"You aren't alone?"

"Two of us. And my friend up the hill has all the money."

I grunted at the gut pain as I swung Junior upright from where he lay on the ground.

He bulged his arms as if lifting a great weight.

"Heavy," I nodded. "*Schwer*," I also offered the German word.

He wrapped a massive meat hook of a hand around Junior's handlebar and rolled him back and forth before offering a clear nod of understanding. There was a number in blue ink across the back of his hand. Is that how they mark criminals here? Or was it a phone number he needed to remember? Was I going to die here on the goddamn Bulgarian border? I began really sweating once I had that thought.

I slowly moved him aside and swung my leg over the bike. I looked down to hide the grimace of pain in my gut.

It was the third and last time on my trip that I feared for my life. The first was when the RV nearly ran me off Big Sur in California. The second was curled up in the Japanese Alps with chills and fevers so bad I couldn't stood up even if there'd been a forest fire.

There was a ride on a small ferry boat through a storm in Indonesia that I should have feared in retrospect as waves broke over our heads most of that night, but for some reason I hadn't. *Jam karet,* rubber time, perhaps.

The third...

It took perhaps five minutes to get him to release his hold on the handlebar, to remove that massive hand I couldn't look away from. Five minutes that I didn't know if a casual sweep of his fist would lay me on the ground and eventually find the money belt tucked into the top of the right pannier with all my money and identification.

When I at last convinced him I had no money and had to go, he released the handlebar and waved goodbye. I pounded up the hill, weeping from the agony in my gut, but I didn't stop until I crested the pass.

Once safely across the border, I turned on Douglas. "Don't you ever dare to leave me again. Nearly crippled by cramps in a foreign country. I could've been killed."

"First, I didn't know they were so bad when I left. Second, we've never made a point of staying together."

I forced out a breath that eased the last of the really bad cramps.

"Okay. You're right. New deal. Until we're out of Eastern Europe, we stick together."

We shook on it. After all, we had heard about the Russian mafia.

Getting Outta There

Bulgaria was a gray country. The open friendliness of Macedonia disappeared at the border. The moneychangers were so pushy that we had to ride away for fear of being robbed. We had plenty of supplies—courtesy of our Greek mis-advisors—and decided to just get through the country without buying anything. The massive housing projects stank from plumbing that had failed and pumped sewage directly onto the street from two hundred apartments per structure.

Douglas rang his bell at a group of pedestrians, and they

leapt aside as if these two crazy cyclists were armed troops in tanks. Not a soul smiled or waved and eventually even the irrepressible Douglas stopped trying.

We rose at dawn, ate, and rode. At dark, we'd simply land somewhere, eat, and crash into our bags. Both of my knees were sending panic signals, my left hand was frequently numb, and it often took an hour to uncrinkle my neck enough to sleep. We didn't need to move so quickly, but it wasn't until a day from Romania that we finally wore down our pent-up energy at the extra months sitting still and cold in Greece.

We stopped at a closed campground, bathed in the icy stream, and shooed away the local cows who kept trying to see if our bikes were edible. After a day spent mostly asleep, we were better prepared for whatever Romania held for us.

Gun Shot

For the first time since the US, we heard guns being fired in the fields and woods as we rode.

The Bulgarians are passionate in their target practice; at times the sounds were nearly continuous. We couldn't get out of there too fast for me. I was spinning along perhaps a dozen yards behind Douglas when I heard a massive gun report from very nearby. Douglas halted and stood astride his bike facing me with the oddest expression on his face.

I slowed to a halt just behind him thinking: "Oh my God, they've shot Douglas."

He then looked down at his rear wheel.

I followed the direction of his gaze. The rim he'd decided not to replace in Skopje had blown, and not just a little. A whole stretch of the sidewall had let go at once, tearing up the tire along with it. Patches and duct tape couldn't begin to fix it; nothing but a new rim would do. Our first attempt to roll it toward the next town shattered it completely. We quickly learned that there were going to be no repairs locally in Vidin for this high-tech set of gear.

Nor in Sofia.

Skopje, Macedonia, was hundreds of kilometers behind us.

Thankfully just a rim rather than a bullet wound.

Plan B. We caught a night train to Sofia and landed at 6:00 a.m. with no sleep. We hadn't dared. There was a train to Budapest, our nearest hope in the right direction, leaving at 11:15 p.m. Douglas took an emergency $100 US bill that I'd carried since Seattle (our only cash and there was a $25 US charge for breaking a traveler's check)—and managed to get it stolen. Our first encounter with the Eastern European Mafia. Here's how the scam worked:

- As Douglas stood at the ticket window, someone waved a stack of $10 US bills. We'd been trying to get smaller bills for paying bribes since Greece and this man claimed he wanted bigger bills.
- Douglas decided this was stupid and turned back to the ticket window. Despite the sign over her head announcing she was an exchange window, she shook her head saying that the bill was too large. The fact that he would be spending $70 of it to buy the tickets from her didn't change her tune.
- The "dealer" and two buddies pulled him aside and grabbed the bill. Doug grabbed it back and slammed it on the exchange window counter. It was now a $1 US bill.
- The quick-change artists were gone. The nearby policeman and ticket clerk simply smiled; they'd get their cut later.
- A local told us afterward that he'd seen people knifed for $5 US, never mind $100 US.
- I changed a traveler's check directly to their leva currency and purchased the tickets. No one cares about leva. Not even the Bulgarians.

The other catch was that the train went through Yugoslavia, right through Belgrade. I walked down to the local embassy and paid a small bribe in leva to get two transit visas.

By the time we reached the train, we were among the last aboard. We locked our bikes to the structure of the packed railcar. A Norwegian slept on the bathroom floor, Douglas slept outside the bathroom, and I slept over the steps to the platform.

Though I was woken every ten minutes or so for the steps to be lowered, my place smelled the least.

Okay, we weren't comfortable, but now it was just a matter of surviving to Budapest. Provided some Serbian didn't dynamite the train.

- On train at 10:30 p.m.
- Departure at 11:15 p.m.
- Ticket control at midnight
- Passport control twice (1:30 a.m. and 4:00 a.m.) Out of Bulgaria and into Yugoslavia.
- Yugoslavian ticket control at 6:00 a.m.
- Pass through Belgrade at 9:00 a.m. Any historic beauty that hasn't been shelled out of existence is nowhere near the train tracks. All I witnessed was a dismal city with towering concrete projects that looked worse than Bulgaria's, if possible.
- Made a mistake. We detrained to get water from a fountain that was three meters away. The conductor didn't want to let us back on the train without a bribe. Forced our way past him; we were too sleep-deprived to care.
- 9:30 a.m. New conductor wants special $42 US fee for each bike. We act desperate and offer him some leftover Greek drachma and Bulgarian leva (the leva was worthless, only exchangeable within Bulgaria.)
- 11:30 a.m. Conductor returns and threatens to throw bikes off the train. No, we weren't allowed to go with them because our visa was only a transit visa, we must stay on the train. Finally, by prearrangement, I borrowed $20 US from our Norwegian friend. The conductor was elated but refused to give me Hungarian special ticket for bikes unless we paid full amount. He waved as he detrained at the border

and patted his pocket. "*Ich trinken! Ich* girls!" I didn't want to know how cheap his prostitutes were. Obviously, we'd paid too much for the bribe as we reimbursed the Norwegian with our last, carefully hidden, $20 US.
- 12:00 noon Ticket control. If I'd known we were this close to the border, I'd have faced him down and saved the $20 US.
- 12:10 p.m. Yugoslavian passport control.
- 12:20 p.m. Hungarian drugs control.
- 12:25 p.m. Hungarian passport control.
- 12:30 p.m. Hungarian ticket control.
- 1:00 p.m. Hungarian conductor, "Bikes. Problem."
- 3:00 p.m. After lengthy negotiations, including her taking our passports for two hours (I felt naked without it), we paid her off with our drachma (about $21 US). She issued us a ticket for the bikes, but put the money in her purse, not the money pouch.
- 3:30 p.m. Budapest.

Welcome to Eastern Europe. The trip had cost us $235 US: $99 US stolen, $25 US travelers check exchange fee, $70 US train ticket, $20 US Yugoslavian bribe, $21 US in drachma Hungarian bribe.

And Eastern Europe wonders why it is having trouble getting into the EU. For all of Greece's poverty mentality and other shortcomings that make it a drag on the EU, at least criminals were not a way of life.

We sold our now worthless leva to a traveler headed the other direction, with warnings.

We hadn't been robbed at gunpoint, but it felt like it.

A Father's View

There is a saying on the road. "Budapest or Prague. Whichever you see first will be your favorite."

Budapest definitely, and not just because I had my first shower and sleep in three days there. Other than some ex-Communist trying to force bribes and some over-perfumed hookers who wouldn't accept "No" for several blocks, I had a great time.

I went to see *La Bohème* for $1 US and *La Traviata* for $2 US. Splendid performances in beautiful halls. (I had studied operatic vocal production for four years during my "I wanna make music" phase and was humbled by the skill I heard there.)

We heard some hot, hot jazz fusion, visited art museums, and even caught a couple of movies. We splurged $10 US each on a Sunday brunch and ate for four hours and then lingered over tea and newspapers in a lovely grand restaurant that had somehow survived wars and occupations to still feel like Old World glory. Years later when I saw the hilarious *The Grand Budapest Hotel*, it felt and looked a lot like that. Good memories.

Most importantly, we found a bike shop to replace Douglas' rim. I bought a new chain and chainring; mine were so worn that they slipped constantly as I climbed hills.

Just outside Budapest, we stopped in the small town of Dömös. Ester, a girl Douglas had been hanging out with in Goa, had asked us to drop in on her parents. They welcomed us with open arms. Karoly was the town's caretaker, he mowed the parks and so on. He was very proud of his town and toured us all around.

That evening he led me into his study and sat before his small writing desk. I could see he was chewing on a question. I waited patiently while he worked around to it.

"Why do you travel? This I do not understand."

"It is a chance to learn about myself. To take the time to think about what I want and who I am."

"Could you not have learned these lessons at home?"

I realized that I was not talking to the kind host, but the worried father of a daughter somewhere in India.

"I might have learned these lessons at home. But not so fast or well. Experiences in my travels have helped me to understand more clearly how this world works and what place I hold in it."

He rested his hand on his Bible. "All the lessons I need to understand are in this book."

We talked for a couple of hours but found no meeting of the minds.

At long last I shrugged.

Weeks later, Douglas called home in Montana. A message was waiting for him. Karoly's daughter, Ester, had just been abandoned by the fiancé she'd followed to India. The fiancé had taken all of her money, left her with room charges, and run off with another girl. She'd called Douglas's father in hopes of reaching Douglas to bail her out because she was too ashamed to admit to her father that she needed to be rescued.

At a loss for what else to do, we finally called Karoly and gave him her contact information. It took a while, but yes, Ester made it back home safely.

What life lessons had she learned? And could she ever explain them to her father?

At the end of that conversation with Karoly, while we all still thought his daughter was happy and safe, I'd felt a sudden chill. An absolute certainty that all my explanations in my last letter to Dad were no clearer to him than Karoly's daughter's would ever be to her father.

A Definition of Not Home

The next day I spoke with my sister on the phone. "I'm just plain tired. Tired of 'Oh. Another cold shower.' and 'Oh. More bad water, another long night of the shits.' and 'Oh. Where am I sleeping tonight?' It's not that I just miss home, I do. But I'm worn out. Three months to America is none too soon."

We pushed north into a powerful headwind holding us back despite a new rim for Douglas, new chain and gears for Junior, and the taste of Vienna ahead.

At sunset we pulled into a secluded spot in the corner of a farmer's field. Mosquito Hell. We dove into our bivy bags. At one point I had to get up and pee. Despite constant slapping, I counted nearly a hundred bites once I dove back in. I shivered with the pain for over an hour before enough of the toxin cleared my system to allow sleep. My one consolation was that Hungary was free of malaria.

Then it started to rain.

Macedonia, Bulgaria, Yugoslavia, Hungary: 17 days / 812 km
(505 mi)
Elevation Climbed: 5.4 km (3.4 mi)
Total Distance to Date: 13,097 km (8,138 mi)
Elevation Climbed to Date: 73.4 km (45.6 mi)

11

AUSTRIA, CZECH REPUBLIC, GERMANY, LUXEMBOURG

18 JUNE 1994 – 27 JULY 1994

German: *Ich fahre mit meinen Fahrad rund dem Welt.*
English: *I travel with (rather than on or by) my bicycle around the world.*
Translation: *(See? Four years of high school German does have some use in later life.)*

Parting of Ways

At the Austrian border we took a wrong turn and crossed with all of the large trucks. Upon seeing our American passports, they waved us through without stamps to get us out of the way. Officially, I went from Hungary to the USA without going through any other countries.

We rode on clean, safe streets. We exchanged money easily at reasonable rates. Something was off. Were all the bribes and dysentery finally behind me? From here on, could I drink the water?

Then I spotted a road sign.

I burst out laughing so hard that I fell off my bike. I lay on the neatly manicured roadside holding my sides until they ached. Douglas turned back to see what was up, then he, too, spotted the sign and collapsed beside me. The bright-green pictogram made a simple message: "Please drive slowly. Frog crossing." We were definitely back in the West. Nowhere else either of us had been in the last year could possibly have such a sign.

Frog crossing. Definitely in the West.

Two more long days dragging upwind and we finally reached our Viennese goal, a clean campground with a shower and a small grocery store. The tent sites were even numbered, the first campsite I'd paid for since Cairns, Australia. Our final sprint from Greece was finally over.

In 23 days, we'd ridden 930 miles, climbed 34,000 feet, and

we still had a week's worth of food on our bikes. We'd spent three of those days in transit by train, with no sleep except in ten-minute snatches. The Tour de France is also 23 days, and only covers twice the distance on bikes that weigh forty to fifty kilos less than ours. We were exhausted.

It was only with supreme effort that Douglas enticed me from beneath my shade tree to explore Vienna the next day.

I spent a week recovering and visiting art museums. He spent the days finding out that he'd only be able to work black market. He'd be broke and starving long before he could negotiate the uncertain ground of a legitimate work visa. And finally it was time to go our separate ways.

He escorted me down perfect little bike paths, with their own stoplights and rest areas, to the banks of the Danube. Thrown together by chance, we'd been together for four of the last five months.

We'd met in the Alleppey Backwaters, visiting Hindu temples and beach resorts across two weeks and two bouts of dysentery. Three months of our time together had been huddled on various Greek beaches waiting for the very late spring to melt out the passes into Europe. Then a massive sprint from Greece to Vienna, bribing our way through Eastern Europe. We'd never once been separated by more than a kilometer, rarely by more than a dozen meters.

We stopped at the edge of town and gave each other a hug.

"If you'd just get out of your head, Matt, you'd have a lot more fun."

"If you'd just stop flailing around like a chicken convinced he's on the wrong side of the road, maybe you'd find the greener grass."

Despite both being the same age, both burned-out, ex-corporate Americans, and both world-traveling cyclists, we were very different people.

"You've been great to travel with, Douglas. We never fought. It's been great and I wouldn't change that. But neither do I think that we shall miss each other over much."

He nodded slowly.

We *were* down to bare bones after our adventures together.

No facades.

No games.

He nodded again with a sad sigh. We hugged again and rode our separate ways.

We're still in touch and see each other every five years or so. I've built a variation of the house we designed while on the freezing beaches of Greece…and lost it in the recession after a lovely eight years.

I thought a lot about him as I worked on it.

The hours we passed together, making our ever-present Greek salads, my total failure at the fine art of spitting olive pits farther away than my own feet, and crouched around a cookstove waiting for that first cup of tea. Perhaps most of all I shall recall lying side-by-side in our bivy bags, each with an elbow or knee against our bikes so we'd wake in case of thieves in the night, watching the stars turn in the sky as we discussed the past and our hopes for the future.

I've been happily married for over two decades. And the last time I saw him, I met his lovely wife and their new son. And yes, he's still an architect in Vienna, legitimate now.

Path Not Taken

It was now May, so I talked to Ken back in Seattle—the friend who wanted to ride with me in Europe.

He'd meet me in Paris, you guessed it, the second week of August. I was so excited by finally having a definite date that I didn't mind so much. Within hours I booked my flights:

Bordeaux to Paris to Boston, and a month later Boston to Seattle. It was late June and I'd be home September 22nd. Three months to home. The kilometers breezed easily beneath my wheels.

I cruised through Prague, but it had already lost the "visited Budapest first" challenge. I rode quickly on.

I climbed the steep pass out of the Czech Republic and into Germany on a beautiful sunlit day. On that hard climb out in the empty countryside, I passed a group of four women standing by the roadside. Their stance and clothing revealed their trade.

I was so slow that one of them was able to walk easily beside me despite her high heels. I wasn't foolish enough to stop, too many stories of diseases and robberies if for no other reason, but neither was I powerful enough to ride away up such a slope.

"East German businessmen used to come all the time to see us." Her English was surprisingly good. "But since the Berlin Wall fell, now they don't come much anymore, and we all worry about money. This is new to us." Her short, blonde hair shone in the sun and tight clothes revealed every curve of her wonderful figure.

I kept grinding up the hill.

"You should come with me. I give you special discount."

I looked around the countryside. Nothing but a barn and an old farmhouse; I'd grown up in farming country and had seen that fieldwork was brutally hard. Maybe this was her only way out.

"No, thanks. I prefer..." How could I tell her I found sex pointless without passion, or better yet, love. "I prefer not to."

"You don't like women."

"Oh, I like them just fine. Do you have any family?" Maybe if I stuck with what was important to me, she'd cease following and I'd quit having the urge to stop. She was exceptionally pretty and seemed both kind and thoughtful.

"They don't like it much, but they like the money. Maybe you like one of my friends better?"

"No, that's not it."

"It's really important to you. You really care who you are with?"

I nodded my head.

"And you're sure you don't want one of my friends?"

They were little more than black dots in my rearview mirror, though I hadn't moved all that far.

"No. If I were to pick one, it would definitely be you. You're beautiful and you have a great smile. But, I'm sorry, the answer is still no." Also, her three friends had simply looked at me like a possible mark; she alone had thought to be human.

"I like you. Not even for free? Just for fun?"

I shook my head and she dropped behind. She didn't return immediately to her friends, but rather watched me as I continued to crawl upward.

I've always been a little odd about relationships. I once explained it this way, "I'm so monogamous that if I have a first date with someone, and it doesn't work out, I can't have another first date for six months without feeling disloyal." Add that to my impressive ability not to notice when a woman really is interested in me...

The fact that I got together with my wife is an amazing thing. And even that took us half a year to navigate from first meeting to first date.

I had turned down, or not noticed until too late, a half dozen offers on the road from other travelers (plus however many more I hadn't noticed). Some beautiful, others stunning. All very nice women.

One thing I knew: part of what had thrown me onto the

road was that I was sick to death of living my life alone. I wanted family so badly that it hurt—often.

What if I were to turn back and offer that lovely woman working along the Czech-German border the golden ticket to the dreamland of America? There would be no doubts either way about who we were. During that long, slow climb, we'd spoken very frankly of many things. Unlike the lovely Suri back in that destroyed Indonesian village, she could easily have adapted to American culture. Could we have made a happy life together?

I more than half think we could have.

Somehow I had ridden for fifteen months and thought mostly of my failed career, my lost first house, and my mother and father. I flip through my journals now and find very few references to thoughts about a future life's companion prior to that hill climb. If mentioned at all, it was generic "family."

It was to occupy much of my journal from that moment on.

As I crested the hill, she waved and I waved back

Then she was gone behind the trees. Was she hoping I'd change my mind, or was she thinking about what kind of relationship *she* wanted in life? For the answer to that question, I almost turned around. But then it would be a long time before I climbed that hill again.

Going to Church

Former Eastern Germany, now just Germany, was in stranger shape than Bulgaria.

Most factories had been condemned by the more advanced West, throwing tens of thousands of workers out of jobs.

Many bridges, some quite scary even to the untrained eye, were closed requiring circuitous routes to get across the country until they could be replaced.

Decaying cities were sprinkled with a sudden influx of shining department stores and other new structures.

I spent a break day in Leipzig. I wandered about town finally stumbling upon St. Nikolas Church. With the lines of a Gothic cathedral and the interior décor of 1930s art deco, it was hard to know what to make of it. Except for the occasional tourist, I appeared to be its sole occupant that weekday.

I wrote a little poem (I suck at poetry, but I was trying my hand at it) about what had this church seen over the centuries before it had been forgotten.

As I was leaving, I spotted a brochure. I flipped open the sheet of paper to the English section. I was sitting in moments and read every word several times to be sure I missed no details.

In the early 1980s, behind the Iron Curtain, individuals gathered together at St. Nikolas to pray for peace. This movement that had started with a few dozen people swelled, gathering adherents from all religions. Despite harsh suppression, beatings, arrests, and death threats, the masses came until the church was crammed to capacity.

On October 9th, 1989, the largest meeting of all was held.

The city was closed by the military.

When the thousand participants exited from their prayers for peace, they expected to be gunned down.

Instead, 10,000 people awaited them with candles held high. It takes two hands to hold a candle, one to hold and one to guard against the wind. No way to aim a gun.

Stasi troops set aside their weapons and walked away—many of them shedding their uniforms as they went, others joining the crowd. Within the month, the peaceful demonstrations had increased to three hundred thousand people.

The Berlin Wall was torn down November 9th and the face of world politics changed. The Berlin Wall, the USSR, the Cold

War, all gone because of people willing to risk their lives to gather in peace. What can *not* be achieved with such passion? Mahatma Gandhi, Martin Luther King, Jr., and many others knew of this power.

Was there something out there that would someday fill my heart rather than my head, fill it so fully that nothing was more important, not even self?

The ultimate answer is yes, but it took me years to understand why I write the kind of stories I do. And that evolution is ongoing. I'm unsure where it will lead me, but I can't wait to find out.

The Sheep and the Bee

I spent a few weeks moseying through Western Germany visiting friends I'd made at different places around the world.

My attitude confused them badly; I was in a great hurry to get home, but I was being terribly lazy. One friend threw me out, not because we weren't having a great time, but for my own good because I needed to keep moving along.

I had become a reluctant rider. I was riding through beautiful country on nicely groomed bike trails. My German was sufficient to remove most of the strains of travel, yet I was a malcontent on the bike.

I had been fortunate. In nearly 10,000 miles I'd never been robbed, never broken anything, never had an accident. I'd had dysentery twice, a bad flu, a couple rounds of stomach cramps, and an incredible amount of diarrhea. I was getting better and worse, both at the same time. My right knee, which had been screaming since my sprint to Vienna, had healed during my German rest stops. But my wrists were shot from pounding over kilometer after kilometer of cobblestones in various European cities.

And I couldn't figure out what was wrong with my right arm

for the longest time. There was a searing pain across the biceps. I began not using it in camp, and I'd often ride one-handed, much to the dismay of my left wrist. It was only when I looked at my slides at the end of my trip that I remembered Helga and Achim's sheep.

I'd met them (Helga and Achim, not the sheep) in New Zealand a few years before. We had planned to spend a month cycling in France, but it had never happened. First, I'd burned out and quit my career. Then, once I ended up on a world tour, Helga became pregnant.

When I visited them in Germany, it was time to shear the sheep. Helga, only two days from delivering their first baby (though we didn't know that yet) was beyond assisting. These were not big, lazy American sheep. These were small, horned, mountain sheep with immense power in their legs.

In rounding them up, I'd managed to catch one by the horn. No big deal, its back wasn't any higher than the top of my knee.

Right?

Of course right.

That tough little beastie flipped me head over heels into a patch of nettles, wearing only shorts and sandals, and kept right on going. I was quite itchy the rest of the day to put it mildly.

I'd also, without realizing it, torn my biceps. A tear that worsened day by cobble-pounding day. It required a month in a sling on muscle relaxants to heal once I got home.

Mid-Life Crisis on Wheels

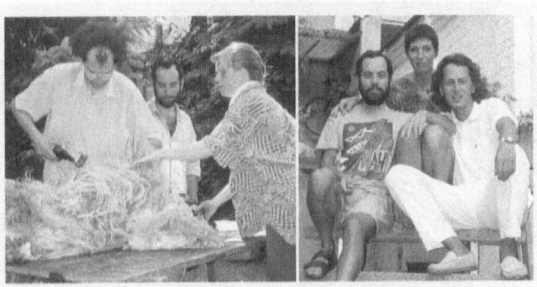

There really is a sheep somewhere under all that wool. Shearing with Achim and Helga (whom I originally met two years before in New Zealand). / Michael and Karin (friends from the Nusa Tigan *losmen* in Indonesia). Michael and I became very close—even if he did tell me to get my ass back on my bike. All part of the community of the road.

But it wasn't just that.

The little injuries kept building up. I was losing concentration. I ran into a park bench along the Mosel River while trying to adjust a strap that had come loose on a pannier—did it while I was riding. I knew better. A bloody knee and elbow were my reward. I burned my fingers on the camp stove not once but twice, and a myriad other minor injuries followed.

The Mother of All Grape Vines

Several days later, still alongside the Mosel, I was riding on a beautiful bike trail through a vineyard-covered valley. A bee flew into my left glove. I tried to scoop it out with my right forefinger before it could sting me. Removing one hand from the handlebar increased pressure on the other, pressing the bee.

He stung me.

I jerked my left hand off the handlebar and now, with no guidance from me, Junior took his own course.

I shot off the trail at twenty-five kmph, wrapped Junior around the mother-of-all grape vines, and plowed a deep furrow through the rocky soil with my helmet. I'm just glad it wasn't the other way around.

I had a very sore neck and blood poured down both my knees, turning my socks a nasty shade of red mixed with brown soil.

The abrasions on my right wrist and ankle and my left shoulder spoke up next.

The bee sting was now the least of it.

As I was daubing at my knees with my antiseptic cream, an elderly German couple rolled to a stop along the wide, straight bike path I had departed so abruptly. I pulled off my helmet and dirt clods fell out of my hair and into my eyes. Gear was strewn about me as I'd had to empty two panniers before finding my med kit. (I'd needed it so rarely, except for the Imodium anti-diarrheal pills, that I'd let it get buried.)

For the life of me I couldn't remember the German word for bee or sting. I tried sign language and finally just assured them that I was okay...and not insane. They looked less than assured on that final point as they rode away down that long, straight, flat path.

Junior taking the hit for me. You can just see the med kit rolled out on the rear pannier. And, if you look closely, you can see his handlebars are planted straight into the dirt, but his front wheel is aimed up in the air. (Thankfully the impact turned out not to have bent the wheel or the front fork.) My helmet plowed the rocky soil between the right-hand stake and a sloping double wire that's by the handlebars. My worst accident on the road; I was very lucky.

Going Dark

In Luxembourg, I spent three days resting and reveling in the joys of reading mail. A friend had sent a T-shirt with a map of Puget Sound. I discarded the remains of my food-stained, blood-stained, torn-up one.

On the last day I checked again and there was a letter from Dad. I sat in the open air of the Place d'Armes where a small band played German folk music for the July tourists.

I tore it open to see what new connections we might make now that my earlier fears were forgotten, dismissed. Perhaps the closeness I felt whenever we had talked of computers could be extended to the rest of our lives' events.

His letter informed me in short, curt phrases that I did not understand the world properly—with a strong implication of my general stupidity. I also did not understand *him* properly. I had ruined my life—with a clear statement that I was an idiot —and he was damned if he was going to bail me out—which I'd never asked for.

I was at a loss.

I desperately wished for a copy of the letter I'd sent from Athens. I couldn't imagine what had elicited this vehement response. I thought back over our letters. It seemed that his had alternated black-and-white. The one in Japan was good, in Australia, terrible. The one in Greece had been great. This one was so awful I couldn't even respond to it.

Who knew what kind of cannonade my next letter might evoke.

If it was a positive response, would I be in for Hell when I actually visited, that being the black part of the cycle?

If I didn't respond and this was the last communication before I visited, what did that portend?

I was too tired, too lonely, and too sore to reply.

I threw it away, aimed Junior westward, and rode toward Ken and France.

Austria, Czech Republic, Germany, Luxembourg: 39 days / 2,287 km
(1,421 mi)
Elevation Climbed: 14.7 km (9.1 mi)

Total Distance to Date: 15,384 km (9,559 mi)
Elevation Climbed to Date: 88.1 km (54.7 mi)

12

FRANCE

27 JULY 1994 – 29 AUGUST 1994

French: Je et vélo voyage de retour, non, autour de monde.
English: I and bicycle voyage homeward, no, around the world.
Translation: I am too tired of travel and new languages to learn the
one language I was most interested in. I had planned three to six
months in your country and I'll be here for only thirty-three days.
Pardonnez-moi..

King of the Road

I reveled in the rolling countryside and sweet air of France as I worked my way slowly toward Paris. The road's shoulders were wide and smooth, and the countryside rolled just enough to get me out of the saddle occasionally but raised no challenges hard enough to strain my aching arm.

I discovered that the massive diarrhea attack of the last few weeks was due to a bad jar of strawberry jam that had been a gift from a German friend. I felt much better after I threw it out.

A heat wave swept Europe, melting roads in Eastern Europe and shutting down nuclear power plants because the river water was too warm to cool the reactors. It was almost as warm as India.

One fine morning I rolled to a stop at a traffic circle with five roads radiating out from it. As I had a thousand times on the journey, I moved against the curb and pulled out a map to contemplate my options. A deep silence descended upon the countryside and I peeked over the top of my map.

All of the traffic had stopped.

The rotary was empty, yet cars waited in each of the entering roads. I looked about but saw no traffic signal that might have stopped them. They were all looking...at me.

They couldn't all be waiting for a solo American cyclist to...

But they were.

Selecting an exit at random, I rode around the circle, turned off, and stopped once again, this time aimed away from the rotary. The traffic roared to life as everyone shot along their way. I learned to move my map consultations farther from intersections to avoid halting others' progress due to their perfect courtesy to someone on a bicycle.

In France, as I was to learn at every intersection and pedestrian crossing, the bicycle is absolute king. A fully loaded touring bike might be closer to emperor just because it was so bizarre.

I can still glance at any bike along the road and tell you how big a tour the cyclist is on, what their rough budget is, and even maybe how long they've been out. There are tons of visual cues: from their gear, the condition of it, and even how they ride and approach traffic. Even for people not used to looking at those cues, after more than ten thousand miles, Junior and I stood out. The scale and wear on the gear and the rider were more than obvious.

France paid full homage to those cues and we were treated fantastically at every turn.

I wondered if my presence would stop the mother-of-all

traffic circles—the Place Charles de Gaulle around the Arc de Triomphe in the heart of Paris.

Once I reached Paris, I assiduously avoided that area on my bicycle, just in case it would. Though I did stand there on the sidewalk and wonder for a while as I watched the five or so lanes whipping around.

Going Gothic

From sixth grade on, I had a favorite report that I redid perhaps every other year right through high school.

I *loved* Gothic cathedrals.

Each time I'd expand my research and once even printed illustrative pictures in my darkroom. It may seem an odd preoccupation for an ethnic Jew, but Mom was an architectural historian and we shared a fascination with the drive to design and build such massive structures during the depths of the Dark Ages. The concept alone was intriguing—planning buildings that took a century or more to construct.

Now, at long last at thirty-six years old, I stood before the cathedral at Reims.

It was...

I felt...

I'll just say that my entire fifty-sixth roll of film was shot there.

I wandered beneath flying buttresses and looked up at the gargoyles Mom would have so loved to see.

I was finally separating my parents; they had resided too long in my mind under the mutual title "The Parents."

Dad would have looked at the engineering necessary for the construction. Then, perhaps, he'd point out that thousands of peasants had starved while some archbishop built this temple to a God who didn't exist anyway.

Mom would have run from stained window to minor altar to entryway admiring the art and recounting the stories.

It was Mom who brought us together for three meals a day. Yes, it was Dad who wanted the image of the "perfect home"—whether or not it was just a pretty facade. Mom tried as well as she could to make it mean something.

Sitting at the rear of Reims Cathedral, I began to understand her and her passion a bit better. She too would have sat and listened to the silence for hour upon hour through that long afternoon.

Mom had passion, but she lacked direction. She'd always wanted to write fiction. When her mother died and left her some money, Mom quit her day job to write the murder mystery she'd always talked about. A few short stories were produced, but no more.

"The novel I always thought was in me, isn't."

I had her passion. Curiously, I think I had spent my whole life to date trying to apply it to my father's path...and been miserable. I always liked my jobs—my utter love of massive projects—but they took a massive toll physically and emotionally.

I'd sold the house, just as Mac had suggested. And by whatever path, I felt that I was finally getting closer to myself.

Yes, it was time to find a new road that was my own, not my father's.

An American in Paris

Despite my dawdling, I arrived in Paris ten days before Ken.

So, I wallowed. And what a city to do it in!

I thought of Rollie as I spent three days wandering through every nook and cranny of the Louvre, another day in the Musée D'Orsay, and an afternoon in Picasso's house. Yes, I found artists whom I enjoyed, but I spent many a hot afternoon sipping lemonade in the cool gardens of the Musée Rodin considering his bronze sculptures of The Thinker, The Gates of Hell, and The Kiss. I'd finally found my artist (and the gardens are lovely as well).

Music of every era from Gregorian chant to Bebop jazz poured forth from street-corner buskers. Did I want to walk the Seine or watch the world from the top of Notre-Dame Cathedral? I did the latter three separate times in those ten days. I was like a little kid trying to do everything at once.

I found little shops on back streets where my meager attempts at French were welcomed and nursed along. People were only too glad to aid my accent and add to my vocabulary. And this was before I would tell them I was on *Le Tour du Monde*. Then they became even more garrulous if possible.

Where were the snobbish, reticent Parisians I had heard so much about?

I found out one fine morning as I walked along the Seine practicing French in my head.

I was accosted by a passerby.

"Where's Notre-Dame?" His tone was sharp and abrupt.

"*Pardon?*" Then, in that instant, I realized what I'd done. I'd responded to an English-language question with a reasonable French accent.

His loud shirt, camcorder, ugly hat, and arrogance identified him all too easily as American.

"Notre-Dame? *C'est cent, non, du cent metres tout droit.*" ("It's 100, no 200 meters straight ahead." Just around a curve in the buildings.) One of my few viable sentences. Then in my most lugubrious English, "Straight ah-head."

He looked to his three companions, "This way." He walked right by me.

I waved to their retreating backs and called out cheerfully, "*Au revoir, Monsieur.*"

No response.

From any of them.

I seethed.

I contemplated accosting him but knew he wouldn't understand. All the goodwill that I might receive as I traveled was being beat out of each country's citizens by tourists like this "ugly American." This isn't the sole province of Americans either, the Germans can be particularly awful as well. And the Japanese are so in their own world when they travel—they aren't offensive, they're just oblivious.

But, *Ooo!* (said with proper Gallic venom), I wanted to throttle that man.

A Fool on Wheels

I rode the fifty kilometers out to Charles de Gaulle Airport and met up with Ken. The first familiar face in eighteen months, I could barely stop touching his arm to make sure he was real.

As we headed back to my campsite at Bois de Boulogne at the edge of Paris, Ken was weaving. He'd been traveling a day to get here, and it was only 10:00 a.m. local time (2:00 a.m. his body's Seattle time). I led him to a little bakery. He recovered quickly enough with a hot croissant in one hand and a fresh baguette in the other.

Little did I know that I'd just unleashed a monster.

It is against the nature of a touring cyclist to sidetrack or even backtrack without good reason. Ken's definition of a good reason included *any* sign saying, "Boulangerie" with a distance of less than ten kilometers.

If they were closed for lunch, we'd wait.

We ate our way out of Paris, around Versailles, to Chartres Cathedral, and past chateau after chateau along the Loire River Valley. We munched éclairs near the house where Leonardo da Vinci had lived out the last of his days. We practiced swordplay with baguettes on winding chateau stairways until our weapons were too short from being bitten off between battles. We sang together as we spun our pedals and nibbled at the ends of baguettes rising from our panniers.

Yes, there is a baguette sticking up out of my pannier. -Photo by Ken

In the Bordeaux region, we sprawled on the fine grass of a campground with a jovial French cyclist. We wore nothing but our bike shorts in the warm evening breeze. The remains of a proper cyclists' dinner lay strewn about us.

Ken, normally a fastidious lawyer from Seattle, mumbled around his dessert pastry as he held the bottle of wine we'd been passing around, "I'm going to have to work on my table manners for the entire flight home or Jean won't let me in the front door."

"It doesn't get much better than this," I mumbled back, relishing the last of my pasta and vegetables seasoned with just a little oil and a sprinkling of fresh cheese.

Ken was always berating himself for not riding stronger or having trained harder. Even pointing out that I'd been training every day for eighteen months didn't calm him down. I put another croissant in his hand and that did seem to help.

Had I been that driven?

Yes. I probably had. Maybe I was changing, or "retuning" as Douglas would say.

Ken was married twenty years with a great wife and two kids. (Something I'd so envied back then. Years later I would find out for myself just how right I was to do so.)

"How did you do that? Me, I'm starting to fear I'll be single until I die."

"Why?"

"I'm short, furry, and funny-looking. Doesn't quite sweep them off their feet." (At least I'd finally trimmed my beard and wild hair neatly, but I was still short and funny-looking, especially on a crazy rig like Junior.)

"I've noticed women checking you out."

"Great, now I'm a freak show on my crazy bike."

Ken pushed on my shoulder until I was facing him. "Matt. You've got French women checking you out—French!—seriously checking you out. You haven't noticed?"

I shook my head. He handed me the remaining half of his croissant as a consolation prize.

"You need this more than I do. Tell you what. I'm riding behind you, letting you do most of the work as we ride." (It's called drafting; riding close in somebody's slipstream is much easier than being out front. By leading, I was balancing our training differential.) "I have more time to watch. Each time some pretty woman looks at you longer than just seeing what's going by, I'll ring my bell."

It rang pretty often.

"It's because I'm a cyclist—in *France*."

Ken finally gave up, but it left me to wonder.

How many wonderful ladies had I turned away from in my life because I was convinced they couldn't possibly like me?

How deep was this lack of trust in myself?

I certainly didn't have the answer then, or the first couple of years after my return.

Molting

On our final night in France we splurged on a hotel room near the airport. For the first time since leaving Seattle, I started throwing out items that had been essential to my lifestyle. I cooked my last meal on the cookstove and burned off the excess fuel. Ken had to force me to dump my spices into the trash. The room reeked of pepper and garlic powder for the rest of the night; should have used the toilet. Even jettisoning the last of the food didn't cover the smell.

I'd had my last major disease, much of my medical kit was now flushed down the toilet.

"Look out for the *le gendarme*," I called out in my worst French accent. "Zey vill be breakink down ze door any moment and emptyink ze toilet pipes to get ze drugs I try to flush away."

Four thrice-patched tire tubes went into the garbage. The broken derailleur I'd kept for parts followed close behind. Ken had to tear a spare tire out of my hands, it had only three minor holes and still had at least twenty percent of its tread.

The baggies that had encased every book and piece of clothing for 11,000 miles were discarded. I felt naked as I reloaded the bike, plenty of space in the last two panniers. For the first time in eighteen months, I could lift Junior easily with my uninjured arm. The other one, not so much.

However, the insult to the hotel room was so nasty that I left a 50 Franc ($10 US) tip on a 150 Franc room along with a note of apology.

We took a short connector flight to Paris. I was headed to Boston first and he was bound for Seattle.

We were plenty early, but I was so eager for home that I left him and went to sit right by the jetway until the first boarding call.

For much of the wait, I worried that I had left behind something crucial, though I had no idea what.

All these years later, I puzzle at what my former self was feeling. Its two-fold nature regarding what I'd discarded seems so obvious to me now.

First, it was the marker in the sand where I was jettisoning old versions of myself and leaving them behind. I haven't stopped growing and learning and I hope I never do, but I threw out far more than a few smelly spices and Ziploc bags worn velvet-soft.

From this release of my past, that wait at the airport had great energy.

But it also had great sadness.

As lonely as it had been, except for some US logistics and seeing my family, my bicycle journey and the peace and the lessons of the road were now left behind me.

I would only ride three miles on Junior in the next month before it was over.

France: 33 days / 1,312 km (815 mi)
Elevation Climbed: 5.1 km (3.2 mi)
Total Distance to Date: 16,696 km (10,374 mi)
Elevation Climbed to Date: 93.2 km (57.9 mi)

13

GETTING HOME

29 AUGUST 1994 – 22 SEPTEMBER 1994

English: *I'm home.*
Translation: *I'm alive? Cool!*

Coming to Terms

Somewhere in the umpteenth hour of my trans-Atlantic flight, the plane began to shrink. No flop sweat soaked my clothes, but the plane definitely shrank against me a bit.

Was it less horrific this time than my experience en route to Japan because I was a better traveler?

Or perhaps mere terror had lost some of its hold on me after all I'd been through.

Would my friends still like me?

Had my so over-imagined land of Seattle moved on without me, leaving me out of sync and with no home?

Seattle was still four weeks away and even from that distance it was being a bit scary.

The parallels with my arrival in Japan continued after my arrival in Boston. Junior was tossed aboard a bus with a minimum of ceremony, or even much care. The bus dumped me in some unknown suburb of Boston some miles from my friend's house. Once again, I went to a service station and purchased a map.

"Can you help me find this address?"

The attendant looked askance at my slip of paper, "Got me." Then he turned away.

I stood in shock at such lack of courtesy for a long moment…until I recalled I was back in America. How rude and uncaring must our country seem to travelers from other cultures?

I think it's part of our individualism. Our country has granted us the ability to pursue almost any interest imaginable. In so many places this is not the case. Even in a First World country like Germany, I was told about a test they had to take at twelve or thirteen. The person I was speaking to said, "That was the day I was bounced out of the high school track and told I was going to be a gardener. I never wanted to be a gardener. But to change tracks is almost impossible once they're set."

However, having the individualistic freedom also often means, "Good luck, you're on your own." Yet another lesson on how I would try to live differently than so many around me.

Once safely regrouped at my friend's, it was time to continue on and face my family.

Mom had died before we could heal the breach between us.

My sister and I had drifted apart over the last ten years, and I didn't want to end up in some kind of similar place with my sister.

"I'm staying for three weeks," I informed her, somewhat to her surprise. I hoped that our reconnection during my trip could be turned into something lasting if we simply hung out together. (I'm glad to say it really did because we decided that, despite our parents, we actually liked each other quite a lot.)

She took me to the Bronx Zoo where we watched the parrots fly about the aviary.

"I was stuck being her caretaker while you cowered on the West Coast. You know what it was like having my life torn up at a moment's notice, time after time—for over three years—each time I had to run to Mom's side? I was so angry with you."

I could do little but hang my head in acknowledgment.

"I thought you were becoming like Dad."

I watched two birds argue over who would get to sit on a particular branch.

"Perhaps I was trying to become like him. I was always told I was my father's son, after all. But I'm not him. In fact, I've learned that I don't understand him at all."

"You aren't him. I thought you were, but you're not."

We watched the birds a while longer.

"What are you going to do about Dad? Hey, don't hunch up like that. It hurts to even watch you."

He was less than an hour away by train. I told her about the letters. "Maybe face-to-face I can clear things up. I could—"

She stopped me, "He isn't going to change. He's seventy and as unchanging as ever. Before our last visit, I reminded him that I don't eat red meat. He made us a London Broil on the grill and said, 'Don't worry, the cows were vegetarian, so this must be as well.' What you need to decide is, can you weather the storm that is our father unscathed, or not. Remember what he said at the one 'family meeting' I called."

" 'I gave up introspection thirty years ago and never missed it'."

"Bingo." That moment had remained so clear in both our memories.

I stared at the parrots for a long time. A macaw watched me closely as it shifted from foot to foot, wondering if he'd struggled to win a branch only to discover it was too close to the bearded stranger.

"I can't do it. I can't face him." I wiped at the tears running down my cheeks.

"There's your answer."

And it was. Whether through cowardice or self-preservation, I returned to the West Coast without contacting him. It's a breach we've never healed. Years later we met again at my sister's wedding—she was finally marrying the great guy she'd lived with for decades. Her bravery, and class, of inviting our father took my breath away, but he and I were barely able to speak civilly. The distance and pain were too great.

He died not long after, bitterly angry at the life and children that had been dealt to him.

He is still a frequent visitor in my thoughts as I explore the world of being a stepfather. But a potential breach was healed, and my sister and I are in constant contact and visit each other when we can.

That was also the exact moment that I swore I would be a very different father if I ever had the chance.

I'm glad to say I did.

I constantly strove for ways to support my stepdaughter—not in ways I'd wished for myself, but in new ways that fit her.

Hours of help with homework, you bet. Teaching her the fun of play, absolutely. Getting our Taekwondo black belts together before she graduated high school, we did. Everyone is always so impressed that I got my black belt in my fifties, but I couldn't care in the least. We did it together for four years and she went out into the world that much safer and, more importantly, that much more sure of herself.

In her late-twenties, her only bigger fan is my wife. I'm *soooo* one of those insanely proud parents—so let's not get me started.

I will just say that I think the woman she's become is one of the most amazing things I've ever participated in and, yes, we're still incredibly close.

Last Entry

I made the final entry in my journal on the plane trip to Seattle:

> 22 September 1994
>
> The last day of my travels!!!
>
> It seems so unreal. The last few weeks now appear as little more than a haze of doing my best to ignore the passage of time. "Here and now," I cry. "Here and now."
>
> I feel as though I'm bundled up in cotton. A numbness before the storm?
>
> The numbness I attribute to many things, the emotional accumulation has been staggering. Striking a peace with my sister. Choosing not to visit Dad. The anticipation and fear of homecoming. Not only of reacquainting with friends, but also "putting my life back together." Purchasing a car. Finding a place to live.
>
> Maybe it's also a cross between numbness and that moment of suspended animation, of untapped potential energy, which proceeds action. I have been ready to start my Northwest life again for months. I have all of this pent-up energy to apply that is going to burst forth in a storm of very Matthew-like activity. Except this time it will come from what I feel and what I want—not from what I think Dad or others want of me. It actually looks as if it will be immense fun!
>
> We'll see!
>
> US: 24 days / 5 km (3 mi)
> Elevation Climbed: 0 km (0 mi)
> (My last three miles were on the right-hand side of flat suburban roads, marked in English, from a bus to a friend's house in Massachusetts. He would ultimately give me a ride to the airport and Junior and I would fly together for the last time: Boston to Seattle.)
> Final Time: 544 days / 78 weeks / 18 months

Final Total Distance: 16,701 km (10,377 mi)
Final Elevation Climbed: 93.2 km (57.9 mi)
(Didn't quite get my astronaut's badge at 100 km up.)
(For a time, I considered calling this book, 60 Miles Up and 10,000 Sideways.*)*

14

AFTERTHOUGHTS (2000)

Witness to Adventure

I completed my journey on September 22nd, 1994, eighteen months after my departure.

Four of the friends who'd stood by me on that cold March day when I'd first kicked my pedal high, greeted me with open arms at the airport. We laughed and cried and laughed again, washing away my fears of homecoming.

Later that night I sat on a couch in Mac and Ruth's house. Their dog, who I'd known since puppyhood, lay with his large head on my lap. At that moment, after eighteen countries and who knew how many languages, I was home. I was in the right place.

Triumphant homecoming. And an old friend who is very glad to see me. – Photos by Ruth and Mac

A dozen friends showed up for a surprise Welcome Home party a few days later. I cried a lot those first days.

I rented a small house in the San Juan islands. It was only a couple miles from where, eight years in the future, I would be building the house Douglas and I had begun in the sands of Greece. But that house and my family were still in my future as I tried to reacclimatize.

Life moved so fast back "in the world."

It unnerved me terribly.

I couldn't spend more than a day or two in Seattle without having to run back to my island. The hour and a half drive took well over two hours because I had to keep pulling out of the high-speed traffic and wait for the shakes to stop. I contacted

Henry and Jo in England, Helga and Achim in Germany, and others. They'd each had the same experience.

"Six months from now it won't be so shocking. You'll get used to it again. Honest."

And I did.

After half a year I went back to computers, but rather than seeking another partnership in a cutting-edge consulting firm, I took the lowest position in Seattle Opera's three-person computer department. I spent my time helping out-of-work actors figure out how to use a computer to sell tickets and market operas.

I focused instead on my writing. My first two novels were published in 1997 and 2000 by a small Northwest press. By 2000, I'd done guest lecturing at the University of Washington on writing fiction and had three more books in the works.

But my definition of home was as yet incomplete.

At least it was until I met a particularly incredible lady and her majorly cool six-year-old daughter. And I found the courage to tell her how I felt. How she made me feel.

In 1998, almost a year after we'd met, we drove along the Avenue of the Giants on our first-ever, experimental family vacation together. I spotted the hiker / biker site where I'd camped so long ago.

We parked along the road and wandered beneath the trees. The forest floor was cool and quiet with gentle puddles of the July sunshine splashing upon the dry needles—rather than a chill April downpour.

A little girl peered eagerly about from her perch atop my shoulders, wondering at the stories of my past, and a lady I was coming to love held my hand.

I tried to picture the man, five years my junior, sick of so many things and huddled in his tent, struggling with the letter that would eventually sever one of the most important relationships of his life.

I may be my father's son, but I am not him. My life is my own.

A pair of local cyclists were lunching at a picnic table (dry and in the sun) and overheard my stories. They too struggled to imagine the world traveler who had passed through the rain and dark seeking so blindly for some sign of light. It did seem fantastically unlikely, but it was true nonetheless.

I had witnessed it.

I had been the only one to do so.

Home

Sometimes I wake at night and move quietly from our bed to stare out the window at the stars. I've always loved the stars and I miss sleeping under them each night.

Yet, I feel no call to return to the road.

I loved my journey and its gift of time and friends, but it has no siren power to drag me crashing forth once more. I have finally found what I'd been seeking all along. I have at last found the thing more important than self, the thing that that fills my heart.

A rustle of sheets behind me and I know, without turning around to look, my wife is smiling.

It took many, many years and 11,000 miles on a bicycle searching, but I am home.

15

AFTERTHOUGHTS (2019)

Junior

I've ridden 40,000 or so miles as an adult (and a whole lot through high school), perhaps half that distance with Junior. Cycle commuting, day camping, three weeks in New Zealand, and, oh, a little trip around the world. He was a staunch companion.

If you figure a high-ish average of ten miles an hour, that's four thousand hours on a bicycle. A full-time job, with forty-hour weeks, is two thousand hours a year. I spent *two full years* sitting on a bicycle seat—actually pedaling.

But times changed. I commuted through Seattle by bicycle for a few years, but once I became part of a family, we never really lived in a good cycling location (tops of steep hills or on small quiet roads...which opened onto busy highways). I rode a few thousand miles after my trip, but no more than a few hundred with my family.

By 2018, I hadn't ridden once in five years. We were moving and space was at a severe premium—we were drastically downsizing. This time it was by choice rather than necessity.

After most of six months of waffling, I decided it was time to sell Junior. My custom road bike (that I'd had built for me before the trip—thank you R+E Cycles of Seattle, it was magnificent) and the amazing GreenSpeed recumbent trike I imported from Australia (also an incredible machine) were long since gone.

But Junior remained.

I ran ads, I asked friends, I talked to bike shops.

With the exception of one bike shop owner (who knew he'd never find my bike a proper home), no one understood just what Junior was. He was a top-of-the-line mountain bike into which I'd poured over $1,000 and untold hours turning into an exceptional touring machine.

Shortly before it was time to just sell it to the bike shop owner for almost nothing, a message pinged in from an ad I'd posted months before.

The guy had been out touring the Pacific Northwest and had decided that it was time to tackle a truly big tour.

But he didn't have a proper bike for it.

I went up to meet him (he only lived a few hours north and I was going to say goodbye to some friends up there). Short legs like mine (a real problem when selling a bicycle), he was perhaps half my age. He'd struggled up out of an abusive past, had avoided the gangs all of his friends had tried to drag him into, and had come off the road to help a girlfriend and her kid get out of a bad situation.

Life had handed him a whole world of suck, but he'd found a way to stand up from it.

Also a trained mechanic, he knew *exactly* what Junior was as we talked over features and configuration choices I'd made.

"Your ad said $325. That's really cheap for all this." I'd thrown in a major bicycle tool kit, spare pedals, parts, cables...the whole bit.

"I'm more concerned that Junior gets to the right person."

He nodded quietly. "I don't have any money." He was giving every penny to his girlfriend to help her out. "But maybe someday. I have a job interview later today at a McDonald's..." He trailed off.

I knew, I *knew* this was the right guy. "Do you have a $20?"

His girlfriend loaned it to him, but he held it out to me uncertainly, not knowing what came next.

I took the twenty, shook his hand, and then gave him my address. "When you have the money, send it here. Don't worry about how long it takes. You were meant to be the next person to ride this bike."

We didn't speak again.

I left him in the parking lot where we'd met, holding Junior in one hand and his girlfriend in the other.

He *couldn't* speak.

My wife, who was there and had chatted with the girlfriend earlier, figured it out: I may have been the first person other than his girlfriend who had ever trusted him—in his entire life.

To most people, he'd probably looked dark and dangerous with his long hair, tattered clothes, and whip-strong tattooed arms. To me he just looked like another traveler, one with a good heart, trying desperately hard to do the right thing.

I made it a mile down the road before I had to pull over and let my wife drive while I cried for a bit.

I cried for the loss of Junior.

I cried because he'd found an ideal home.

And because of what I now understood of the near-heartbreak on his new owner's face as I shook his hand—which said some sixty-year-old short Jewish guy trusted him and believed in him.

But I think, most of all, it was for actually releasing that piece of my past. For finally, twenty-five years after I'd started, I had completed that journey that had started when a bicycle almost clipped me and gave me the idea to travel.

I think the reason I was never able to finish this book properly was that I'd been holding onto that last piece of my journey. So, if you see a short guy with long dark hair tooling along on a crazy-ass touring machine, tell him I said hi. Offer him a meal and a place to roll out his sleeping bag. Ask him for his stories. You won't be sorry.

The rest of the money arrived a month later.

The Writing

I've mentioned my writing only a few times in this journey, but it tied so much together for me.

I set out to write a bicycle-around-the-world narrative. Which meant that for the first time, since one week when I was fourteen, I kept a daily journal. I was dutiful to that task and didn't miss a single night in 544 days. With the best of intentions to continue it, there's one additional journal entry in my logbooks—dated two months later. (It mostly states how bad I am at journaling. No additional entries follow.)

In addition to the daily journal, I wrote a "chapter" about each country after I left it without referring to my journal. I wanted to capture what thoughts, people, and places had stuck in my memory as important.

I wrote down the location and content of every single photograph I took: all 2,500 of them (averaging five a day—I saw some amazing places in addition to meeting such incredible people).

I also tracked every book I read and movie I saw, just in case it would somehow fit into the book.

But it was that silly little vignette that I started on the flight from Korea to Singapore that was to change my life. I worked on the first draft of that book every day with few exceptions from the Australian Outback in August until the following

March in Greece. I read excerpts to various people when they asked, but I kept it mostly to myself.

Dominic, the recovering heroin addict / dealer in Indonesia, asked me about the story. After I described what I knew up to that point, he said, "Wow! You're very creative." For reasons passing understanding, I managed not to hear that, though it's in my journal for November 29, 1993. It would take designing and building two houses, writing my first dozen novels, and years of my poor wife constantly beating me about the head with that supportive word before I managed to hear it.

We are *all* creative people. I think that too many of us have been allowed to have that trained out of us. School systems, parents, life circumstances... I won't try to analyze the "why" here. But learning and *accepting* that I'm a creative person was a very hard road to travel. I now watch assiduously for any "I'm not..." phrases in my life and always question them as they go by.

I finished the first draft of *Cookbook from Hell* in 1994 in Greece, somewhere near my thirty-sixth birthday—a full year on the road. I tucked it away and focused on designing a house with Douglas.

After my return to Seattle, I pulled it out and tried to edit it. It was a strange, awkward bit of satire of which I was immensely proud. I knew it needed fixing, but I didn't know how to tackle that. So, I gave it to my four best friends to read. Which earned four very distinct reactions:

- One suggested that perhaps I might want to hire a book editor. I did. She knew nothing of science fiction, fantasy, or religious humor writing (all elements of the book), but she assured me that was no problem. She was expensive and useless.
- My closest friend at the time, who I know reads some number of my books even now years later, has

never spoken to me about that first draft or any other book since.
- Another friend said, "This is such shit! Whatever gave you the idea you could write?" She claims that she then went on to give me a lot of other advice. I didn't hear a word of it. It was over six months before I could bear to look at the manuscript again after that. I finally decided that I didn't need people who could say things like that any more than I needed someone who could make me feel as awful as my father's sharp remarks often did.
- The fourth friend said, very tactfully, "Perhaps you should take a class."

It was the best advice I've ever been given in writing. Over the years since, I've taken dozens and dozens of classes and workshops. My career has advanced to the point (now that I'm a full-time writer) where far more of the workshops are about the business of publishing rather than the craft of writing, but I still take a few of the latter.

That first class opened up so many concepts for me about the craft. I took my little hundred-page quixotic snarl and turned it into a three-hundred-and-seventy-page first sale to a tiny publishing house. It went on to be the bestseller for the house that year (except that isn't saying much, at least not to anyone but me). I've since redrafted it into *Cookbook from Hell: Reheated*—the same story, just much better told.

My second book met with very little success as the press was on its way out of business (and it was still neophyte writing best forgotten about). Ten years and over four hundred rejections later, I finally sold the first book in my Night Stalkers series, *The Night Is Mine*. That title received rave critical reviews, garnered a follow-on 5-book contract, and launched an entire universe of titles and spinoff series.

But that didn't mean it was clear sailing.

Shortly after that book's release, I was laid off from my corporate job at the bottom of the recession. We were broke, I couldn't find a new job, and desperation was fast approaching.

I then released a little Christmas book, *Daniel's Christmas*, launching the first spinoff series: The Night Stalkers White House.

And it sold.

It sold well. Not spectacularly, but well.

My mentor had a fascinating idea...if we dared.

Suddenly, a number of the tools from my trip became completely relevant.

"Are you willing to take a risk?" That one I had down.

"Are you willing to think out of the box?" A mid-life crisis on wheels taking me around the world seemed pretty out of the box.

"And are you willing to bust your ass just like you always have?" A hard-work ethic is something my wife and I, and now our kid, share very deeply.

"What if you slashed expenses and wrote your ass off? Choose an amount that you're willing to risk and make it your writing goal to need less than that. Assume that you'll lose money in the first year, break even in the second, and pay yourself back in the third."

On the two-hour drive back home, my wife and I were shaking, literally. We probably weren't safe to drive, but we couldn't afford a hotel.

Forty-eight hours later, we'd dumped the house we'd been trying to sell for years for half its market value (bottom of the recession, remember?). At least this time I had found the family *before* I built the house. It was the one based on the design that Douglas and I had done on the chilly beaches of southern Greece. The kid was already off to college at this point.

My wife and I gave notice on our apartment, I sold my

entire library of project management books to a used bookstore and went looking for a cheaper place to rent out on the Oregon Coast. We moved in nine days later. Done.

It was a disaster. The place we'd hastily rented: untold layers of mildew, frequent visits from buyers looking for the drug dealer who'd just moved out, ticked-off policeman dropping in at odd hours, not knowing we were new tenants.

On that first day, standing in a sea of boxes and both weeping at what we'd done, my wife pointed at my small office —the first room we'd set up.

"Go write. That's your job now."

"No, I'll help you unpack first."

"No, Matt. We're doing this to support your dream. This is your big chance. Now go grab it. I can do this part of it."

It almost broke my heart, but I left her in that disaster and went and wrote.

Without her and her belief in me, I would never have pulled this off...and I *love* what I do. She's given me so many gifts that...well, I'll just leave it at that.

If nothing else, that moment proved that writing isn't about mood or muse or whimsy.

Successful writing is about intense hard work. Daily, consistent hard work, like climbing on a bicycle to keep crossing the Outback despite the bloody sores from your bike seat.

It's about taking personal beliefs and challenging them on the printed page. It's about not knowing where you're going *or* how you're going to get there but having faith that if you keep spinning the wheels in a forward direction, you *will* get there.

The learning curve, in the midst of the indie-publishing revolution of the early-to-mid-2010s was horrendous—often harder than learning Greek or finding a safe meal in India.

The fears made the claustrophobic flight to Japan seem trivial. Our future—my family's future—was in *my* hands.

Computers hate my wife, quite literally, and the feeling is mutual—they'll crash just to spite her. But she learned how to market and upload books, how to engineer audio, and how to wrestle with the multi-fanged mess that is administering and tracking a startup publishing corporation.

We persevered.

We made plenty of mistakes, but we learned and kept moving in the right direction.

This is my seventh year as a full-time writer. We paid off our three-year plan in twenty-nine months. The next year I retired my wife from her business to be my assistant.

By no means has the road been easy since then, but it is easier. The wheels are spinning smoothly. We've traveled far enough that we can see the sharp curves *before* we slam into them—though there are sometimes still baby elephants and occasionally seriously peeved mama elephants around those corners.

We've journeyed a long way together.

But when we look at each other, the question we ask is, "What's next?"

Truly Home

I've written this book most of four times trying to get it right... and I think I got close this time. At least as close as I ever will.

I wrote the first version in the fall of 1995, freshly returned from my travels, hoping to capture the prestigious Barbara Savage *Miles from Nowhere* Memorial Award. It included publication by The Mountaineers—a Pacific Northwest activities club of magnificent scale. The award was set up by the proceeds of her incredible book of that title (completed shortly before her death in a car-bicycle accident while on a training ride)—absolutely worth the read. I was told (very quietly and off the record) that I placed first, but the publisher had decided not to grant the award that year. Disheartened, I had moved on.

In 2001, I had published my first two novels and revisited the manuscript. Now I understood why the publisher hadn't agreed to publish it. With some distance, and far more skill, I tackled it again.

In 2006, I threw it out and tried again from scratch to capture the emotional ride of my journey, but my skills still weren't up to the image in my head. I gathered some publisher and agent rejections, but nothing worthy of note.

In 2019, now with a significant full-time writing career that has spanned sixty novels, a hundred short stories, and many awards, I stumbled onto my old 2006 manuscript again.

I hadn't forgotten about it exactly…perhaps I'd been avoiding it.

One night in March of 2019, twenty-six years to the day after my departure around the world, I cracked open the file and peeked inside.

It was surprisingly good. There was some real heart and emotion here. Much of it was hidden by insufficient writing skills, but it was there.

Intrigued, I read further.

I was soon deeply involved in this story of my younger self and his / our amazing adventures through the past. I could also see the struggles and battles that are so much clearer now.

Perspective is an awesome thing.

Is this trip still a part of my daily life?

Curiously…pretty much.

Certainly, the person I've become was greatly reshaped by this trip. And, while I can't see a piece of world news and not think of its impact on the people I met and the ones I didn't, that isn't the big portion.

It's I myself who was *most* profoundly affected. I constantly remind myself of the lessons I learned on the road:

- "Perfection is not required—good is triumph enough." – Noah's Beach, FNQ, Australia
- "I give myself permission to feel good about feeling good." – Trinity Beach, FNQ, Australia

Journal excerpt from Trinity Beach, Australia Sept 24, 1993

- "Acknowledge, even celebrate the successes." (I used to really suck at this. I'm up to mediocre now.) – Cairns, Australia
- "Trust myself, I'm good at what I do." – Darwin, Australia
- "Remember to slow down." Advice from a young man over a cup of tea during a brief break as I rode across Indonesia. I thought I already had by then—apparently not enough. I do *try* to slow down and appreciate what's around me more.
- "Am I pursuing my parents' dreams or my own?" – Singapore
- Antonio's rule: "Good Heart. Good thoughts. Automatic good actions." I do my best to remember this one *every single day*. To always act from a place of heart and truth. – Maumere, Indonesia
- "Just because something is a big challenge, it doesn't

mean that I have to do it. (Especially if it isn't fun!)" – Flores Island, Indonesia
- "It is not your problem. Don't make it your problem." – Indonesian bus conductor
- "Preferences beat the hell out of expectations." – Flores Island, Indonesia
- *Jam karet.* Rubber time. "Waiting is." – Rainer, a German traveler in Indonesia
- "I try to live each day better than the day before. That is my goal, and look how far I have come." – Bali shop owner, Indonesia
- "Maybe it's a good thing I'm not good at music; it's one less choice I have to worry about making." – Goa, India
- "Find the joy in every day (even when all I can find are the small ones)." – Israel
- "You strike me as someone who stays the same through your travels. You come across as knowing very clearly who you are." – Rabbi Mordecai, Israel, and Douglas, Vienna
- "Live, love, and laugh like today is the only day." – from *Zorba the Greek* by Nikos Kazantzakis. (Read while sitting by his grave on Crete, Greece.)
- "A little effort a lot of the time beats the crap out of a lot of effort all the time." (This one still seems counterintuitive, but I'm convinced that it's true. Living at max effort as I did for so many years left me little bandwidth to collide with opportunity, take a chance with circumstance, and just plain old have a bit of fun.) – Greece
- "The past is memory; the future is possibility." – Greece
- "How do I do my trip? Easy! Strong legs, weak

mind." – my birthday, camped on Crete by a three-thousand-year-old ruin.
- "I crossed the Luxembourg-France border this morning. I was feeling so strong and I wish there had been a photographer to take a picture of me waving my arms over my head and shouting like an idiot." – Verdun, France. (There is a full page note in my journal where I circled this part of the entry and wrote, "Remember this feeling. It was REAL! It IS important."—and it *is* important to remember that I *am* strong when I need to be rather than some weakfish at the whim of whatever life or some corporate boss, or parent, wants to throw at me.)
- "Just ride through it." Because if I do, at some point I'll come out the far side. That adage had gotten me through the first day of my trip and stills helps me through the hard patches.
- "No worries." – Australia

I pat myself on the back, literally, when I make a particularly good batch of fajitas. I do a little happy dance when I finish a draft or even just a good scene. I take the time to unpack a copy of every single title I've ever written and reappreciate the story within and why I chose to tell it.

I willingly drop everything if my wife has a question or my kid calls. I never begrudge a friend an interruption. People are far more important than any task and I know this for sure.

My family isn't on my to-do list...they're the reason *for* my list.

I live by these and a hundred less-conscious guides I gathered on the long road.

Am I still a socially awkward introvert? Perhaps more than ever. It's a part of being a writer—living so deep in my head with my characters for hour after hour. But that doesn't change the priority I give to those around me.

And I really did find home. Like Claud in Indonesia, I don't need to turn around to see my wife's smile. She *knows* she's my home and I tell her every day how grateful I am to be hers.

I'll leave you with the words of a good friend who helped change my life so much for the better: *Sell it all. And go now.*

And a few of my own:

Kick the pedal high!

4 July 2019
North Shore Massachusetts

APPENDIX I

WHAT IS REQUIRED TO GO TOURING, ANYWAY?

Um, a bicycle. No, really? Every bike book I've read has a list, a different list. A lot depends on the length of your tour, what climates you expect to encounter, and how much money you have.

You can climb on a $300 bike with less than $500 of equipment and have a fine year-long tour. You may even get away with having no problems (beyond the normal stuff).

Others will invest thousands in the best equipment. If you can afford to, you'll be glad you did. Fewer breakdowns, less space needed, less weight, and more comfort will be your rewards for each dollar you spend. The trick is to find where your budget and your plans meet. I had the luxury of enough money to buy the best in most cases (still under $5,000 all told).

Where you are traveling also makes a significant difference. India and Indonesia, among others, are so cheap that cooking gear and camping gear are totally nonessential. I never used mine in those five months. Europe, the US, and Japan are so expensive that cooking equipment is required for financial survival.

There is a rule called the "One-Hand-Rule" in Barbara

Savage's book *Miles from Nowhere*. It states that if you can't lift your bike, at least a little, with one hand, then get rid of something. Good advice, I didn't quite follow it. I traveled a bit heavier in favor of comfort. I only regretted it when going through airports or getting a room that was a fourth story walk-up and I didn't dare leave half the load in the lobby. Ugh!

Traveling with two people also saves you weight. One tent instead of two, one cook kit (with an extra plate), one medical kit, one set of bike tools, and so on. The solo tourer is in for a heavier ride.

I stockpiled things at home and had them sent to me: extra bike parts, water filters, guidebooks, etc. Some things I bought when I needed them and sent them home when done: mask and snorkel, cold-weather clothing, tent in the rain but bivy sack in the sun.

One more essential tip: get a good supplier. You know, man, a "supplier." Just kidding. I often picked up the phone (from Japan, Australia, Indonesia, Greece) and said, "Derek, Buddy, I need some more tires, a new rear rack, and, you won't believe this, I broke a seat rail, too." Derek would have parts waiting for me anywhere in the world on two weeks' notice. It often wasn't cheap, but it certainly made the ride more enjoyable as these parts were often very hard to find...very. Thanks, Derek and R+E Cycles of Seattle. Thanks.

Here's what I carried:

COOK KIT

It can save 50-75% on your food budget in First World countries.

- MSR International cookstove. It burns 4 different fuels.
- 2 1-quart fuel bottles. It was often hard to find the

good fuel and there is nothing worse than running out in mid-soup.
- 5 small plastic spice bottles in a zippered case. The spices varied depending on country and taste. I usually had salt, pepper, red pepper, tarragon and oregano (pre-mixed), and garlic powder.
- Swiss Army knife. Not one of the monsters, take something you can use.
- A real fork and spoon. Even heavy-duty plastic ones break.
- A plastic pancake flipper, great for eggs, toast, pancakes, etc.
- 1-quart pot.
- 7" fry pan. It also served as a plate and a pot lid.
- Large "thermos" mug. Make tea with your first hot water and it's still hot when the spaghetti is done. This was an essential.
- Water filter. A must for serious bike travel. I started with MSR and finished with Katadyn. Drinking 8–10 liters a day in Third World countries where even the water in the plastic (yuck!) bottles couldn't be trusted. Make sure the filter will remove bacteria as well as larger particles. This will make life much less worrisome. I created clear, potable water from Indian sinks, Indonesian mandis, and even a French mud puddle. It also saved me once when I accidentally kicked over the spaghetti pot with the last of my water when I was camped alongside a stream in Japan. (But I had diarrhea all the time? Not really. It was a common occurrence, but I was always able to trace it to food or the "unfiltered water incident" on Flores Island.)
- Water bladder. I had an MSR 5-liter bag and would fill it with fresh water prior to riding across the

Outback or through areas where clean water wasn't available.
- Various plastic containers, Nalgene bottles, Ziploc baggies, etc. for food storage.

CAMPING GEAR

- Tent. Great for extended wet or cold travel. Due to bad planning, three of my first four months were in the rain! I used the North Face Firefly, a self-standing tent, and was never disappointed. I've also traveled with the Flashlight tent, but it requires staking, which is hard to improvise on sandy beaches or concrete parking lots.
- Bivy bag. Once well out of the rain zones, I sent my 7-pound tent home and substituted a 1-pound bivy. I wish I'd done it much sooner. This is a raincoat for a sleeping bag that I used throughout Europe. Smaller, much lighter, and no "tent charge" in European campgrounds. It was great.
- Mosquito net. I bought a freestanding one and, frankly, just get one of the lightweight, tie-up kind. Cheaper and easier. In the countries where you need it, rooms are so cheap that there is no point in camping, and they all have some way to hang a net.
- Sleeping bag. I used a North Face Chrysalis down bag. Keeping it dry was sometimes tricky but it sure rolled up small and it sure was warm. Most people travel with polyfill bags of some sort. The advantage is they are warm when wet but they are a little bulkier and heavier.
- A twin-bed sheet folded over and sewn across the bottom and part way up one side. Use as a liner to

keep your sleeping bag clean and it often saves a "sheet-charge" in youth hostels.
- Therm-a-Rest ground pad & Therm-a-Rest chair. The pad rolls up to the size of a large bottle, inflates quickly, and is immensely comfortable. It also fits into the chair, a must for those long days trapped in a tent by rain and those lazy afternoons camped alongside a river.
- Candle lantern. For those nights you just can't sleep, or you started cooking too late. (No LED lanterns in 1993.)
- A small backpack for tramping around and getting through airports.
- Patch kit for tent, mattress, and sleeping bag.
- A small flashlight.
- Compass. Rarely used.
- Emergency whistle. Never used, thankfully.
- 30 feet or so of parachute cord or lightweight Dacron line. I used it to hang clothes to dry, tie my tent to a tree during windstorms, suspend my bike in the air to ease maintenance, tie together shattered bike racks, etc.

CLOTHING

Each piece in a separate Ziploc baggie; if one gets wet, the rest are OK. I can't speak to a woman's additional needs from any experience, so I won't even try.

- 2 pair non-cycling shorts. Wash one while wearing other.
- 3 pair socks. Replace them as they wear out.
- 1 pair neoprene socks. When worn with sandals, they make great cold-weather camp shoes.

- A T-shirt or two.
- A nice shirt. A must for embassies and borders, etc. It should be light-colored and long-sleeved so that it can be worn after sunset in the mosquito-filled tropics. Mozzies don't attack white as much (especially when it's sprayed with DEET).
- Light-weight hiking boots. I used these a lot.
- Cycling shoes – see cycling clothes.
- Sandals for camp and walking around cities.
- Bandana. It can be dipped in water and worn as a cooling hat, can also be worn as a face mask in very polluted or pollen-filled countries.
- Polar fleece jacket and pants. Stays warm no matter how wet it gets and odor-free, too. I was always glad for them and never sent them ahead. Rolled up they were my pillow for eighteen months.
- 1 pair long pants (not jeans). Jeans are bulky, take a long time to dry and, worst of all, weigh a lot. I used khaki, but now there are these great lightweight synthetics. I traveled for almost a year with no long pants except my fleece.
- 1 sarong. A very thin, beach towel-sized piece of cloth. Worked as a beach towel, a portable changing room when wrapped around my waist, even in airports—much to a shocked Singapore official's dismay—and as a sarong to cover knees in countries where bare ones are offensive.
- Rain gear. In the first wet months this included: jacket, pants, booties, and neoprene gloves. Once it became warmer and drier, I sent all this home and bought a good poncho. A poncho was essential in Third World countries as a bottom sheet to protect me from bedbugs.

CYCLING CLOTHES

I always wore Lycra to ride and was glad of it no matter how ridiculous I looked.

- 2 pair of cycling shorts are essential.
- 2 Lycra jerseys. The kind with pockets in the back.
- Helmet. Many Europeans and Americans will disagree with this, but I've been saved a concussion in both of the two accidents I've ever had. I've heard many stories from people who attribute being alive to their helmet. Oddly I hear very few stories of, "Boy it was an ugly wreck, but I was fine without a helmet."
- Goggles with both clear and dark lenses. The clear ones for when you need glasses to keep the rain or exhaust fumes out of your eyes on dark, overcast days.
- Cycling gloves. Make sure they're well padded. There are some very rough roads out there.
- Cycling shoes. For me, cycling in sneakers just isn't good enough. I count the day I went to "clipless" pedals as the second most important upgrade to my bike after cycling shorts. The day I started using them, I became much more powerful and my knee problems due to misalignment went away. I rode with the Shimano SPD's and a Shimano shoe designed so that it was still quite comfortable to walk in; the cleat was recessed.

BICYCLE STUFF

- Raleigh Peak Mountain Bike with Shimano Deore

XT components Mavic 231 steel rims (36 spoke). Fantastic bike. I loved both the bike and the gear, and they gave me a minimum of problems over some very rough trails.
- Avocet Cross K 26 x 1.5 tires at the start. Ended up with Continental Touring. When the Avocets were overheated by heavy braking, the bead separates from the sidewall. Blowouts suck. I lost three that way crossing the Japanese Alps.
- Scott AT4-B aero bars with wrist risers.
- Rear triangle reflector.
- Flashing rear light for foggy days, massive rainstorms, and long, dark tunnels.
- I didn't ride at night, so no front lights.
- Avocet Alt 50 cycle computer. Distance and pedal rpm (both essential) and altimeter, which was amusing, but also useful as a barometer when I was in camp. If the altitude started climbing, I knew the pressure was dropping and I was in for a wet day the next day. Once it rose 200 feet in 6 hours. I went out and double-pegged the tent as well as tying off to a few trees. In the middle of the night, I was slammed by a storm and was glad to not have to crawl out in it to do the tie-downs then.
- Bruce Gordon racks. Much stronger than the Blackburn racks, which shattered in the first months.
- Mountain Minded saddle bags. Built on Lopez Island, WA, by a couple of cycle-tourists. They are simply the best bags I've ever seen. I was the envy of every cyclist that really looked at them. Regrettably they are no longer made at this writing.
- Good air pump. Be kind and get one that can do

both Schrader and Presta valves. Your stranded fellow cyclist will love you.
- 3 water bottles.
- Rearview mirror.

TOOLS

Take all the tools necessary to take your bike apart and put it back together. Even if you don't know how, you may meet others who do.

- 6" adjustable wrench.
- 2 cone wrenches.
- Complete set of hex wrenches.
- Chain tool and spare links.
- Crank puller.
- Bottom bracket tool. I don't recommend the Cool Tool as it stranded me badly on the Oregon coast. I finally went to a sealed bottom bracket (which was awesome) though I still, needlessly, carried the adapter to remove it.
- Rear cluster remover. Essential in case of breaking a rear spoke.
- Spoke wrench.
- Good lubricant. Tri-Flow is great.
- Good grease. Phil Wood is my favorite.
- The weird little tool to take apart my pedals; I had to re-grease those bearings only once.
- A good chunk of duct tape.

SPARES

- 12 spokes (taped upright to the seat post).

- 4 tubes and a patch kit.
- Spare tires. I carried between one and four depending on which country I was in. I used up three in a month due to faulty sidewalls before I changed brands and rode the rest of the way home on the new ones with no further failures.
- Brake pads. I used up six sets.
- Cables and cable housing. At least one spare set and a few universals just in case.
- Extra shifters and rear derailleur. A point of some debate, but I'm glad I took them. If you're going way off the beaten track, take 'em.
- A full set of bearings for your entire bike. Even if you don't know what to do with them. I changed them all in Germany and I saved another cyclist's pedal in Eastern Europe.
- Miscellaneous nuts and bolts. Something will loosen and fall off. Use nylon locking nuts and Loctite.
- Spare axles and seat-post locking bolts. These don't often break but I have heard stories of them being stolen.
- Many miscellaneous straps. At one point, four of these held together my shattered rear Blackburn rack for over 300 miles. Rough roads out there.

My brilliant bike tip (that I figured out somewhere in Japan): Find two trees a couple meters apart, and hang your bike between them by the handlebars and seat, using a bit of line. It makes an absolutely brilliant work stand.

TOILETRIES

All in a zippered, bright-red bag so it's easy to find when you need it.

- Aspirin.
- Preparation H.
- Cortisone cream (I'm allergic to poison ivy) or Calamine for nasty bug bites.
- Scissors, for my beard and hair.
- Nail clippers.
- Bug juice. DEET may be nasty, but it works great; careful, a 100% solution will melt some plastics. After I returned, researchers were finding life-threatening allergic reactions in 1 / 100,000 people or some such. Check it out and decide for yourself, but take bug juice in some *very* potent form.
- Sunscreen. Use it. I met a long-term traveler who

didn't use it and ten years later is "having pieces of his face removed" due to skin cancer.
- Cotton swabs.
- Toothbrush and toothpaste.
- Brush or comb. Cut off the handle to save weight.
- Needle and thread for fixing stuff. It can be used for open wounds in emergencies. Something I thankfully didn't have to try.
- Antidiarrheic. Imodium A-D, a true lifesaver many times over. Carry lots.
- Moleskin for blisters.
- A towel. I had a small chamois towel, they're great and dry quickly.

MEDICAL KIT

This varies a lot depending on where you go. I went loaded.

- A good, small medical book. *The Pocket Doctor* by Dr. Stephen Bezruchka is excellent. I used it many times and often loaned it to other travelers. It was the only book to travel the whole distance with me. It may not have saved my life, but time and again it felt as if it did.
- Syringes. Many countries reuse them, bring your own. Travel Medicine Clinics will gladly give you prescriptions for them.
- Band-Aids.
- A couple regimens each of two different antibiotics. I carried a big gun for dysentery and a little one for severe flus, etc. I used one regimen of the small one and both regimens of the big one. Two bouts of dysentery during my six weeks in India will do that to you.

Appendix I   349

- Oral thermometer.
- Gauze.
- Tape.
- Condoms. You know why.
- Malaria pills. Many people now carry a malaria cure rather than taking a prophylactic medicine.
- I chose to get many vaccinations before I left. Talk to your local Travel Medicine Clinic. If your local university or hospital doesn't have one, there are government ones in most cities. The University of Washington Travel Medicine Clinic was simply fantastic. The one in Heidelberg, Germany, where I purchased one of the one-year boosters that I needed, was also excellent.

OTHER STUFF

- Journal. I mailed it home in 2–3-month installments so I couldn't lose too much if it went astray (again, pre-Internet era). I lost one, only a week of entries—not in the mail, but off the side of a tiny Indonesian ferry boat in a nasty storm.
- Camera. Back in 1993, I was shooting film with a water-resistant Pentax Zoom 90-WR. Whatever you use, unload the images often to somewhere that you know is safe.
- Whatever guidebook, map, and phrasebooks were currently relevant and usually the next country's as well.
- 1-2 "fun" books. (Plenty of trading goes on in campsites to keep your tiny library fresh.) Now they have apps for this. Have something preloaded,

there's often a lot of wait time in very obscure and unconnected locations.

LUXURIES

- Small shortwave / AM / FM radio. A ham operator suggested this for when I wanted to follow the news or just hear the English language. Thank you, Radio Australia, Radio New Zealand, BBC World Service, and the Moscow jazz station.
- Business cards with mailing address and "Traveler" as occupation. Especially if going to Asian countries.
- Mask and snorkel.
- Therm-a-Rest chair. I blessed it the many days I sat in the tent, reading, and watching the rain pour down. Well worth the extra half pound.
- Something to write down your journal. Keep it current. Years later you'll be glad you did.

And, yes, all of this fit on one bike. I got to weigh it all at every airport. At the beginning, with no food or water, my bike weighed 33 pounds and another 90 pounds of gear for a running weight of 123 pounds. I did shave off 10–15 pounds by the end of the trip, but it was not light by anyone's standard. Add another 20 pounds when carrying a lot of water like Indonesia or the Outback, and 10 more for food. Remember the motto: "Strong legs, weak mind."

OTHER LUXURIES I'VE SEEN ABOARD BICYCLES

- 6" chef's knife.
- Polypropylene cutting board.

- Real dinner plate.
- 14" cast-iron frying pan! (I was assured that it was a "life essential" item.)
- Chess, backgammon, Scrabble, cribbage, etc.
- Frisbee, paddle ball set, Hacky Sack.
- Every kind of musical instrument including: tambourine, guitar, didgeridoo (carried one myself for a while until I lost it on an Indonesian night bus), fiddle, flute, harmonica, and penny whistle.
- Fancy clothes: I saw many dresses but no jackets or ties... Hmm, I'll avoid exploring the insanities of societal expectations here.
- Hand mirror.
- I even saw an electric hair dryer once on the California coast. She never did find a place to plug it in at that wilderness campground.

APPENDIX II

THOUGHTS ON LEARNING A LANGUAGE IN THIRTY DAYS

I am no linguist and I am sure that there are far better methods for learning a language, but I'll tell how I learned them. It may offer some insights that will be helpful, especially because a traveler down at this level needs language to survive—in a unique way.

I worked out this method in Japan because, for my first month on Hokkaido, I either spoke Japanese or I was silent. I met no English speakers there but one, and that wasn't until my third week in-country.

The first things I always learned were: *please, thank you*, and how to count. Believe it or not, how you count on your fingers is far more important than how you say the numbers. In the US, we ask for three of something by holding up the three middle fingers. In Japan, that will only elicit a blank stare. Three is a thumb and the first two fingers.

I created a crib sheet, reproduced below, and looked up all of the words I could in a Berlitz or Lonely Planet language guide. I paid special attention to the pronunciation tips. In many countries, a few words pronounced properly engendered far more patience and assistance than a whole slew of mangled vowels.

I finally selected four essential sentences and did my best to fully understand the grammar behind those sentences. I could then plug my vocabulary into those basic structures and achieve quite a bit of communication.

BASIC SENTENCES

- "My bicycle and I are traveling around the world together."
- "Could you please tell me where there is a ferry to the next island?"
- "Yesterday I was in Larantuka and tomorrow I'm riding to Maumere."
- "Thank you very much for your help."

Notice the types of substitutions that can be done within these basic structures.

- "I am traveling to learn about myself," or "I liked the hot waterfall (hot springs) more than the temple."
- "Could you tell me where there is a grocery store...laundry...bike shop?" or "Do I turn right or left for the airport?" (Sometimes it literally translated as "Airport do I right or left turn?" but people always smiled and pointed the way.)
- "Last month I was in Australia and in December I'm riding in India." or "Last year I was a computer programmer and next year...(shrug)."
- "Thank you very much for your help." No substitutes. Learn it and use it.

Appendix II

The foremost rule is to keep it simple. I often found that I could be understood because I was speaking in kindergarten language, but I was lost when they replied. I soon added one more sentence to my repertoire:

- "I speak in French (or whatever), you speak in English please."

If they had even the most basic English, I could always understand them. Communication was often slow, but it could also be quite fun. This worked everywhere except Japan, where they were too afraid of losing face with poor pronunciation. On my very last day I discovered that, in Japan, the secret was to write down the word. They could often read but were unwilling to speak incorrectly.

I was constantly amazed, as I talked around subjects, how much I could communicate with only a few hundred words.

- "Why are you traveling?" "Bad job. Heart sick."
- "Do you like traveling?" "(Make a sad face.) Friends. America. (Point far to the west.) Me. (Point to ground.) (Then big smile.) Macedonia. Ahhh. Good."

I was able to discuss why and where I was traveling and something of what I had learned within weeks of entering a new language. My worksheets were normally a single piece of paper that was folded and refolded in my pocket until I knew enough words, or the paper disintegrated, whichever happened first. Only my second one, from Indonesia, survived and is reproduced below. I have included the word lists that I used to learn Bahasa, though I have spared you the translations.

| Bahasa crib sheet

Please note that the category headings are loose at best, I put the words where I expected to find them on the page, which is not always under their proper heading. Also, the ordering may seem bizarre. It was mandated by a mixture of what I needed first, the order in which I learned them, and the alphabet, not of English, but of the language I was learning. This forced me to think in the language all the sooner to find the words I wanted.

The word selection can also vary by country, often a single word translates as a whole, essential phrase. In Bahasa, *jalan-jalan* literally means "travel-travel." But the proper translation, in context, "walking to no particular purpose" and is the only phrase that will convince a *bemo* driver that you want to see the town on foot and don't need his minivan's services. There are also many ways to say "please" depending on the type of request. But, go ahead, use the wrong "please." At least the thought is there, and the listener may well be charmed or even offer an interesting language lesson.

Also learn the parts of the day. In the outer islands of Indonesia, hours are meaningless. Time is broken down into parts of the day: morning, late morning / heat of the day (when everyone stops moving), late afternoon / evening (when people start moving again), and evening (when the towns are most lively and the night markets are open). Try to learn these cultural language features as well as the literal ones. The best way to learn the nuances is to be friendly with the native-speakers and they will gladly spend time tutoring you in their tongue.

These two hundred or so words served me well in Japanese, Bahasa (Indonesia), Greek, German (along with my rusty high school German), and French. I learned about fifty in Hungarian, a dozen or so in Russian, and a smattering of Hindi.

One problem was that, upon my return to the US, I spoke to airport officials and bus drivers in only this limited word set. I had become so used to not using complete sentences that I was tongue-tied for days after my return, much to the officials' initial frustration and later amusement.

WHO

I, me, you, we, they, friend, father, mother, my father, my mother, sir / official, brother, older brother, sister, older sister

POLITE

please, thank you, very much, please help, please (giving permission), please try, sorry, excuse me

VERBS

To: work, walk, arrive, forget, pass by, sit, try, listen, rest, leave, stop, stand, run, be alive, live, fall, shop, study, drink, eat, come, go, die, read, chat, dance, do, play, cook, reserve, wash, carry, pay, like, love, follow, meet, go, hope, wait for, know, draw, rush, look, look for, exchange, visit, meet, wait, bargain

QUESTIONS

what, how much, how many, where is, where from, when, who, how, how far, how long, how old, marry (I was often asked if I was and learned it early), wife

TRAVEL

sell, house, travel, leave, job / work, journey, world, ship port, airport, United States of America

TIME

times of day, days of week, months of year, past, future, yesterday, today, tomorrow, now, time, for a long time, last, next

DIRECTIONS

"numbers," N / S / E / W, where, where from, when, why, approximate, a half, a third, first, second, third, near, far, want to go to

NOUNS

map, market, table, floor, door, window, roof, shirt, dog, school, price, money, person, heart, place, bed, room, toilet, dictionary

ADJECTIVE PAIRS

long / short, this / that, expensive / cheap, big / small, open / closed, here / there, left / right, fast / slow, young / old, rich / poor, fat / thin, thick / thin, new / used, bitter / sweet, happy / sad, fresh / stale, before / after, sick / healthy, empty / full, clean / dirty, inside / outside

CONJUNCTIONS

and, or, but, if, because

MISCELLANEOUS

of course, a moment, only, also, too, guests, okay, wrong, perhaps, outside country, hungry, thirsty, with, glad, good luck, what news, news good, what is this, what is that, please repeat, speak slower, no meat, very, too, rather, again, for the fun of it

APPENDIX III
BOOKS

E-books have changed the experience completely. However, one of the great things I did was having a friend at home cut up the complete works of Shakespeare (cheap from a used bookstore), and send several plays per mail stop, slender and light. These were immensely popular, both in camp for group readings, and later as trades.

I've made a list of the books I read about cycling and cycle-touring prior to my travels. These do not include the numerous books I read about the countries I traveled through.

CYCLING BOOKS

- *Bicycling Magazine's Complete Guide to Bicycle Maintenance and Repair,* Bicycling Magazine. I recommend reading several books on bicycle maintenance, the more the better. This is one of the best.
- *Greg LeMond's Pocket Guide to Bicycle Maintenance and Repair,* Greg LeMond.

- *Bicycling the Pacific Coast,* Vicky Spring and Tom Kirkendall.

TRAVEL ESSAY

- *The Roads to Sata,* Alan Booth.
- *The Road of Dreams,* Bruce B. Junek.
- *Full Tilt,* Dervla Murphy. One of the best cycling chronicles.
- *Miles from Nowhere,* Barbara Savage. A pioneer in modern bicycle travelogue.
- *Seeing Myself Seeing the World,* Sally Vantress-Lodato.

ESPECIALLY USEFUL FOR UNDERSTANDING CULTURES

- *The Songlines,* Bruce Chatwin.
- *Philosophers of East and West,* E.W.F. Tomlin.
- Anything by Joseph Campbell.

TRAVEL BOOKS

- *The Pocket Doctor* by Dr. Stephen Bezruchka. Absolutely essential. I will never attempt extended travel without it. It is still my first choice for home reference as well.
- *Weather Patterns of the World,* Times Books (out of print). Consider Fodor's *World Weather Guide.* An excellent guide for understanding where the rain, monsoon, winds, and winter typically are and are

not. Of course, with the changing world climate, it is harder and harder to predict.
- Language guides. Berlitz were consistently the best for major languages. Lonely Planet for the less common languages.
- Guidebooks. Lonely Planet series is excellent for the budget traveler. In Europe I also often bought the Blue Guide as it emphasizes historical rather than logistical features of travel. "What does the inscription on the arch of Hadrian's Gate in Athens mean anyway?" is a Blue Guide question. By the way, one side states: "This is Athens, the ancient city of Theseus." Upon the other: "This is the city of Hadrian, and not of Theseus." In case you were wondering.
- *Richard Hittleman's Yoga: 28 Day Exercise Plan*, Richard Hittleman. Some form of stretches must be pursued to balance the muscle building of cycling or toting a heavy pack.

ABOUT THE AUTHOR

M.L. Buchman started the first of over 60 novels, 100 short stories, and a fast-growing pile of audiobooks while flying from South Korea to ride his bicycle across the Australian Outback. Part of a solo around the world trip that ultimately launched his writing career in: thrillers, military romantic suspense, contemporary romance, and SF / F.

Recently named in *The 20 Best Romantic Suspense Novels: Modern Masterpieces* by ALA's Booklist, they have also selected his works three times as "Top-10 Romance Novel of the Year." NPR and B&N listed other works as "Best 5 Romance of the Year."

As a 30-year project manager with a geophysics degree who has: designed and built houses, flown and jumped out of planes, and solo-sailed a 50' ketch, he is awed by what's possible. More at: www.mlbuchman.com.

Other works by M. L. Buchman:

Thrillers

Dead Chef
Swap Out!
One Chef!
Two Chef!

Miranda Chase NTSB
Drone
TBA

Romantic Suspense

Delta Force
Target Engaged
Heart Strike
Wild Justice
Midnight Trust

Firehawks
Main Flight
Pure Heat
Full Blaze
Hot Point
Flash of Fire
Wild Fire
Smokejumpers
Wildfire at Dawn
Wildfire at Larch Creek
Wildfire on the Skagit

The Night Stalkers
Main Flight
The Night Is Mine
I Own the Dawn
Wait Until Dark
Take Over at Midnight
Light Up the Night
Bring On the Dusk
By Break of Day
and the Navy
Christmas at Steel Beach
Christmas at Peleliu Cove

White House Holiday
Daniel's Christmas
Frank's Independence Day
Peter's Christmas
Zachary's Christmas
Roy's Independence Day
Damien's Christmas
5E
Target of the Heart
Target Lock on Love
Target of Mine
Target of One's Own

Shadow Force: Psi
At the Slightest Sound
At the Softest Word

White House Protection Force
Off the Leash
On Your Mark
In the Weeds

Contemporary Romance

Eagle Cove
Return to Eagle Cove
Recipe for Eagle Cove
Longing for Eagle Cove
Keepsake for Eagle Cove

Henderson's Ranch
Nathan's Big Sky
Big Sky, Loyal Heart
Big Sky Dog Whisperer

Love Abroad
Heart of the Cotswolds: England
Path of Love: Cinque Terre, Italy

SIGN UP FOR M. L. BUCHMAN'S NEWSLETTER TODAY

and receive:
Release News
Free Short Stories
a Free Book

Get your free book today. Do it now.
free-book.mlbuchman.com